Velocity

SUPERCAR REVOLUTION

JOHN LAMM

MOTORBOOKS

For Holly Lamm

First published in 2006 by Motorbooks, an imprint of
MBI Publishing Company, Galtier Plaza, Suite 200,
380 Jackson Street, St. Paul, MN 55101-3885 USA

MBI Publishing Company titles are also available at discounts in bulk
quantity for industrial or sales-promotional use.
For details write to Special Sales Manager at MBI Publishing
Company, Galtier Plaza, Suite 200, 380 Jackson Street,
St. Paul, MN 55101-3885 USA

Library of Congress Cataloging-in-Publication Data

Lamm, John.
  Velocity : supercar revolution / John Lamm.
    p. cm.
  ISBN-13: 978-0-7603-2596-4 (hardbound)
  ISBN-10: 0-7603-2596-0 (hardbound)
  1. Sports cars. I. Title.
  TL236.L354 2006
  629.222'1—dc22

                              2006018892

Edited by Darwin Holmstrom
Designed by Mandy Iverson
Jacket Design by Tom Heffron

Printed in China

On the cover:
Ford recreated a legend with its GT.

On the endpapers:
Lamborghini's Miura and Ferrari's Daytona kicked off the whole
supercar movement.

On the frontispiece:
Steve Saleen's S7 is an all-American supercar.

On the title pages:
The Mercedes-Benz SLR of 2004 remained faithful to the company's
Vision show car of 1999, right down to the flip-up doors.

On the back cover, top to bottom:
Ferrari Daytona
Lamorghini Countach
Porsche 959
Pagani Zonda
Bugatti Veyron

CONTENTS

FOREWORD

Exotic Cars cars are near and dear to my heart. I have been involved with them since the 1970s, and I have delighted in driving them and writing about them for *Road & Track* during these many years. I have also very much enjoyed working with John Lamm for more than 30 years. He is a special talent in the world of automotive journalism, because he is both an excellent writer and among the most highly respected automotive photographers in the world.

John and I have traveled the world together on many assignments, and his knowledge and understanding of these exotic cars is without parallel. Add to that his enthusiasm for going anywhere to get the job done, his love for his craft, and his determination to do it right, and the result is this remarkable book you hold in your hands.

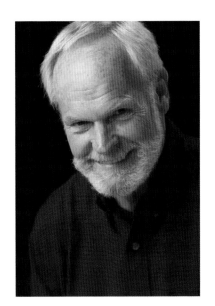

Thos L. Bryant
Editor-in-Chief
Road & Track Magazine

ACKNOWLEDGMENTS

This book covers the work of three decades so the chances are I've forgotten someone who helped me and to them my deepest apologies. Thanks to Bill Baker, Chris Bangle, Richard Baron, Michael Baumann, Toscan Bennett, Klaus Bischof, Thos L. Bryant, Luca Dal Monte, Ian Callum, Harry Calton, Anne-Hélène Casse, John Clinard, Geoff Day, Pietro DiFranchi, Bill Donnelly, Jeffrey Ehoodin, Leonardo Fioravanti, Sergio Fontana, Paul Frere, Marcello Gandini, Jack Gerkin, Antonio Ghini, Joe Grecco, Bernd Harling, Phil Hill, Dominik Hoberg, Patrick Hong, Georges Keller, Davide Kluzer, Doug Kott, Ralph Lauren, Richard Losee, Rob Mitchell, Rob Moran, Sandro Munari, Gordon Murray, Ken Okuyama, Horace Pagani, Chuck Queener, Mark Reinwald, Allan Rosenberg, Alois Ruf, Joe Sackey, Steve Saleen, Michael Schimpke, Murray Smith, Ken Sodowsky, Frank Stephenson, and Bert Swift. A special thank you to Jay Leno for his personal comments about many of the cars. Thanks also to Tim Parker for his help in developing the concept for this book.

INTRODUCTION

VELOCITY: swiftness, quickness of motion, speed imparted to something

We were headed downhill, so when the throttle fell open we quickly gained speed and things got tense. The brakes were questionable and the wheels were making a funny noise. Thank goodness world driving champion Phil Hill was driving or we might have ended up . . . I hate to think about the last part of that sentence. Velocity can be scary stuff when it gets out of hand.

By the way, we were in an 1893 Benz Victoria that topped out around 30 miles per hour, which was also scary because velocity is also a relative thing. Relative velocity is also relatively inexpensive in any era, but if you want to test the upper limits you need to slip into the somewhat rarified air of supercars or, as some prefer, exotic cars.

There have been super and exotic automobiles from the beginning. In its time, Gottlieb Daimler's 1886 huffing and puffing single-cylinder Patent Motorwagen was exotic, and it must have been super to get from point A to B without looking at the backside of a horse. Automotive history is riddled with other examples of great machines such as Stutz Bearcats, Mercedes-Benz SSKs, Bugatti Type 57s, Duesenberg SJs, 8C2900B Alfa Romeos, and generations of hot rods that will get your heart pumping faster than a gallon of espresso.

After World War II, the line never lost speed, with Chrysler 300s, Mercedes-Benz 300SLs, Maseratis, Jaguars, and—of course—Ferraris.

It can be argued that you can't get any more exotic than the Ferrari Superfasts. Very exclusive, they were built as one-offs or in small series. The very first one in 1956 was wrapped in Pininfarina bodywork that would stop you in your tracks. Its drivetrain was straight out of a Ferrari 410 Sport Spyder race car. Talk about velocity. . . .

Some would argue that this book should begin with the start of series Ferrari production, with the 250GT Lussos, the 275/330 GTCs, and 275 GTBs, while across town in Modena, Italy, Maserati was crafting the beautiful Giorgetto Giugiaro–designed Ghibli. Others would suggest that we throw in the Cobra Daytona coupe and Corvette Grand Sport.

Yet somehow the modern era of super and exotic cars seems to flow from one day in March 1966, when the Lamborghini Miura was unveiled at the Geneva Auto Show. On this day, everyone's attention was diverted from Ferrari by what some still consider the most evocative automotive shape ever penned, and by the fact that a 320-horsepower engine sat sideways behind the driver and when you'd gotten through all five gears, you were at 163 miles per hour.

Ferrari was shaken. There was an honest alternative to the Prancing Horse . . . the charging bulls of Lamborghini.

The modern supercar and exotic car wars were on . . . and that's where *Velocity* begins.

SECTION I
THE FIRST WAVE
1967–1978

155–190
MILES PER HOUR

CHAPTER 1

Lamborghini's Miura (left) and Ferrari's Daytona mark the beginning of the modern supercar era. Lamborghini took the engineering lead by giving the Miura a mid-mounted transverse V-12 engine.

LAMBORGHINI MIURA AND FERRARI DAYTONA 1967

163 AND 173
MILES PER HOUR

As the crow flies, Enzo "Commendatore" Ferrari and Ferruccio Lamborghini worked only 17 miles apart, but their thinking was on different planets.

Enzo Ferrari was conservative, so his 365 GTB/4 Daytona had a front engine and rear drive. Ferrari always said the horse belongs in the front of the chariot. The car drove like a traditional Ferrari, with wonderful mechanical noises from the V-12 ahead of you, a tall shift lever in a metal gate to your right, and when you punched the throttle you were pulled along by powerful forces. With speed, you sensed you were in the last car of the roller coaster.

No photo can capture the sound of the Miura's V-12 hunkered down under those amazing rear window louvers.

Ferruccio Lamborghini was a former Ferrari owner who badly wanted to trump the Commendatore. So he approved the nontraditional Miura with a mid-mounted engine and a low nose that offered a widescreen view of the road. The Lamborghini's snarling V-12, sideways in back, seemed to propel you ahead. You were in the roller coaster's front car.

Such different racehorses from basically the same breeding grounds. . . .

Great cultural changes influenced automobile design in the early 1960s, and different countries seemed to lead the way in various sectors. The English headed the mid-engine movement in race cars. Porsche did the best job of cheating the wind. American tire companies seemed to make their products wider each week. And with a few notable exceptions, like Jaguar's E-Type, the Italians held the high ground in exterior design.

This latter trend wasn't a new one and it was surprisingly localized. Perhaps because their grandfathers were famous for shaping metal pots, suits of armor, and gun barrels, young men in the area around the northern Italian city of Torino seemed to have a way with forming automotive bodywork. Giovanni Angelli had established Fiat in Torino, giving the locals plenty of metal to shape. It was no accident that automotive design houses Pininfarina, Bertone, Ghia, and Italdesign are a short drive from each other in greater Torino.

Let's narrow it down even more. Between January and August 1938, three male *bambini*, Leonardo Fioravanti, Marcello Gandini, and Giorgetto Giugiaro, were born near Torino. Combined, this trio of designers was responsible for—among many others—the

One of the more shocking things about the Miura design is the car's size. Overall length of the Lamborghini is 171.6 inches and width is 69.3 inches, but the Miura's height is a mere 41.5 inches.

The Miura first appeared as a bare chassis at the Turin Auto Show in late 1965. Engineers Giampaolo Dallara and Paolo Stanzani worked after hours with Bob Wallace to create the spectacular mid-engine chassis.

A transverse 60-degree V-12 resides under the Miura's rear cover. In the original Miura, the engine spun out 350 horsepower.

Lamborghini Countach; Ferrari Dino, Boxer, and 308; Lotus Esprit; Detomaso Mangusta; DeLorean; BMW M1; Alfa Romeo Carabo; Lancia Stratos; Lamborghini Miura; and Ferrari Daytona.

Now move ahead to mid-1964, as Lamborghini engineers Gianpaolo Dallara (who makes Indy Racing League chassis today) and Paolo Stanzani conspired after hours with ace mechanic and test driver Bob Wallace to create a mid-engine exotic car. Though ever more common in race cars, this powertrain layout had not yet been used in a series production sports machine—yet Ferruccio Lamborghini approved the project.

A chassis was ready for the Turin Motor Show in late 1965 and labeled the P400 (*posteriore* 4.0-liter engine). Based on a boxed central frame of sheet steel, with extensions front and back for the drivetrain and upper and lower A-arm suspensions, the platform looked simple and elegant with its lightening holes. The company's 4.0-liter, twin-cam V-12 was mounted transversely behind the driver, the five-speed gearbox combined in a cast-housing with the crankcase and their mutual lubricating oil. While considered a fascinating and promising study, the chassis was missing two crucial elements: bodywork and a name.

Designer Marcello Gandini was only in his 20s when his boss, Nuccio Bertone of Carrozzeria Bertone, brought him the challenge of the new Lamborghini. He remembers,

"After the P400 was presented at the Turin Motor Show in 1965, Mr. Lamborghini, with engineers Dallara and Stanzani, contacted Carrozzeria Bertone for a body for this chassis, which had a racing car definition. At first glance it was clear that we could make a very sporty car out of it."

What were his instructions? "There was no brief at this time, but we all agreed that the body had to underline—and not hide—the evident and aggressive muscles of the frame."

Gandini, who later designed the body for Lamborghini's Countach, calls the Miura "a good synthesis of the tradition of the famous sporty car from the 1950s and 1960s, but interpreted in a modern way. And that's why everybody liked it. This car was interesting and new enough to amaze, but with soft shapes that gave to the eye a certain pleasure." He adds, "This wasn't the case with the Countach, which was more bothering, at least at a first glance, in its unusual shapes."

Designer Marcello Gandini calls his Miura, "A good synthesis of the tradition of the famous sporty car from the 1950s and 1960s, but interpreted in a modern way."

When the Geneva Auto Show opened in March 1966, the P400 had its exotic bodywork, including retracting headlamps with eyebrows and flaming orange paintwork, and a name—Miura—from a breed of Spanish fighting bulls. The reviews were excellent and the car established Lamborghini once and for all as a potential rival for Ferrari.

There has been some controversy over the part Giorgetto Giugiaro played in the design of the Miura. The first person to dispel such rumors is Giugiaro himself, who quickly points out that he left the company in November 1965 for Ghia. Gandini took his place, and the Miura was unveiled at Geneva the following March.

JAY LENO ON THE *LAMBORGHINI MIURA*

This is going to sound dumb," Jay Leno begins, "but I think the most important part is its fatal flaw. The Miura is sort of like, well, you know there are guys who are white knights. They meet a beautiful waitress who has problems or a stripper who is screwed up and they just have to rescue them and save them. The deeper they get, the more in love they fall, the more problems there are. It's the same thing with the Miura."

Example?

"I've got an early production car and every time you go around left-hand corners the oil pressure drops, so you learn how to deal with the problem. Consequently, it makes you more involved with the car.

"It's what I call the Betty Crocker theory of automotive involvement. In the '50s, the Betty Crocker people came out with a cake mix where all women had to do was add water and mix it up. They couldn't sell any of them. Then someone said, 'Why don't you make them break two eggs, add milk and water.' They did and women bought them and were making cakes left and right because they felt like they were really baking a cake.

"When you're driving a Miura and it breaks down and you fix it and you get home, you feel like you've won a race. You're involved and there's a great deal of satisfaction with that sort of thing.

"I have two Miuras, one being the early car, a 1967. It was Dean Martin's. He bought the car new for his son who took it to school, went over a berm or something, cracked the crankcase and the engine seized. Then it was given to a friend of mine who was a school teacher at the time. He couldn't afford to fix it and to show you how little Miuras were worth—this was back in the early '80s—he said, 'Do you want it? The engines gone.' I took it, fixed the motor and got it running, but it's a really primitive car. The chassis flexes

Giugiaro had, however, spent six years at Bertone working with its team, creating a mid-engine style for the design house that has been part of the Miura's legacy. He recalls that the strong economy of the 1960–1963 period prompted many new automobiles, and that several automakers wanted to be in the race to build the first mid-engine production car.

Giotto Bizzarrini was a likely candidate, but lacked funds. Alessandro De Tomaso also wanted Giugiaro, by way of Bertone, to create a mid-engine model, but money proved to be a problem there too. Nuccio Bertone, being a good manager, realized that the logical automaker to build the first mid-engine car was Lamborghini.

and things you wouldn't tolerate now, like no crash protection, aren't included. It's all done for the sake of good looks.

"Get going real fast, anything over 125 mph, and you can actually sort of move the steering wheel on a straight road and the car doesn't turn. It gets that light and a little bit scary. Modern supercars have such high limits they aren't scary until you've crashed. You're driving along and you're going, 'Oh, I'm doing 180...it doesn't seem like 180.' Whereas in the Miura you're doing 110 and, whoa, things are moving."

"The 1969 Miura S is a much better car.

In its era the Miura was a styling sensation, Leno remembering, "When you open an old *Road & Track* and see a Miura going down the highway in 1966 with the cars of the period...'55 Chevys, '57 Cadillacs...it looks like it could go under them. I remember seeing a picture in one of the magazines of a Miura on Sunset Boulevard at a light and all these enormous cars—even cars from the late '40s were around in 1965—and thinking, geez what is that?

"And it cost $22,000, which barely gets you a Solstice now.

"I remember I was driving my Miura one day and I looked in the rearview mirror and I go, 'It's raining...damn.' Then I looked out the front and it's not raining in the front. I realized what had happened was that one of the carburetor hoses had popped off and was spraying the rear window with gas. I pulled over, opened the back and heard 'ping...ping...ping' as gas hit the exhaust manifold. All I've got is this stupid little Haylon fire extinguisher. Luckily the car didn't start on fire.

"People just don't have those sorts of adventures anymore."

The Miura interior styling matched its exterior, with seats that look straight out of the 1960s, an arcing top to the center console, and the lever for the five-speed transmission set in a metal gate.

Before Giugiaro's departure, Nuccio Bertone asked him to design a mid-engine car. He was given the car's dimensions, the packaging of the engine, the pedals, and the steering, but not a name, though he suspected it might be Bizzarrini. He points out that the transition to a mid-engine sports-car layout was more of a technical problem for engineers rather than designers. And like several men involved in the first mid-engine designs, Giugiaro reveals, "The Ford GT40 [the early racing version], with respect to the development of sports cars of the time, was very important to us."

What did Giugiaro think when he first saw the Miura? "It was an impressive work, a brand new kind of sports car." He explains, "You can say many things about the Miura; you can like it for some things, you can dislike it, but the greatest achievement is that he found a way to put sporty racing cars on the street in a very successful way and for the first time.

"The Miura was the first to have the driver's position put so far forward," Giugiaro adds. This presented a new ratio between fundamental dimensions, like front and rear overhang and the placement of cockpit and engine bay, so "optically it was a real breakthrough." The Lamborghini also provided a psychological impact, according to Giugiaro. "The idea of a long hood was associated with prestige and luxury, so taking the engine back and changing this proportion while still having a serious, racy car really was a breakthrough."

After Giugiaro went to Ghia, Alessandro De Tomaso finally got his Giugiaro-designed mid-engine car, the Mangusta. Giugiaro points out that because he had already given his ideas to Bertone for the earlier mid-engine car, he was constrained when it came time to design the Mangusta. He wanted it to be different from the rounded shapes he had done at Bertone, and made an "absolute effort"—laying the windscreen back, moving the B-pillar—to visually separate the two cars.

Where the Lamborghini Miura pointed ahead with both its chassis layout and exterior design, the Ferrari Daytona was more conservative but also designed in such a way as to separate it from its predecessors.

The Daytona's is a simpler story than the Miura's. It was 1965 and Leonardo Fioravanti was a young designer at Pininfarina with a very active imagination and a lot of independence to do what he liked, when "one day there arrived at Pininfarina in Grugliasco a mechanical chassis complete with wheels, engine, steering wheel, and fuel

tank. By chance I saw it immediately after it was discharged from the truck. I was shocked, thinking that until this moment we were completely wrong."

Fioravanti can't recall the project he was working on at the time, but he immediately put it aside. "I was driven by an extreme desire to design a new Ferrari. So I worked one week continuously. My wife only saw me late in the evening. Finally I finished my work . . . three to four views, some perspectives."

Presented with the drawings, Sergio Pininfarina was a bit surprised, and the designer recalls him saying, " 'A Ferrari? But there is no plan for a new Ferrari.' I explained why I did it, and finally he looked at the design and was very impressed. Soon after, Mr. Pininfarina met Mr. Ferrari and told him, 'We have a possibility to propose to you— a new GTB.' "

For all the Miura's power and potential, the factory never raced it. Some critics argue that Ferruccio Lamborghini's refusal to go racing kept this company from challenging cross-town rival Ferrari.

Enzo Ferrari was interested, possibly because his current grand touring model, the 275 GTB/4, wasn't selling that well. In this decade when a very nice GTB sells for $400,000, that seems so odd, but those were the times.

Fioravanti explains it from his perspective: "To me the 275 GTB/4 wasn't the best Ferrari. Now it is considered one of the best, but to me it was a bit too old, not with the best proportion on the side. It was strong evolution on all the themes from Ferrari's past."

Ferrari gave permission to start on the new car using the GTB chassis, which meant

The staff of *Road & Track* admitted the Daytona was not the most exotic car in the world, but declared it to be, " . . . the best sports car in the world. Or the best GT. Take your choice, it's both." When new, a Daytona cost $19,500, a small percentage of what one is worth today.

a steel tube frame, independent upper and lower A-arm suspension at both ends, and that most sublime of powerplants, the Ferrari V-12, now in 365 twin-cam form with 4.4 liters and 405 brake horsepower. While that classic layout meant the new car would be technically less interesting than the Miura, it brought with it a heritage and almost mystical aura that Lamborghinis had never had, thanks to Ferruccio Lamborghini's anti-racing policy.

As it turned out, the most difficult part of the Daytona design was the front, because the GTB chassis proved to be too narrow for its length. Seen on a 1:1 model, the original design looked quite nice, but as Fioravanti recalls, "the main criticism was the front. Very disappointing. Too thin. Too high from the ground. In my view, too old."

On one of his rare trips outside of Maranello, Enzo Ferrari visited Pininfarina in Torino to see the full-size Daytona model. He liked what he saw, Fioravanti recounts, "but he said, 'Wider track, please.' I don't remember if it was 6 or 8 centimeters, but in any case it was enormous. More than in the tradition of Ferrari, where modifications were very small."

Another fundamental change being made on the Daytona involved the use of a grille other than the traditional oval egg-crate type. While it wasn't easy to convince Enzo Ferrari to agree to the changes, perhaps the slow sales of the 275 GTB swayed him.

Fioravanti also designed the new GTB's interior, but he explains, "Like the other Ferraris I did, there are no drawings of the interior. I put in the car what I got from the

Ferrari people: the best driving position possible, the dials, gearbox, steering wheel, changing as little as possible." There were drawings for seat stitching and vent holes, but that was about it.

"Finally we went for the official launch at the 1968 Paris Auto Show with a new metallic red," the designer continues, and the 365 GTB/4 ". . . was a very big success."

But the Daytona, its nickname derived from the 1-2-3 win of Ferrari 330/P4s at that track in January 1968, was also criticized. Its sin? A front-mounted engine. Ferrari already had the mid-V-6 Dino 206/246—also with bodywork by Fioravanti—and the press expected a mid-big-engine Ferrari answer to the Miura, which was already two years old.

These harsh criticisms were expected at Pininfarina. In fact, many of the influential people at Pininfarina had been trying for years to convince Enzo Ferrari to do such a mid-engine car. "We discussed this with the Commendatore many times," Fioravanti recalls, "and we were ready to design a big Ferrari with a mid-engine, but the Commendatore was not absolutely sure."

What was his objection? "He was against it because the legend said the horse is in front of the chariot."

When the P400 (Miura) chassis was presented at Turin in late 1965, "We [Pininfarina] were completely destroyed. This was a chassis for a very innovative design. We spoke immediately with the Commendatore. At the beginning he was even more contrary about the mid-engine car because Lamborghini was an ex-Ferraristi."

In March 1966, the complete Miura was unveiled. "I was very impressed. This was a new car, like the Dino, but bigger." And yet Ferrari's resistance was such that it wasn't until 1968 that Pininfarina responded to the Miura with the Fioravanti-designed P6 mid-engine V-12 show car, which would prove to be the prototype for the Berlinetta Boxer.

These days, Fioravanti ranks the Daytona as his favorite design, but then makes a somewhat typical designer's comment about this beautiful Ferrari. "When I finished this car in 1965, I was terrified. Horrible. Now when I see a Daytona I like it, but I see only the faults."

In the Daytona design, Giorgetto Giugiaro found what he calls the huge legacy of a great sports edition of the period ". . . and it was a very rich period. It was an appealing and impressive sports car with a great emotional impact. It was really a reference to building a sports car, as was the Jaguar E-Type."

This Daytona has the traditional Borrani wire wheels, which were a feature of the earliest cars. Later cars featured alloy wheels designed for Ferrari by Cromodora that became so famous the shape was used on other cars, where they are simply called, "Daytona wheels."

Road & Track (R&T) found both the Miura and the Daytona to be benchmark exotic cars. In its May 1968 road test, the magazine called the Lamborghini, ". . . the most glamorous, exciting, and prestigious sports car in the world." Okay, the mid-engine Miura wasn't perfect, particularly the gearbox, but with 0–60-mile-per-hour time coming up in 6.3 seconds (the S version would cut that to 5.5) and a top speed of 163 miles per hour, the magazine concluded the mid-engine Lamborghini, at $21,000, ". . . has its faults but every enthusiast should have at least one Miura."

When *R&T* tested Ferrari's 365 GTB/4, it admitted this car also wasn't faultless, but nonetheless concluded it was ". . . the best sports car in the world. Or the best GT. Take your choice; it's both." Maybe it was the $19,500 car's stunning looks, the 5.9 seconds in

In its day, a Daytona would get to 60 miles per hour in 5.4–5.9 seconds, with a top speed around 175 miles per hour, depending on the car's specifications. Ferrari didn't officially name the car Daytona, but the nickname was started to commemorate the Ferrari 330 P4's 1-2-3 win at that famous Florida track in 1967.

Leonardo Fioravanti designed both the interior and exterior of the Daytona.

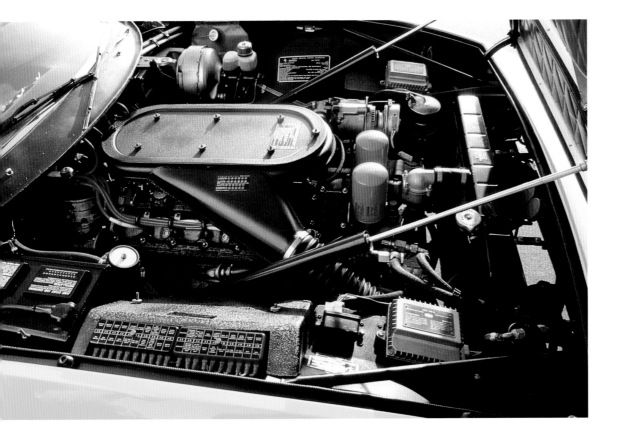

The 4.4-liter, 60-degree V-12 in the Daytona develops 405 horsepower. Six Weber 40DCN20 carburetors reside in the center of the vee.

Under that Pininfarina bodywork is a classic Ferrari chassis with unequal-length A-arm coil spring suspensions, recirculating-ball steering, and vented disc brakes.

the 0–60 or the 173-mile-per-hour top speed; whatever the reason, *R&T* loved the car and took a shot at those who objected to its front-engine layout by subheading its Daytona road test: "The fastest—and best—GT is not necessarily the most exotic."

Let's update the Miura–Daytona controversy by dropping it in the lap of two young American designers.

Freeman Thomas designed the Audi TT, moved to Chrysler to head its advanced design department, and is now the strategic design director for Ford. He loves both cars, calling the Daytona, "The last great hurrah of the great V-12 cars, and the body design expressed that, though very modernistically. The elements are classical, the long nose and the cockpit set far back, but the graphics on that form were brand-new."

As for the Miura, it was "an argument against Ferrari. It was all about being rebellious. The styling of the car is nothing short of glorious."

Leonardo Fioravanti was just 27 years old when he took on the assignment to design the Ferrari that would become the Daytona.

While the design of the Daytona has become a classic, at the time of its debut the critics were disappointed Ferrari hadn't done a mid-engine car like Lamborghini.

Though technically quite different, the Lamborghini Miura and Ferrari Daytona were successful for both companies. They showed great optimism from the Italian automakers at a time when new emissions and safety laws were making life difficult for small, specialized car companies.

The designer of Porsche's Boxster and the exterior of its Carrera GT is Milwaukee-born Grant Larson, who figures, "The Miura set a standard for future generations of mid-engine sports cars as far as the way the lines flow, especially the cut-off ducktail. It established a new form of language for mid-engine sports cars."

He admits to being a bit put off by the Daytona at first because "it represented a departure from my favorite era of Ferraris, which are those with more flowing lines up to about 1966. Regardless, I love the car because it has a very strong stance and it was a complete departure."

Which would you choose? ■

Oppostie page: Ferrari built 15 competition Daytonas, while privateers produced others. While not designed as race cars, Daytonas proved solid runners in the GT class. Here the Luigi Chinetti North American Racing Team competes in the 1973 24 Hours of Le Mans.

CHAPTER 2

Though arguably not the sort of car that tickles the imagination like Ferrari's Boxer or Lamborghini's Countach, the Maserati Bora is an undeniably handsome machine. The U.S.-mandated nose suffered slightly from the buck tooth "safety" bumpers that jutted ahead.

163
MILES PER HOUR

MASERATI BORA 1971

Thanks to its V-8, Maserati's Bora had a vaguely American sound that seemed to get more powerful the closer you got to the redline. This was 1973 and supercar acceleration wasn't as explosive as today, so you had to work harder when you drove the big Maser into a corner, then tried to top 100 miles per hour on the next straight. Work your way through the gearbox, can we make it to 100? . . . Now hard on the brakes.

The Bora was a 163-mile-per-hour car but it took a while to get there, so we tended to play in the 70–110-mile-per-hour range, which was quick enough in the canyons north of

Maserati's venerable V-8 resided behind the passenger compartment. The big carbureted twin-cam 4.7-liter engine, which had seen service in earlier race cars, was rated at 300 horsepower and 325 ft-lb of torque in the Bora.

A driver can't complain that there aren't enough dials, switches, and levers on the dash of the Bora to keep his attention. The seats lay the driver out like a chaise lounge, but provide a very comfortable ride.

Los Angeles with their gravel-strewn corners. When those cars slipped on the fallen scree there was no intervention from electronics tapping brakes or pulling back throttle to save us; they just kept slipping. We wore seatbelts, but didn't have an anti-lock braking system (ABS) or traction, and airbags were just a rumor.

Were we nuts?

Actually, Chuck Queener and I were in our late 20s, a couple of young magazine car guys thundering through the canyons in someone else's expensive (for then) Italian exotic car.

What, me worry?

It helped that the Bora had the unassuming torque of its V-8, so you could work your way up a tight and twisting hill road in just a gear or two, not having to spend much time shifting about to stay in a power band, as was necessary with some exotic cars in the early 1970s. And comforting, because driving these cars quickly took a lot of work and concentration.

And the Bora did it without growling at you. Where other mid-engine supercars would let you know their powerplant was just aft of your head—sometimes to your pleasure, sometimes not—Maserati insulated the Bora's cabin more from the V-8. The engine sound was still there, but it accompanied you and never intruded. Like a respectful friend.

A very nice automobile, but . . . .

It so happened that 1971 was the year of Italian mid-engine exotic cars and, at the Geneva Auto Show in March, Lamborghini stunned the audience with the Countach, leaving pundits to speculate how soon Ferrari would launch its big mid-engine model.

Over on the Maserati stand, almost lost in the speculation, the Bora was being tossed into the mid-engine mix, and if the Lamborghini and (expected) Ferrari were creating a splash, the Bora was kicking up ripples.

Too bad, because Maserati's early-1970s attempt at mid-engine stardom deserved better.

It certainly had the heritage, and for many years Maserati had been better known in the United States than upstart Enzo Ferrari.

The four Maserati brothers built their first race car in 1926 and produced competitive racing machines through the 1930s. When the Germans took over much of the European Grand Prix scene late that decade, Maserati found a home for its 8CTF at the Indianapolis Motor Speedway, where Wilbur Shaw drove one to win the 500 in 1939 and 1940. Masers were still competitive at the Brickyard after World War II, so when Ferrari was still just a rumor in the States, the name Maserati was familiar.

For all the corporate wealth seen on the exotic car front these days, in the decades after the war things were economically tenuous for the likes of Maserati and Ferrari. In fact, the Maserati brothers had sold out to the Orsi family in the mid-1930s and stayed on to design and build cars, but no one was getting rich.

Postwar, Maser was successful with its small A6GCS sports cars and, later, the booming V-8–powered 450S. Fangio won the Formula 1 championship in a Maserati 250F in 1957 and the company's innovative Birdcage race cars caused Ferrari fits . . . when they stayed together. It seemed that racing was the Italian specialist automaker's purpose for being, and road cars almost a necessary evil.

When the Orsi family wanted out in 1968, it sold its interest in Maserati to the French automaker Citroën, creating—at best—an odd couple.

Not wanting to miss the mid-engine exotic car craze, Citroën put Maserati's chief engineer, the highly regarded Giulio Alfieri, to work on the project that resulted in the Bora.

Giorgetto Giugiaro was commissioned to do the exterior design and his firm, Italdesign, summed up in its press release that Maserati wanted a car ". . . devoid of the exotic look that unnecessary decorations can create, strikingly sporty but not inordinately aggressive . . . innovative but not revolutionary." In other words, the French didn't want a Countach. That sort of flamboyance wouldn't be the Gallic way. By the way, how many great French exotic cars have you found in this book? And is the Bugatti really French or German?

After the French automaker Citroën bought Maserati, it wanted to get in on the mid-engine craze. Citroën hired famous designer Giorgetto Giugiaro to design the body, but the car company made it obvious it wanted to avoid the glitz and glamour of cars like the Lamborghini Countach.

The Giorgetto Giugiaro-designed Ghibli, predecessor of the mid-engine Bora, was one of the prettiest sports cars of the 1960s.

Citroën certainly got its wish. No adult male's jaw dropped open or any kid's knees went weak with delight upon seeing see a Bora. Unlike the Lambo or Ferrari Boxer, teenage boys never decorated their rooms with posters of the big Maserati.

Nonetheless, it is a beautiful piece of sculpture. Conservative and a mid-engine next-step from the front-engine Ghibli that Giugiaro also penned for Maserati, the Bora is possibly best known for its brushed stainless-steel roof and the fact that it is unerringly handsome. Whether that latter quality was enough for an exotic car was another matter altogether.

Maserati certainly stayed traditional with the engine, a 4.7-liter version of the venerable twin-cam 16-valve V-8 used way back in the 450S sports racing cars. In the Bora, it had 310 horsepower at 6,000 rpm and a sweet 325 ft-lb of torque at 4,200 rpm. For the Bora, Maser chose a ZF five-speed transmission with an ungated shifter.

Maserati's V-8 was an impressive hunk of an engine under a large one-piece rear-hinged cover, a real mechanical beaut back in the pre-fuel-injection days when the V-8 was fed by four big Weber carburetors.

For the U.S. market, Alfieri installed a 4.9-liter version of the V-8, which had been used in the Ghibli and was tamed for modernity and U.S. emissions rules in 1973 to 300 horsepower at 6,000 rpm and 310 ft-lb of torque at 3,500. That nice torque and the sound of the V-8 gave the Bora an almost American feel and sound.

Maserati had to abandon its preference for DeDion rear suspensions with the mid-engine layout, opting for the traditional upper and lower A-arm design front and rear. The brakes were unusual in that, while they were vented discs, the 9.4-inch-diameter fronts were smaller than the 9.8-inch rears.

Citroën was famous for its master hydraulic systems and applied them to the Bora, not just for the brakes but also to adjust the driver's seat and move the foot pedals 3.5 inches front or back. Though not so unusual these days, this ability to move the pedals, combined with the steering column's fore/aft and up/down adjustability, made the Bora amenable to just about any driver's physique.

In 1971 the Maserati Ghibli cost just over $22,000, about three times as much as a Corvette.

Maserati's Merak, the Bora's little brother, borrowed much from the Citroën SM. With a mid-mounted V-6 engine, the Merak cost about $10,000 less than the Bora.

Citroën borrowed the instrument panel and steering of the SM for the Maserati Merak.

You would expect to see the Bora's seats in a *Jetsons* episode, lovely long shells with leather upholstery you could settle into and that would support you well out to under your knees. The dashboard had an array of eight gauges—with a big tachometer and speedometer—and a row of rocker switches that placed the Bora in the early 1970s.

Road & Track tested a 4.7-liter European Bora that had been certified to U.S. standards at an estimated 300 horsepower and 325 ft-lb of torque. It wasn't a light car, with a curb weight of 3,570 pounds, and geared for a top speed of 163 miles per hour; nowadays its 0–60-mile-per-hour acceleration of 7.2 seconds doesn't look all that impressive.

When it went on the market in late 1971, the Bora's price was around $25,000, but by the time it was certified for the United States with the dollar dancing around European currencies, the prices elevated it into the mid-$40,000 area. Apparently between 1971 and 1979 Maserati produced 530 Boras.

While Ferrari had its big 12-cylinder Boxer and its distinctly different, smaller V-6 and then V-8 models, the Bora had a more direct little brother. Called the Merak, it shared the chassis and much of the body of the Bora, with its own flying buttress upper rear bodywork. Little brother inherited much of the equipment of the odd-but-interesting Citroën SM, including the instrument panel, the strange little bulb brake pedal, and the SM's Maserati V-6 front drivetrain turned front-to-back and mounted aft.

Price at about $10,000 less than the Bora, the Merak wasn't very quick—about 9 seconds to 60—but it was a comfortable machine.

Boras weren't necessarily automobiles to fall in love with it, but they were cars to be appreciated. Unfortunately, exotic cars need more than that for most drivers. They need to get your heart beating faster, give you a little rush, leave you a little breathless. ∎

Ferrari had the more famous name when the Bora was launched, but at one time Maserati was better known to many racing fans in the United States. The Maserati 8CTF *Boyle Special* driven by Wilbur Shaw won the Indianapolis 500 in 1939 and 1940.

CHAPTER 3

Ferrari finally made the move to a mid-engine sports car layout when it created the 365 GT4/BB, the last two initials standing for Berlinetta Boxer. The prototype was presented at the 1971 Turin Show, while the car went into production in 1973.

188
MILES PER HOUR

FERRARI BOXER 1973

Enzo Ferrari was taking a lot of heat.

Lamborghini had set the exotic-car world on fire with the mid-engine Miura in 1966, and here it was, mid-1971, and there still was no 12-cylinder mid-engine road-going Ferrari.

British race car constructor John Cooper had been the main force in the modern European move to mid-engines in the 1950s, and had done the same at the Indianapolis 500 in 1961. Throughout the 1960s, sports racing cars had shifted the engine to the rear, and the trend was being taken up by high-performance sports cars for the streets . . . but not yet by Ferrari.

Ferrari built the Pininfarina-designed Boxer at the Scaglietti factory in Modena, Italy. At the time Scaglietti, now owned by Ferrari, was an independent constructor of cars for Ferrari and other car companies.

Why go mid-engine? As winning race cars were proving, there were significant handling advantages and, with the engine in back, the frontal area could be cut significantly. It made more sense from an aerodynamic standpoint and it was easier to fit big rear tires on mid-engine machines. There were disadvantages, like minimal luggage space and poor visibility to the rear, but they were not crushing problems in exotic cars used only occasionally. Just as important, perhaps, was image. Mid-engine was the proof you were technically advanced; it was the next new thing.

Enzo Ferrari would have none of it in his road cars. He had always been conservative about engineering changes, a classic case being his refusal to adopt mid-engine technology. He'd resisted the move to disc brakes in the late 1950s, and Ferrari was the last major Grand Prix constructor to situate the engine of its race machines behind the driver. There had also been a slow transition to mid-engines with his sports racing cars, and it seemed he was making his point in June 1962 when Phil Hill and Olivier Gendebien won the 24 Hours of Le Mans in a front-engine Testarossa.

Ferrari always made the necessary changes, eventually, and when he did, he won. Hill drove Maranello's initial mid-engine GP car to a World Driver's Championship in 1961. And the mid-engine sports cars were quickly competitive, from the 1961 246 SPs, through the beautiful 330 P4s in 1967, to the victorious 312 PBs in 1971–1972.

But where, pray tell, was the 12-cylinder, mid-engine Ferrari road car?

Actually, it was at the Turin Motor Show in the autumn of 1971 as a concept car. This was another battle in the turf war being fought between local rivals Ferrari and Lamborghini. One-time Ferrari customer Ferruccio Lamborghini had again stunned the automotive world the previous spring by showing Bertone's dramatic Marcello Gandini–designed Countach LP500 show car at the Geneva Auto Show. Ferrari shot back that fall in Turin with the Berlinetta Boxer, shaped at Pininfarina by Leonardo Fioravanti on the theme of the 1968 P6 show car.

As it was, the 365 GT4/BB (BB for Berlinetta Boxer, though its common name is simply Boxer) needed two more years before deliveries began in 1973, while the Countach wasn't ready for customers until 1974. But enthusiasts certainly had something to talk about in the meantime, and both final production models were almost identical to the show cars.

At Pininfarina's design center outside Turin, Italy, Leonardo Fioravanti, designer of many famous Ferraris, poses with the Berlinetta Boxer and the car that was the inspiration for its exterior design, the Ferrari P6 show car.

It isn't just great automobiles that separate Ferrari from others, but the fact it is the only automaker that fields its own winning Grand Prix cars, building both the engine and chassis. In 1983, the Boxer's GP companion was the 126 C3 with a carbon fiber/Kevlar frame and a turbocharged 600-horsepower 1.5-liter V-6.

From a styling standpoint, the Boxer was an interesting contrast to the Countach. There is no denying the Lamborghini is spectacular, jaw-dropping, cool, and memorable, looking as though it could go nose-up and head for the moon. Arguably, however, the Boxer is more beautiful and ultimately more sensual.

Its designer was Leonardo Fioravanti, and if you worship Ferraris of the late 1960s and early 1970s, he is your idol. He penned the Daytona in his 20s and went on to shape the Dino, Boxer, and 308 GTB. And he's still at it in his 60s, working independently and getting credit for the clever folding glass top on the 2005 Ferrari 612 Superamerica. Fioravanti also designed Pininfarina's 1968 P6 show car and made the production version of it into the Boxer.

Pininfarina has been the designer of almost all major Ferraris since the mid-1950s. Integral to the design of the modern cars is aerodynamic development in Pininfarina's wind tunnel, which was one of the first modern examples in Europe.

With a long nose, great haunches, and a flying buttress rear window, the Boxer had a more graceful form than the aggressive Countach. It was also rather easier to drive as there wasn't so much automobile around you, so you didn't feel quite as encapsulated in it. It also had rather large windows that made outward vision better than in other exotics.

The interior was just what you'd expect in an exotic car: easily read gauges set deep enough to avoid glare and switchgear that, today, looks a bit archaic, but took up little room and, for the most part, had a firm, positive feel. As an example of how simple things were then, the sun visors rolled up and down like window shades and, when unrolled, were held in place by suction cups. In fairness, road testers of the day complained about the lack of flexibility of the interior, forcing the driver to adapt to it rather than the other way around. No eight-way power seats or adjustable lumbar supports in the Boxer.

It was important that as Ferrari's mightiest road car, the Boxer should have a 12-cylinder engine. There was a mid-mounted V-12 in the P6, but the BB had a flat-12, otherwise known as a "boxer" engine: hence the car's name. Ferrari race cars had been using flat-12s

With the 512 version of the flat-12, the Berlinetta Boxer could scoot to 60 miles per hour in just over 5.0 seconds, on its way to a top speed of 188 miles per hour. For its final three years, the 512 engine was fitted with Bosch fuel injection, allowing it to meet ever-tightening emissions laws.

since 1964, and they were particularly successful in the early 1970s with the 312 PB race cars, which won the World Sports Car Championship in 1972.

Why a flat engine? Its shortness lowered the aerodynamic profile of the car and put the engine weight lower in the chassis, dropping the center of gravity.

Although Ferrari adopted the flat-engine layout for the Boxer, it didn't adapt a racing engine to the production car. Instead, engineers basically took the company's aluminum V-12, with its traditional 60-degree vee between cylinder banks, and opened that angle to 180 degrees.

As the car's official designation 365 GT4/BB suggests, the Boxer had the same 4.4-liter displacement as its predecessor, the 365 GTB/4 Daytona, even keeping the 81x71-millimeter bore and stroke and 8.8:1 compression ratio of the V-12.

It was an impressive engine, particularly with the air cleaners off, its two banks of paired three-throat Weber carburetors standing rather proudly atop it. Where the factory claimed 352 horsepower for the Daytona's V-12, it pegged the Boxer's at 380.

Just as the Countach had a unique engine-transmission layout with its five-speed ahead of the V-12, the Boxer was also unusual in that the five-speed was located below the flat-12; it was actually a part of the engine.

The frame of the Boxer was a cage of steel tubing, and while the Boxer's hood, rear deck, and doors were aluminum, the remainder of the body was steel. Its suspension had upper and lower A-arms at each corner with coil springs and tube shocks. The brakes were discs inside Cromodora wheels.

As exciting as the Boxer might have been, it wasn't meant for the United States, in which Ferrari never officially sold the car. In the early 1970s, huge automakers, such as General Motors and Ford, were struggling with new laws meant to lower engine emissions and increase road safety, but small companies like Ferrari and Lamborghini were downright flummoxed by the rules.

Other men weren't. As automobiles like the Boxer and early Countach were kept from the United States, a small industry was created to certify them for sale there. It was complicated work. New structures had to be created inside bumpers to absorb the shock of mandated crash tests, hopefully without making the cars' ends butt ugly. Huge Weber carburetors had to be retuned, camshafts often reground, and catalytic converters plugged into exhaust systems in an attempt to get engine emissions down to the federal limits.

To power the Berlinetta Boxer, Ferrari engineers took the company's famous 60-degree V-12 and opened the angle between cylinder banks to 180 degrees, making it a flat or "boxer" engine, a layout the factory had been using on race cars since the 1964 512 Formula 1 engine.

Some of the men who did these conversions were very clever and their work was impeccable. Some were scam artists. Some managed to make the conversions without adding huge masses of weight to the cars' ends (not the best thing for handling) and draining too much horsepower. Some made a mess of the "safety" bumpers and created monsters that met the legal emissions standards, but would barely run in everyday traffic.

The feds kept an ever more vigilant eye on this business of "grey market" cars and, by the mid-1980s, had almost eliminated it with ever stiffer laws and penalties. By the time the very desirable Porsche 959 came along in 1989, no one was even trying to certify it. That would wait for new rules at the turn of the century—but more on that in the chapter about the 959.

Back to the Boxer. In 1976, Ferrari increased the displacement of the flat-12, opening the bore 1 millimeter and the stroke 7 millimeters to create the 5.0-liter Boxer 512. It also

A classic photo from Ferrari's Fiorano test track, as a Boxer kicks sideways coming out of the hairpin. The automaker opened this advanced test facility in 1972 and the 512 Boxer was one of the first production Ferraris to benefit from development on the track, which the engineers share with the company's Formula 1 team.

Inside, the Boxer was typical for its time, with complete instrumentation set tightly in a pod and the expected tall shift lever.

changed its number system: while the 365 designation in the previous model referred to the displacement of one cylinder (so 12 x 365 = 4.4 liters), the new one meant a 5-liter, 12-cylinder engine.

Anti-emissions laws were taking hold throughout Europe, too, lowering pollution and horsepower. So despite the greater displacement and a 9.2:1 compression ratio, the 512 BB had 360 horsepower—down 20 from the 365—but with about a 10 percent increase in torque. Ferrari also made this version a dry sump engine to lower it a bit in the car to take better advantage of the flat engine's low center of gravity. The car was also a bit wider at the back to accommodate rear tires that were now larger than the front ones (215/70VR-15 front, 225/70VR-15 rear). There were also a few exterior changes, like a new front spoiler and added ducts.

Road & Track tested both 4.4- and 5.0-liter Boxers in the United States: the former uncertified (and, as a result, getting the owner in trouble with the feds when they saw the road test), and the latter nicely reworked to meet the rules. Both cost around $40,000 new, while the 512 BB had some $45,000 in conversions to make it legal.

For the sake of the 365's clutch (and owner), the tester had to ease the car off the line, so the 0–60 time of 7.2 seconds was neither impressive nor truly representative . . . but that was the way supercars were in the early 1970s. They didn't like drag-racing starts, being much happier ripping their way past 100 miles per hour. These cars were happiest when run at or near maximum velocity.

The 512 was up to the task, and got to 60 in 5.5 seconds. The 365's top speed was estimated at 175, the 512 at 188, and I know for a fact that the latter achieved 155 with little strain and with plenty left. The guy who did it for *Road & Track* on a quiet Orange County highway just couldn't wipe the smile off his face.

R&T did another test—one of its most famous—when it pitted a 512 BB against a Countach at the high-banked Transportation Research Center track in Ohio. Both cars were legalized machines, so they were a bit down on factory-claimed power but proved quick nonetheless. *R&T* cut the Ferrari's 0–60 time down to 5.1 seconds against the

In the 1979 24 Hours of Le Mans, this was the best-finishing Ferrari 512 Berlinetta Boxer. Drivers Steve O'Rourke from England and Belgians Bernard de Dryver and Jean "Beurlys" Blaton, one of the most famous Ferrari GT drivers, came in 12th overall and 5th in the IMSA class.

This is one of the factory-built "silhouette" 512 Berlinetta Boxer race cars. Compared to the street 512 BB, the "LM" (Le Mans) versions had Pininfarina-smoothed bodywork, added inlets, a rear spoiler, and an extra 16 inches of length. This car was first sold to an American, Bob Donner; it finished ninth overall at Le Mans in 1981.

In addition to being lighter than stock at somewhere shy of 2,400 pounds, the racing Boxers got a horsepower increase to 480–500 horsepower, which was enough to propel the spectacular-looking Ferraris to just over 200 miles per hour.

Lamborghini's 5.7 seconds, after which race driver Sam Posey took the Boxer to 168 miles per hour and the Countach to 150.

With another nod at still stricter emissions laws around the world, Ferrari did one more variation on the Boxer: the 1981 512 BBi, the little "i" meaning it now had Bosch K-Jetronic fuel injection. While this helped meet the rules and made the cars easier to maintain, it cut another 20 horsepower, bringing the 5.0-liter engine down to 340.

This would be only a three-year model, leading up to the Testarossa.

In a Boxer it always felt odd that the tall shift lever and the slim rim (by today's standards) steering wheels should be attached to such powerful stuff. It might have been the fact that this engine seemed to growl more than most exotic cars, sounding as though it was trying to attack you from right behind the cockpit.

Today's supercars are meant to feel like they are of one chunk—hefty, buffed up, and packed like a fighter jet with electronics that will help you go faster, yet save your backside if you get stupid.

The Boxer had a more athletic feel to it, less like a power lifter than a sprinter. You didn't so much power off the line as let the engine wind out while the revs climbed. Exotic cars then weren't as blindingly quick or sudden as they are today—not so much immediate gratification off the line. Instead, they tested you down the road as it bent left and right, rose and fell, the car on narrow, less grippy tires and with no electronic aids to save your bacon if you screwed up. You didn't go as fast in those days, but to be truly quick you had to be more talented than today.

Sorry, boys, but that's the truth.

Even though the Boxer wasn't sold in the United States, the first attempts to race a 365 GT4/BB were based there. Long-time U.S. Ferrari importer and three-time winner of Le Mans, Luigi Chinetti prepped a pair in the mid-1970s, but other than a sixth at Daytona in 1975, the effort wasn't terribly successful.

The factory stepped up in 1978 to build three 512 BB LMs (Le Mans) for that French race. With only minor body modifications, they were good-looking race cars that had shed weight down to around 2,700 pounds and had 440 brake horsepower, though none finished the race.

Pininfarina got involved the following year when regulations allowed GT race cars more variation from the stock versions. Shaped in Pininfarina's wind tunnel, these Series II and III 512 BB LMs were wider and 16 inches longer—mostly at the tail—and had smoother, much more aerodynamic bodywork. Horsepower was upped to 480–500, weight was cut still more, but as spectacular as they looked and despite a top speed of just over 200 miles per hour, they were never as successful as they looked like they should be.

The Pininfarina mid-engine design set the pattern for a generation of Ferrari sports cars.

In 1984, Ferrari replaced the Boxer with the Testarossa, retaining the mid-flat-12 layout. Still a supercar, it was fully certified for sale throughout the world. Many of us went "Wow" when we saw the Testarossa's Pininfarina styling, which was spectacular and somehow seemed to cater to the inner tingles that made Countachs so popular.

A great car, but somehow it made us miss the Boxer. ▥

CHAPTER 4

This is the second Countach prototype and the oldest existing Countach. It was originally red, but Lamborghini repainted the car green for presentation at the 1973 Paris Auto Show.

180
MILES PER HOUR

Today there's too much traffic to rush along that road near the Lamborghini factory, but not in 1988. Then there was plenty of open space for Sandro Munari to show me how Lamborghini test drivers scared the daylights out of the clients of their 180-mile-per-hour Countachs for years.

Munari is a four-time world rally champion and one of the world's great car control experts. For several years he also led Lamborghini public relations, which is why he was driving the Countach as we hurried down the dead-straight road toward Modena.

Race cars of the late 1960s, which were shaped more for function than for beauty, influenced Italian Marcello Gandini's design of the Countach. Gandini said of his design that he wanted "people to be astonished when they saw the car." They were.

We left the factory briskly, to say the least—down somewhere around the 5.0-second 0–60 time—and kept up a good head of steam as we crested a small rise in the road. The Lambo felt a bit lighter and then . . . *good grief! There's a hard left turn ahead!*

I knew it was coming and Sandro could handle it, but I gulped nonetheless. Hard on the brakes, he drove us forward into our seatbelts and pitched the big Countach left through the tight turn, smoothly caught it and, bang, back on the throttle. The hunk-of-a-V-12 was wide awake and we squirted down a short straight to a 90-degree right

Like any true big Italian exotic car of its day, the Countach has a V-12, which began as a 4.0-liter, was increased to 4.7 liters, and then to 5.2. The latter version had four valves per cylinder, and horsepower rose to 455. The engine sits "backward" in the car, its transmission jutting forward into the cockpit.

where Sandro deftly nailed the apex and we were quickly out the other side, flying toward Modena.

I had always wanted to do that.

In automotive history, there have been exotic cars with more impressive engineering, a flashier time to 60 miles per hour, a greater technical portfolio, and even higher top speeds than the Lamborghini Countach, but none have captured the public's attention like the big Lambo.

Stunningly sleek as a show car, tarted up in its later years, the big Lamborghini stole and broke hearts around the world. It was the poster boy for all supercars; it was their Elvis.

With the Miura, Ferruccio Lamborghini began seriously sparring with Ferrari in 1966, and now came back with what might have been a serious body blow if only it hadn't taken so long to land the punch.

Lamborghini had outmaneuvered Ferrari by showing the mid-engine Countach LP500 at the 1971 Geneva Show, six months before the similarly laid-out Berlinetta Boxer debuted. Even before the public saw the big Lambo it had apparently stunned onlookers. Other Lamborghinis had been named after famous fighting bulls. Countach is a somewhat off-color Piemontese (language spoken by many people in northwest Italy) expletive of surprise uttered by one of those who saw it early on.

The forward-leaning top edge of the rear wheel opening is a signature of designer Marcello Gandini. Behind those alloy wheels are vented disc brakes. The tires of the early 1970s look almost impossibly narrow today.

Marcello Gandini takes the credit for that surprise, having shaped the Countach while working for the design firm Bertone. This wasn't a one-trick pony for Gandini, who also gets credit for such important automobiles as the Maserati Khamsin, Fiat X1/9, Ferrari 308GT/4, Lancia Stratos, and the car that first used the now famous swing-up doors, the Alfa Romeo Carabo.

Those first LP 400 Countachs earned their glory, so low and wide, arcing strongly from front to back, the two-seat jet fighter cockpit, just enough louvers, Gandini's signature forward-leaning rear wheel arches. Later, Lamborghini would yield to faddish spoilers and other add-ons that corrupted what Gandini first drew.

The Alfa Romeo Carabo, first seen at the Paris Auto Show in October 1968, is arguably the most influential exotic show car of the modern era. Like the Countach, it was designed by Marcello Gandini.

BMW's design director, Chris Bangle, echoes the feelings of many of us when he says, "A Countach in anything other than its original form is so *Pimp My Ride* it's almost impossible to discern the original."

Bangle refers to supercars like the Countach as having a look of "post-atomic technology. How did Gandini do cars like the Lamborghini Countach or Bertone Stratos show car I thought were so cool?" he asks. And then he explains: "He took the things you could exaggerate—like the wheel-to-car relationship, the lowness and wideness of the car—and exaggerated the hell out of them. Getting in and out of the Stratos [concept car]—a car that could drive underneath my chair—would be difficult, but you were expected to go through some agony to get in and out of them, and that agony was pleasurable."

To Bangle, true supercars are those that shock us—that make us take extra notice. "Cars that are so politically incorrect, no possible physical reason for being, they are the supercars."

This taillight is the view most drivers saw of a Countach in its early days. Few automobiles have managed to match the public impact of the Countach.

Gandini drew his inspiration for the big mid-engine automobile from the sports racing cars of the day. He thought that race cars had changed in the late 1960s, and while they had improved, they had become more functional and were no longer beautiful for the sake of beauty. They needed lovely lines less, aerodynamics more—to keep them from flying off the road at high speed. Such race cars became wild-looking, in the manner of the long-tail Porsche 917s. Gandini said, "If there was a car that inspired the Countach a little bit, it was the Lola T70 Coupe." With the new Lamborghini, the designer went for a feeling of these sports racing cars and how they pushed their mechanical parts to the limit. Gandini wanted "people to be astonished when they saw the car."

He certainly succeeded.

Styling wasn't the only unique feature of the Countach. Chief engineer Paolo Stanzani (later of the Bugatti EB110) had this big V-12 to fit in the chassis. The Miura had a sideways transverse V-12, which was great for a short wheelbase, but could be a wide package with one cylinder banked up close to the bulkhead and a need for a very specific, very expensive drivetrain to get the power to the rear wheels.

A north-south longitudinal layout, with the engine ahead of the gearbox, is common in mid-engine automobiles, but lengthens the wheelbase and puts accessory drive belts next to the firewall.

Continued on page 64

JAY LENO ON THE *LAMBORGHINI COUNTACH*

The sexiest cars have a male and female side to them," Jay Leno explains. "The Miura's engine is very masculine, but its styling is very sensual. The Miura and Jaguar XK-Es and XK120s are cars women think are very sensual." They may go "oh" or "ah" when they see one, but, Leno explains, "I've never seen a woman think the Countach is attractive.

"If you're trying to impress 12-year-old boys, the Countach is the greatest car in the world, because they jump up and down and go crazy. I would get letters from kids writing that they knew I had a Countach and, 'If you could take me to school one day it would be the coolest thing.'

"So I wrote back and did that a couple of times. One kid lived in Huntington Beach. I picked him up in the morning, pulled in front of his school, the door goes up and all his friends are watching. I said, 'So long, Jimmy.' It's fun doing that, and in that sense the car is great.

"The Countach suffered from what a lot of the early supercars did in that most of them were fairly primitive, with a tube chassis. It's a big, heavy car that's not nearly as fast as it's supposed to be. I guess in its time it was pretty quick. Now it seems fairly agricultural. It is fun to drive and I enjoy it. It's just not modern fast."

Originally Leno's Countach had a rear wing, but, "I didn't like the wing so I took it off. I mean the chances of you getting airborne on the street are fairly remote.

"I like the Countach, but not as much as the Miura. I would have preferred to see the Miura perfected, the next generation of the SV."

This 1976 Countach is the super Lamborghini in its cleanest form, before extra spoilers and wings sprouted. BMW design chief Chris Bangle says, "A Countach in anything other than its original form is so *Pimp My Ride* it's almost impossible to discern the original."

Getting into a Countach means stepping over a wide sill and then dropping down into a reclining leather-upholstered seat. The shift lever is attached directly to the forward-facing transmission.

The earliest versions of Lamborghini's Countachs could hit 60 miles per hour in the mid-5.0 second range, while the later cars did the same in the mid-4.0s. Top speed for the mid-engine supercars ranged from 175 to almost 200 miles per hour, depending on engine and body configuration.

Stacks of V-12 blocks and heads await assembly in the Lamborghini factory in 1988. At this point the company was owned by Chrysler and looking very neat and clean, but in the lean years, the assembly line could be dusty and feel almost deserted.

Opposite page: As much as anything else, the Countach is famous for its flip-up doors, which are now adapted to custom cars and trucks. They aren't just a visual attraction; conventional doors on a car of the Lamborghini's size would have been quite long and difficult to open and close.

As the years progressed, the Countach design was modified with added wings, spoilers, and lower sill extensions, as on this 1988 version. To some fans the additions were cool, while to many others they tarted up the basic excitement of the Countach design.

Continued from page 57

Chris Bangle, who heads design for BMW, explains that Countach designer Marcello Gandini, " . . . took things you could exaggerate—like the wheel-to-car relationship, the lowness and wideness of the car—and exaggerated the hell out of them. Cars that are so politically incorrect, with no possible reason for being . . . they are the supercars."

So Stanzani turned the engine around, with the accessory belts to the back and the transmission sticking forward into the cockpit's center tunnel, with the clutch between the V-12 and the five-speed. There were several advantages to this layout, like shortening the wheelbase and putting the shift linkage right on the gearbox.

One problem: how did he get the power from the five-speed gearbox rearward to the differential? Stanzani routed it off the transmission countershaft to a shaft that spun in bearings under the clutch and transmission, then through the engine's sump to the limited-slip differential, which was in its own compartment aft of the engine's sump.

Over the Countach's 1974–1990 lifespan, the V-12 was in three power forms. Its original 4.0-liter edition had 375 horsepower at 8,000 rpm and 387 ft-lb of torque at 5,000. When displacement increased to 4.7 liters the horsepower stayed the same (remember, these were the power-killing emissions years), but torque rose a bit to 409 at 4,500. The increase to 5.2 liters also brought four valves per cylinder and horsepower progressed to 455 at 7,000, torque to 502 ft-lb at 5,700 rpm.

It all depended on gearing, of course, but 0–60 times started in the mid-5-second range and were down near the mid-4-second range with the four-valve engine. Top velocity varied from the 175-mile-per-hour area up to almost 200 miles per hour, with the winged versions generally more stable but slower.

Under the Countach's amazing aluminum body was a tubular space frame. Under that was the suspension, upper and lower A-arms with coil springs and tube shocks at the front, while in back were upper links, a reversed lower A-arm and a pair of coil springs and shocks per side. Vented disc brakes were used all around, while the tires—at least on the early cars—looked narrow for a car with so much potential.

Those flip-up doors were more than just a design gimmick, because conventional swing-outs would have been impossibly long, and that was true even if you weren't in a parking lot. Even with them, it was a stretch to get in and over the wide sill, so you tended to climb over and drop into the seat, which laid you out like a chaise lounge. Getting out was more difficult.

What you faced was a short but wide rectangular instrument panel and seven purposeful gauges. Radio and climate controls were another stretch forward at the front of the center console. There was no mistaking the car's huge size as you stretched again to reach up and pull down the door.

It's a good thing the Countach was fast so you could stay ahead of most automobiles, because rearward visibility was minimal. I always envied the factory mechanics who had this marvelous trick for sitting on the driver's sill, door up, and looking backward as they worked the pedals and steering to reverse a Countach. I have never been that dexterous.

There was big stuff rumbling behind you at the turn of the key, and when you moved the shift lever down and left into first, it was like an extraordinarily hot knife cutting

through an anvil. You were always aware that it was a large, wide car, weighing as much as a National Association for Stock Car Racing (NASCAR) stock car, but that didn't take away from the fun. Okay, it wasn't the most refined supercar in some respects and you never forgot all the power behind you, but it went like the wind. Besides, you were driving a Countach, poster boy of the exotics, and that alone was worth a lot.

Countachs have been at the center of so many stories about driving quickly. Here's my favorite:

Tom Bryant, now editor in chief of *Road & Track*, was a young editor assigned to write a multiexotic car test, which included the Countach. The crew headed for the desert and a quiet, isolated public highway loop to do some high-speed comparison testing. Every lap they sedately passed a Highway Patrol officer who finally couldn't stand it and stopped the Countach and all the cars behind it.

Uh-oh. The Highway Patrol officer looked the Lamborghini over, walked over to Tom, and said, "I don't know what you're up to, but *stop it*."

They did. Wouldn't you? ■

In the Lamborghini factory, employees build the final Countach, while in the background the first examples of its replacement, the - Diablo, take shape. Here you can see the basics of how the cars were made, as the aluminum body panels are fitted over the steel tube frame.

CHAPTER 5

Porsche has often made special editions of its Turbos, like this 1993 lightweight model. Although the basic shape of the 911 Turbo from its first iteration in 1975 to the latest might look similar to an outsider, the exterior design has been through many variations.

PORSCHE 930 TURBO 1975

155
MILES PER HOUR

When the speedo needle slipped past 150 miles per hour I knew everything was going to be okay. Up on the banking at what was then called Transportation Research Center, off in the Ohio countryside, the Porsche Turbo felt snug and secure at speed, maxing at 155.

I'd already had a chance to rush the Turbo to 60 miles per hour. It needed some 6.7 seconds, which isn't quick today, but there were extenuating circumstances. We were just learning how to spool up a big turbocharger off the line, and even when we did, it could be tough to launch a Turbo.

Who cared? This was 1975 and after a half decade of watching horsepower in performance cars disappear like smoke, thanks to (badly needed) anti-emissions laws, the Turbo gave me the feeling that there was hope after all. Speed was back.

It's a fact that when you mention going quickly in an automobile, the subject of Porsche Turbos is close at hand. No one is too picky about which vintage is mentioned. No big concerns about 930 or 996 or rear-wheel drive or twin turbos or the size of the tail. It's just that Porsche Turbo equals speed. Simple as that.

There are entire books devoted to the subject, so think of this as paying homage to the type, to more than 30 years of Turbos.

That first supercharged 911 was a two-year model, the 3.0-liter version of the famous flat-six equipped with a big turbo that boosted it to 234 horsepower at 5,500 rpm and 246 ft-lb of torque at 4,500. Even with that now-middling 0–60 time, it felt like a handful and heaven help you if you thought you could get on or off the throttle quickly in a corner.

Porsche's original Turbo was known inside the company as the 930 Turbo, an internal code it carried until the introduction of the 964 for the 1990 model year.

Who cared? We loved the Turbo, and it came with that great "whale tail" rear spoiler.

During 1978–1979, Porsche dramatically picked up the pace with a revised Turbo, which had a displacement increase to 3.3 liters and, possibly more important, an intercooler neatly designed into the whale tail. Horsepower got a nice boost—so to speak—to 253, torque to 282 ft-lb, but it was a much quicker car, to 60 miles per hour in just 5 seconds while we hung on for what felt like a rocket booster lighting off just shy of 4,000 rpm.

Peter Gregg, driving for the Brumos team, was one of the finest Porsche drivers in U.S. racing history. He won more than 40 races in the 1970s, 8 of them in 1979 driving this twin-turbo, 700-horsepower Porsche 935.

And then Porsche abandoned us. They pulled the Turbo from the United States, and it was even rumored the 911 series was doomed by emissions and such. How depressing.

Those of us in the States were supposed to be happy with 928s and 944s while Europeans still got Turbos, which were headed for 300 horsepower. Some Americans weren't put off and brought gray market Turbos and had them certified (or at least claimed to be) by private firms.

We were saved by an American, Peter Schutz, who ended up in charge of Porsche and ordered the Turbo back into the States, where it returned in 1986. The engine was still at 3.3 liters in the 930 platform, and while horsepower was up by almost 30, anti-smog laws had kept performance from improving. But we had the Turbo back and that counted for a great deal.

The 994 version of the 911 Porsche came along in 1991, still at 3.3 liters, but in 1993 it was increased to 3.6 and things got serious again. The 0–60 time was down in the mid-4-second range and Porsches were being tamed, losing their reputation for getting tail happy.

Come 1995, Turbo horsepower was at 400 and Porsche put all-wheel drive under the car to make things even more manageable. The 0–60 times were under 4 seconds and top speeds in the 175-mile-per-hour range.

With the 996 design the Turbo took another step forward, and while performance numbers weren't all that different, there were such technical advances as Porsche Stability Management; now Porsches were eminently manageable.

There's just one thing about Porsche Turbos that generally does *not* look impressive: the engine compartment. The powerful engine is flat so it is lost well down in the bodywork, and the plumbing tends to disguise and cover up the good mechanical bits.

By 1984, the Turbo had a 3.3-liter engine, an intercooler, and enough power to get to 60 miles per hour in 4.9 seconds. But not for the United States, as emissions control problems kept the car out of that market from 1980 until 1986. Seen with this car are World Driving Champion Phil Hill (left) and Le Mans winner Paul Frere.

Ratchet forward to early 2006 and the 911 Turbo based on the 997 chassis. Turns out the engine is still at 3.6 liters, but look what they did: 480 horsepower at 6,000 rpm and 457 ft-lb of torque on a broad base . . . if you don't buy the Sport Chrono Package that extends boost for an added 10 seconds and drop-kicks torque to 502 ft-lb.

Ach du lieber!

The all-wheel-drive system is now lighter, electronics refined again, brakes still larger, and a very tricky variable turbine geometry system changes the pitch of the turbo's blades to best take advantage of the exhaust flow.

So now we are looking at a 0–60 time of 3.5–3.6 seconds with a manual six-speed, a tick quicker with Tiptronic if you have time to notice on your way to 195 miles per hour.

That's a Porsche Turbo for you: a hero car for more than three decades. And we haven't even touched on the fact that Porsche put its racing where its mouth was, its Turbos an assumed winner around the world for decades.

Several years ago *Road & Track* was invited to Germany to drive 911s from over the years. Included in the stable was an original Turbo. We had an 8-mile circuit through the forests

Early in 2006, Porsche presented the sixth generation Turbo, based on the 997 chassis. While the engine remains at 3.6 liters of displacement, the horsepower pops to a whopping 480 horsepower at 6,000 rpm, with 457 ft-lb of torque from 1,950–5,000 rpm.

Photo by Jeff Allen/Road & Track

One of the developments Porsche adds to its 2007 Turbo is turbochargers with variable turbine geometry for better exhaust flow over the turbo impeller. *Photo by Jeff Allen*/Road & Track

near Zuffenhausen and the chance to let the cars go. After two laps in the original Turbo, I asked Klaus Bischof, the amiable leader of Porsche's historic section, "Is that car really up to spec?"

I couldn't imagine Klaus giving us anything save a perfect car, but the Porsche felt so slow. He laughed and said I wasn't the first to ask that question . . . and, yes, the car was in excellent tune.

Continued on page 77

After the flat-nose-flip-up-headlight look became popular on Porsche's all-conquering 935 race cars, it was adapted to production versions of the Turbo. The car seen here is a 1985 model.

Porsche has long had a program under which it will do special modifications of its cars for customers. Requests have run from gold shift knobs to special leathers to, as you can imagine, still more power. In the mid-1980s it was common for owners to have the factory convert their Turbos to the flat-nose look.

Opposite page: What says Porsche Turbo better than that big whale tail with its intercooler? This 1988 version had the 300-horsepower 3.3-liter engine.

The interior of a 1988 911 Turbo displays classic Porsche design.

In 1990, Porsche presented the Turbo based on the 964 chassis. The single-turbo 3.3-liter flat-six was rated at 320 horsepower at 5,750 rpm and had a top speed in the high 160-mile per hour range.

Continued from page 70

By the mid-1990s, Porsche had an all-wheel drive version of the 993 Turbo and 400 horsepower and 400 ft-lb of torque on tap. This "oomph" came from a 3.6-liter version of the famous flat-six with a pair of turbochargers and intercoolers.

   To a modern right foot that felt any sports car over 0–60 in five seconds was lagging, the vintage machine was just that. But to think of any Porsche Turbo as anything but a hero car would be as historically lame-brained as dismissing Babe Ruth, Bill Haley and the Comets, or Chuck Yeager as irrelevant. ▮

Opposite page: Imagine having this red 1994 Turbo out in the Arizona desert with plenty of straight road and not a soul in sight. This version puts 360 horsepower under your right foot, thanks to an increase to 3.6 liters.

This Turbo, with a rear spoiler that seems to hug the bodywork, can whoosh to 60 miles per hour in just 3.7 seconds on its way up to 190 miles per hour.

In 2000, Porsche presented the 996 rendition of the Turbo, with the 3.6-liter engine now producing 415 horsepower at 6,000 rpm. Top speed is around 185 miles per with 0–60 under four seconds. Important to hard drivers was the availability of Porsche Stability Management system.

CHAPTER 6

According to BMW's testing, a new M1 would get to 60 miles per hour in 5.3 seconds, and its top speed was a few ticks over 160 miles per hour. While not necessarily impressive today, those numbers got plenty of attention in 1978 when the BMW supercar was launched at that fall's Paris Auto Show.

162
MILES PER HOUR

BMW M1 1978

There is a vintage, welcomed, and honest sound to the BMW M1's six under acceleration. Much of it seems to be induction noise, the sound of air being drawn into the injector rams, with some exhaust rap. For being so close behind the cockpit, the engine's sound isn't obnoxious and two people can converse without raising their voices too much.

If you're driving quickly, you'd probably be too busy to talk. Supercars in the late 1970s didn't have the ability to unleash today's megahorsepower. There was no point, push, and hang-on driving with electronics to save your bacon if you screwed up. In a BMW M1 it was more about a balanced interplay

Lamborghini was contracted to design and develop the M1 chassis and then build the cars. However the Italian automaker fell on difficult times, and the project had to be pulled from them. As a result, the frames were made by an Italian firm and the bodywork added by Italdesign, with final assembly done in Germany by Bauer.

between power, steering, brakes, tires, and handling, which had to be treated with more respect than today.

You built momentum and then maintained it. Nowadays you can zip though a supercar's gearbox and be at 130 miles per hour with ease. In the BMW M1's day you *earned* 130 miles per hour.

For all the supercars BMW has built, from snarling little 2002 tiis in the early 1970s to modern V-10 M5s, it has only done one automobile you could officially classify as a supercar: the mid-engine M1.

It was the mid-1970s and BMW was already racing the 3.5-liter CSi coupes, which were wonderful to watch, always a bit out of shape as their drivers pushed them to the limit . . . and still not quite quick enough to stay with Porsche's latest.

BMW dearly wanted to beat its German archrival in the international Groups 4 and 5 racing classes, but needed a new weapon. And that new BMW would have to be homologated for competition, which meant building 400 examples of the car within months. Rather than trying to make a race car out of another of its production cars, BMW went the other way, creating a race car that would then be productionized to meet the homologation rules.

BMW management signed off on the program, but what followed was a classic case of best-laid plans going awry.

Already too busy to design and build the M1 on its own, BMW farmed out much of the project. While the all-important engine would stay with BMW Motorsports (who better?), the rest of the project was sent south to Italy.

Giorgetto Giugiaro at Italdesign was contracted to design the body. There had already been one sensational mid-engine BMW, the gullwing-door 1972 Turbo created by well-known designer Paul Bracq to celebrate the (now infamous) Summer Olympics in BMW's hometown, Munich. There were hints of Bracq's car in the M1, particularly in the rear three-quarter view, but the M1 had more in common with other cars being designed in that era by Giugiaro, like the Lotus Esprit and DeLorean.

Lamborghini was contracted to develop the chassis, which assigned design responsibilities to one of the most prolific of all chassis men, Gianpaolo Dallara, who had done the Miura and Countach. Dallara still builds IRL race cars today.

Lamborghini was also meant to build the cars, but here came the first hiccup. It may be owned and supported by Volkswagen via Audi these days, but in the 1970s and 1980s Lamborghini was like a ship in heavy seas, sliding deep into a financial trough before being saved, only to slip away again. It was during one of those deep slips that BMW had to pull the M1 project from the Italian automaker. A firm called Marchesi welded the frames together, while the fiberglass bodies were made by Trasformazione Italiana Resina. Bodies were fitted to the frames by Italdesign. Each car was then shipped to the well-known German coach-building company, Bauer, for final assembly and the addition of the BMW Motorsport engine and ZF gearbox.

There's nothing too fancy about the dashboard of the M1, but then the cars weren't meant to be design exercises, but the basis for race cars. Note the redline of 6,700 rpm for the BMW six, with the speedometer reading to 280 kilometers per hour (174 miles per hour).

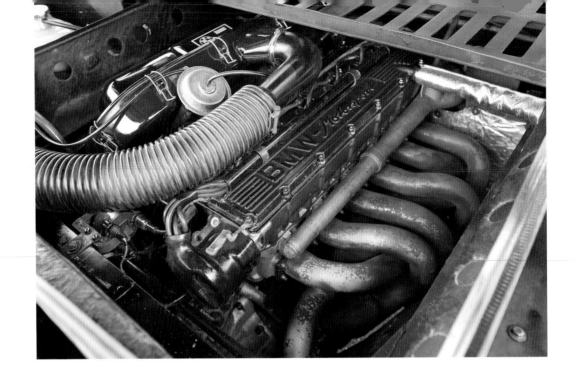

BMW Motorsports developed and built the twin-cam straight-six engines for the M1s. Based on the 635 CSi coupe engine, they added a 24-valve head used in IMSA racing in the United States. In the M1, the 3.5-liter six developed 277 horsepower at 6,500 rpm and 243 ft-lb of torque at 5,000 rpm.

By twenty-first century standards the M1 interior doesn't look particularly aggressive. Compared to the often overly firm seats in some supercars, the M1's are downright comfy, and they get the job done in hard cornering. The sound of the classic BMW six behind the cockpit at speed is music to the ears of an enthusiast.

The BMW M1's philosophical predecessor was designer Paul Bracq's 1972 Turbo concept car, done to commemorate the Munich Olympics. Creation of the final production M1's design was given to Italian Giorgetto Giugiaro, though hints of Bracq's Turbo shape remain in the BMW.

It was a promising package. Motorsport tuned the 3.5-liter inline-six to 277 horsepower at 6,500 rpm and 243 ft-lb of torque at 5,000 rpm. Starting with the engine from the 635 CSi coupe, they added 24-valve twin-cam heads designed for use in the 635 coupes that raced in the U.S. International Motor Sports Association (IMSA) series in 1974, along with Kugelfischer-Bosch fuel injection and electronic ignition with no distributor, something common today but new then.

Set longitudinally behind the cockpit and bolted to the ZF five-speed transmission, the BMW six motivated the M1 to 60 miles per hour in, by BMW's timing, 5.3 seconds, on its way to a top speed of 162 miles per hour . . . not impressive today, perhaps, but enough to turn heads in 1978, when the car was launched at the Paris Auto Show in October of that year.

The rest of the chassis was de rigueur for the time: upper and lower A-arms suspensions (the rears with radius rods), nonassisted rack-and-pinion steering, vented disc brakes, and alloy wheels, here fitted with the famous Pirelli P7 tires.

Famed Italian chassis engineer Giampaolo Dallara was responsible for the underpinnings of the M1.

M1s were raced by Grand Prix drivers in the Procar series, and one won the U.S. IMSA GTO championship in 1981. Easily the most memorable M1 race car, however, was this Le Mans entry. Its fame came because it had been painted by Andy Warhol as part of a BMW art project.

Enter hiccup number two. With all this fussing around to get the car built, its original purpose was slipping away as the homologation rules were revised. The great plan to take on Porsche with an 850-horsepower turbocharged Group 5 M1 fell apart. There were M1s built for Le Mans—the most famous being painted as part of a BMW art project by Andy Warhol—but they were never a threat to Porsche.

To garner some notoriety with the M1s, BMW created the Procar series, pitting Grand Prix drivers against each other in 470-horsepower Group 4 M1s as curtain raisers to many Grand Prix in 1979 and 1980. This was the European version of International Race of Champions (IROC) and just as competitive.

Most prominent of the M1's racing honors came in the United States, where David Coward and Kenper Miller drove one to win the 1981 IMSA GTO Championship. By which time BMW was off on another racing tack, building Formula 1 turbo engines for Brabham.

In the end, BMW built around 400 M1 street machines with an additional 45–50 as race cars. Today, a nice one brings $200,000. What few M1s were originally imported for sale in the States were then certified by independent firms to meet safety and emissions rules, bumping the price back then to around $115,000.

BMW has M1s in its collection in Munich and brought one for our day in the southern German countryside. It's still a great-looking automobile, arguably Giugiaro's best wedge sports machine.

We're now used to seeing engines hidden under styled covers and panels, so it's nice to lift the M1's large rear panel, look in, and see a naked engine. Mind you, it's a stretch, well forward in the bay, but there is BMW's beloved straight-six, injectors under a small air filter on the left, headers snaking down and forward to the right. How nicely uncomplicated.

The M1 interior looks so period with a squared-off instrument binnacle containing little gauges. The steering wheel feels slim and looks to modern airbag eyes to be a bit lethal, but it is the perfect shape for the racer's hands at a nine-and-three grip.

While the Recaro seats don't have the aggressive visual appeal of those in today's performance cars, they are arguably better. For some reason or other, modern interior designers seem to believe sport seats need to be very firm and high sided to hold you in. By contrast, the M1's are surprisingly soft, like sitting on a comfy cushion. While that may not be the best on those occasions when you're cornering hard, it certainly makes this one of the more comfortable-riding high-performance cars of its day.

Shifting the M1 is a vintage matter, with a little hitch in the neutral slot as you change up or down, combined with double clutching to ease the process. That was expected then as automakers were less than a decade into building production mid-engine cars in any numbers. Thus getting that shift pattern duplicated way back there behind the engine

involved a lot of levers and linkages, including bushings or whatever to keep them from being noisy.

But rhythm is the key and once you get into the rhythm of shifting the M1 is quite easy.

Another odd thing: back then German automakers insisted on putting first gear in their five-speed transmissions in the lower left slot, down below reverse. This was a racing tradition because first was a launch gear and it was more logical to put the four working gears in the H pattern.

Nowadays, most cars are developed so all the driver inputs are well balanced—steering, brake effort, throttle. The M1's nonassisted steering, by contrast, is a bit heavy at low speed, but lightens nicely as speed rises and is about right and nicely direct at speed. Brake and clutch efforts seem quite logical for a 25-year-old high-performance car.

Too bad timing and the times seemed to trip up the M1 project. It had the right styling pedigree, one of the best chassis designers in the business, and the beloved BMW straight-six. Even after two and a half decades it stands out in the exotic car crowd like an honored, dignified middle-aged statesman, still quite athletic . . . and with an excellent tailor.

A supercar among BMW's many super cars. ▪

When BMW could no longer get enough speed from its 3.5-liter CSi coupes to beat its German rival Porsche on the racetrack, the Munich firm decided to create the mid-engine M1 to uphold the company's honor in competition.

SECTION II
THE GROUP B CONNECTION
1983–1991

163-220
MILES PER HOUR

CHAPTER 7

While the mid-engine 288 GTO has its own fan club, the original front-engine GTO is a legend. The 250 GTO was based on the Testa Rossa sports racers that had won so many victories for Ferrari, a tradition the 250 GTO continued by winning the FIA's Manufacturer's GT Championship in 1962, 1963, and 1964.

189
MILES PER HOUR

FERRARI 288 GTO 1983

Got 10 million bucks? That's the least you'd need to buy an original 1962 Ferrari 250 GTO. Probably more, but probably enough to buy all the original Pontiac GTOs still worth owning.

Or for about $400,000 you could have a 288 GTO, a limited-edition Ferrari that will outperform the other two. One that turbos to 60 in 4.9 seconds, to 125 in 15.2, and doesn't want to stop until you hit 189 miles per hour.

First, a bit of history: Based on the Testa Rossa sports racing cars that almost dominated international racing in the late 1950s, the 250 GTO (for *Gran Turismo Omologato*) won the Federation

Internationale de l'Automobile (FIA) Manufacturer's GT Championship in 1962, 1963, and 1964, plus the hearts of so many of us. With arguably the most beautiful front-engine GT shape ever created, strong and reliable V-12 power, and a predictable, unbreakable chassis, GTOs rose to the top of the Ferrari list—hence their eight-figure price tags.

All Pontiac did was steal the name. And then Ferrari reused it.

As with Porsche's 959 and Jaguar's XJ220, the Ferrari 288 GTO was aimed directly at the FIA's Group B race program. Like the Jaguar, the new GTO became a historical postscript to that short-lived racing class, but is still highly regarded among Ferrari owners.

It was 1983 when Ferrari said it would build the GTO. Unlike Jaguar, which created entirely new automobiles for Group B, Ferrari based its machine on an established production car, the 308. By doing this, the automaker was starting with a known commodity and there could be marketing spillover to support sales of the normal production car.

Admittedly, there wasn't much of the 308 left when the 288 GTO was finished. The standard semimonocoque structure had been replaced by a lighter steel tube frame and separate body panels. While it had the same upper and lower A-arm suspension as the 308, the GTO's arms were of tubular steel, and the shocks and springs firmer for the added engine power.

Pininfarina sculpted the bodywork for the 288 GTO, the racing version of the production 308. The slanted cooling ducts in the rear fenders, which vented air from the brakes, were reminiscent of those used in the original 250 GTO.

Originally Ferrari intended to race the 288 GTO in the FIA's Group B class against cars such as Porsche's 959 and Jaguar's XJ220. The class was short-lived, and this modern GTO was never raced in anger.

Pininfarina, which designed the 308, did the reworking for the GTO, buffing up the original design with muscleman fender flares, adding serious spoilers front and rear, and plugging in four huge driving lights. A holdover from the original 250 GTO was a set of slanted air vents, which had been behind the front wheels on the 250 GTO but vented air from the rear brakes in the new car.

Even the bodywork material was new and was kept lighter for the race/road car. Using steel only for the doors, Ferrari molded fiberglass for the major body panels (as it had for the very first small run of 308s). Kevlar was used for the hood, combined with carbon fiber for the roof and with Nomex and aluminum honeycomb for the firewall.

In perhaps the most fundamental change from the production car, the engine was turned from its lateral side-to-side placement in the 308, to a longitudinal fore-aft layout for the 288 GTO. In swinging the drivetrain around, Ferrari had to extend the 308 wheelbase by 4.3 inches, making it 96.5. This rearrangement meant it could use the more conventional race car engine/transmission layout, which would be crucial for situations like quick gear ratio changes. Also, one of the turbos didn't have to be fitted in between the engine and firewall.

Ah yes, turbos, because to get the sort of power one needed for an exotic car in the early 1980s, adding turbos and intercoolers was a logical solution. In the GTO's case, it was a

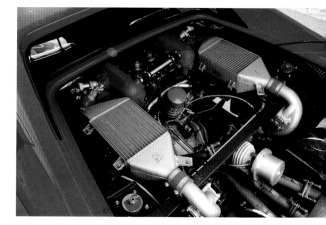

Ferrari lowered the displacement of the 308's V-8 to 2,855 cc so it could then turbocharge the engine. With a compression ratio of 7.6:1 and running 14.5 psi of boost, the 288 GTO engine was rated at 400 horsepower at 7,000 rpm and 366 ft-lb of torque at 3,800 rpm.

To get the 288 GTO ready for racing, Pininfarina squared its shoulders with wide fender flares and added spoilers under the nose and atop the tail. Four driving lights were plugged into the grille.

The seat style, the stitching, the steering wheel, the gated shifter are all pure mid-1980s Ferrari style.

pair of IHI-made turbos, one per side and kept small to lower inertia so they could spin up easily and minimize lag. Using turbos meant Ferrari had to lower the V-8's displacement to 2,855 cc, because the rules said that if you multiply the displacement by a "turbo factor" of 1.4—the FIA's mathematically calculated advantage of the little exhaust-driven superchargers—the result had to be less than 4,000 cc.

While the GTO's twin-cam, 32-valve V-8 was derived from that in the 308, it understandably had major internal changes to allow for the turbo-charging and increased horsepower. The compression ratio was lowered to 7.6:1, the boost set at 14.5 psi, and it got new Weber-Marelli electronics for fuel injection and ignition.

On the dyno, the results were impressive: 400 horsepower at 7,000 rpm and 366 ft-lb of torque at 3,800. With the help of a five-speed gearbox and a curb weight of just 2,555 pounds, *Road & Track* managed to get a 288 GTO to 60 miles per hour in 4.9 seconds. Terminal velocity topped out at 189 miles per hour.

Sadly, while Ferrari had no trouble selling the 287 Ferrari 288 GTOs it made, the cars were never raced in anger. Rule changes and corporate priorities kept the GTOs out of the race garage. Stillborn.

And then one day in 1987, we were working at Ferrari's Fiorano test track on a story for *Road & Track* when a rather amazing-looking 288 GTO showed up in the pits. Was it a competition car? Sure looked the part, but Ferrari told me its correct name was the GTO Evoluzione.

Hmm, we'd never heard of it. Ferrari went on to explain that it was one of three such cars made and it used turbo V-8s that were a development of the GTO. Actually, Ferrari had developed two engines, both with boost pressure set at 24.7 psi. The first, called the 114 CR, pumped out 530 horsepower while the second, the F114 CK, produced 650 horsepower.

Hmm again, when they told us the more powerful GTO/E got to 60 miles per hour in about 3.5 seconds with a terminal speed of 240 miles per hour.

There were other changes, too, like a tube frame chassis that was reinforced with carbon fiber—the latter material used for a body that created a machine 40 percent lighter but three times stiffer than a GTO.

A test driver did any number of laps with the GTO/E, its right seat filled with instrumentation, hanging the back end out for me. Wow. And then the car was gone.

What I didn't realize until later was that I was looking at one of the prototypes for the soon-to-be introduced F40. Using the GTO/E as a yardstick against Porsche's 959, Ferrari was developing the first of its limited-run exotic cars. ▪

While Ferrari's 308 has a semimonocoque structure, the 288 GTO uses a steel tube frame with separate body panels. The doors have steel skins, with the major body panels in fiberglass, while some components are in Kevlar, carbon fiber, and other lightweight materials.

CHAPTER 8

By the early 1990s, when the 512M version of the Testarossa was produced, the big mid-engine machine had been developed into a strong handler that could generate mid-0.9g handling around a skid pad. Here World Driving Champion Phil Hill plays with a 512TR on a damp racetrack.

185
MILES PER HOUR

FERRARI TESTAROSSA 1984

" **At 175 miles per hour or so**—this feels like cruising speed—the car is stable, the handling feels taut and secure. Pushing up over 180 miles per hour you begin to detect just a hint of lightness in the front end and there is a dramatic awareness that you are going incredibly quickly. With sufficient room the powerplant eventually nudges the redline in fifth gear and you flash past the (racetrack's) lighted sign that shows your speed: 185 miles per hour. Back off a little, the speed drops into the 170s, and the sure-footedness returns as though you were cruising along the Interstate."

Been there, witnessed that from the passenger's seat.

The preceding is a description of what it was like to peg the tach—world champion Phil Hill driving—in a Ferrari Testarossa. This was over 20 years ago at a *Road & Track* World's Fastest Cars event, back before exotic cars got the wind tunnel time and aerodynamic attention they receive today, so very high speeds could get your attention.

Despite that speed and the fact that it's difficult to be lukewarm about any Ferrari, that word—lukewarm—is how many of us remember the Testarossa, or TR.

Mind you, Ferrari sold a fair number of TRs, and they were solid, reliable automobiles, but they weren't exactly enchanting. Sorry to burst any bubbles.

They also weren't that quick in their initial iteration, *Road & Track* needing 6.2 seconds to get a U.S.-spec first-generation TR to 60 miles per hour. (European TRs were almost a second quicker, back when emissions controls often caused a dramatic difference

When Pininfarina designed the Testarossa—successor to the Berlinetta Boxer—it created a controversial big-hipped shape with flip-up headlights and a stack of horizontal "strakes" that fill the air intakes in the rear fenders.

in Euro versus U.S. horsepower. This disparity disappeared in the early 1990s as government rules between the two continents became more similar and techniques, particularly electronics, improved.)

There is no denying the Testarossa is fun to drive. Power from the flat-12 behind your back is eager to punch you down the straight and to the next corner, and you can guide a Testarossa with surprising ease given its potential . . . and its size.

If you have ever driven on the roads in the hills behind Ferrari's factory in Maranello, Italy, you would understand why the automaker's cars handled so well. They have nicely paved two-laners that twist over the hilltops, down into valleys, and through towns like Serramazzoni. It isn't unusual to see a Ferrari test car or camouflaged prototype in the hills.

On these roads you would find the TR drives "narrower" than it is; it is easier to maneuver than expected, given its 77.6-inch width (0.6 inch wider than a Range Rover).

Testarossa means "red head" in Italian, a reference to the color of the engine cylinder heads of this mid-engine Ferrari exotic. The name was inherited from the highly successful Testa Rossa sports racing cars of the late 1950s and early 1960s.

While the width of the Testarossa might be a problem when driving, it brings the benefit of a broad interior. Once over the wide door sill, you can settle into very comfortable, leather-upholstered seats.

Like the Boxer, the Testarossa is propelled by a flat-12 engine. In its original form it displaced 4.9 liters and generated 380 horsepower and 354 ft-lb of torque. With the 512M version in 1992, horsepower increased to 421.

But you are always aware of its big backside, something the limited visibility to the rear reminds you of every time you checked the mirrors.

Many bicycle riders cycled on those winding roads behind Maranello and, with the TR, you are aware of the potential for sweeping one into the weeds.

And then there is the car's exterior styling.

Ferrari's first mid-engine car, the Berlinetta Boxer, is a better automobile than the Lamborghini Countach and, some would argue, just as attractive in its own not-in-your-face way. The styling of the Countach, however, so captured everyone's attention that it seemed the Boxer's successor would have to make a strong statement.

It did. When Ferrari distributed the first photos of the Pininfarina-designed Testarossa, we were all amazed. It was a big-hipped shape, the front smooth with pop-up headlamps, but what is that along the side? Slicing into the rear side duct were five . . . what are they? Some critics named them strakes, while others called them a stack of little fins. Was it a cheese grater? In any case, it got our attention, as did five similar lines across the back of the car.

Technically, the TR has a lot going for it. Out back is the flat-12, 48-valve, twin-cam boxer engine displacing 4.9 liters and producing 380 horsepower at 6,300 rpm and 354 ft-lb

of torque at 4,500 rpm—plus red cylinder heads as Testarossa means "red head." Behind it is a five-speed manual gearbox that is shifted up front through a traditional, handsome shift gate.

Classic chassis specs: upper and lower A-arm coil-spring and tube-shock suspensions, rack-and-pinion steering, with vented disc brakes (12.2 inches) all around. The Goodyear tires are on alloy wheels with the famous five-spoke Daytona pattern.

While you have to be aware of the TR's width when driving, its benefit is a generous cockpit, at least in width, as the design's low height makes it a bit tight for those over 6 feet tall. Once you have climbed in over the wide sill, the interior's leather ambiance and scent are (at least when new) enticing, the gauges classic.

Exotic cars had lost much of their fussiness when the first TR was introduced in 1984. Clutches were no longer too heavy and the threat of stalling the car on launch (how

If there is one overriding feeling when driving a Testarossa, it is that you are guiding a very wide car. This is, of course, a result of putting a large flat-12 powerplant amidships and building a supercar around that layout.

Ferrari champion Phil Hill wrote of the 512TR: "At 175 miles per hour or so—this feels like cruising speed—the car is stable, the handling feels taut and secure. Pushing up over 180 miles per hour you begin to detect just a hint of lightness in the front end, and there is a dramatic awareness that you are going incredible quickly."

embarrassing) was minimal. Steering effort had leveled out and the air conditioning actually worked on cool days.

By 1992, the Testarossa was a bit long in the tooth and upgraded to the 512M. Displacement didn't change, but horsepower certainly did, up to 421 at 6,750 rpm. Torque was up only 6 ft-lb, but the curve was broader, adding to driving flexibility. The brakes were better, the tires bigger, and the car would circle a skid pad in the mid-0.9 g area. It got off the line smartly at just 4.7 seconds to 60 miles per hour with a top speed of 192.

Pininfarina designs tend to be better known for the manner in which they establish a long-term trend rather than follow a fad, but the TR seemed to do the latter. You won't find the car on many (if any) "Best Ferrari" lists. When its successor, the 550 Maranello, turned out to have a front-engine, rear-drive layout, no one was disappointed. ▪

You couldn't fault the Testarossa's pedigree. By the time it was launched in the early 1980s, Ferrari had been successfully racing mid-engine cars for two decades.

CHAPTER 9

At the debut of the F40, Enzo Ferrari explained the car's name: "It is 40 years since the first Ferrari left the factory. On March 12, 1947, the 125 S was presented to the public for the first time. On May 25 of the same year, Franco Cortese won the Rome Grand Prix."

201
MILES PER HOUR

FERRARI F40 1987

July 12, 1987, Maranello, Italy.

When Enzo Ferrari arrived, the place went nuts. Journalists—normally cool, reserved, standoffish—stood to applaud and cheer the Pope of Maranello. Photographers rushed toward the table behind which Ferrari was to sit, and the repeated flashes from their strobes gave the darkened hall a strange disco feeling.

"Please, no flash photos," the public address system asked. Now there were more than ever.

They had to be kidding. This was Enzo Ferrari. Predictable pandemonium.

Enzo Ferrari was the real star the day the F40 was presented to the public. The famous man is off in the shadows to the right, a photographer taking aim at him. It was a hot, sweaty day in the presentation auditorium, but no one cared because they had a chance to see Ferrari . . . and the F40.

I was sitting well up in back in Modena's small Centro Civica auditorium in Ferrari's museum, watching all this unfold like a strange comic opera. It was grand entertainment. You have to understand that we attend numerous press conferences each year, and in most cases, those putting on the event are just happy to have journalists attend. This, on the other hand, was a command performance.

The invitation was almost informal: "If you happen to be in Modena this particular day you might be interested in seeing this new car." We journalists pitch some engraved press invitations in the trash, but this quiet invite from Ferrari was enough to cause us to drop

everything to be in Maranello on the appointed day. We knew it had something to do with the rumored new model dubbed the "Le Mans," successor to the 288 GTO, but beyond that it was a mystery.

The bar of Modena's Fini Hotel the night before the press conference had sounded like a session of the United Nations, with many languages being heard all around. No one was about to miss this meeting.

Ferrari added to the mystery the next day when we entered the hall to find a lovely draped shape sitting under spotlights. Starting time was promised as 11 A.M., but then it was said Mr. Ferrari would be 10 minutes late. Despite the heat inside the building, no one minded. Finally, a side door opened, adding a corner of bright light to the dimly lit hall. Mr. Ferrari, now 89 years old, was helped to the table. That's when the place went nuts.

Ferrari forsook aluminum for the F40's body, going instead with carbon fiber and Kevlar. That big front deck weighs a mere 39.6 pounds, while the huge rear engine cover tips the scale at just 48.5 pounds. Each door is only 3.3 pounds, complete with hardware.

The Commendatore began:

> On July 6 last year I asked my research department to look into the feasibility of building an exceptionally powerful sports car incorporating the very latest developments in engine and assembly technology. Only six days later, the directors gave the project their blessing, and now, barely a year later, the finished car stands before you. It is 40 years since the first Ferrari left the factory. On March 12, 1947, the 125 S was presented to the public for the first time. On May 25 of the same year, Franco Cortese won the Rome Grand Prix, driving a Ferrari. Now, 40 years later, the Ferrari F40 demonstrates that Ferrari is still a byword for technological excellence and exceptional performance.

Everything went nuts again as the red drape was pulled from the F40, Ferrari's response to Porsche's 959.

There followed speeches by Giovanni Razelli, president of Ferrari; Dr. Leonardo Fioravanti, who led research and design for Pininfarina; and the man who had a great deal to do with the engineering development of not only the F40 but also the GTO and Evoluzione, Nicola Materazzi.

Razelli acknowledged that the F40 was a direct product of racing, using what Ferrari could learn on the track to test ideas for production cars.

Fioravanti explained the design development of the F40. Naturally, Pininfarina's famous wind tunnel was used to develop the shape of the F40, which has a coefficient of drag of around 0.34 combined with low lift figures front and rear.

But forget all the facts and figures, because first of all the car is damn exciting. In describing the F40, Fioravanti, who is a fan of vintage automobiles, harkened back to Ferraris of the 1960s. Consider the shapes of the F40 and 959, and then remember the form of the two companies' race cars of 1960. Porsches featured round, organic shapes, while Ferraris had that specific Italian look, sleek and racy. The descriptions still apply.

In front, the F40 has one major opening, which doubles as an intake for both the oil cooler and the optional air conditioning. Outboard of this are brake-cooling holes. The NACA ducts on the hood provide the breeze to cool the interior, while the pair on each flank of the car cool the brakes and engine compartment. Behind each flared front fender is a duct to release hot air. That big rear wing is there for adding downforce, while the back window was specifically shaped to direct flow onto the wing.

When doing the interior, function was the point of Pininfarina's design. There was a choice of three types of seats for the new owner, who had to visit the factory or his dealer

Ferrari was developing the F40 near the end of the era when turbochargers were often used on supercars, a technology only Porsche has continued to use. Ferrari tacked two turbos on the F40's 2.9-liter V-8 with air-to-air intercoolers and got the engine to whoosh 478 horsepower at 7,000 rpm and 425 ft-lb of torque at 4,000 rpm.

to be fitted for it. The plastic composite seats weigh about 3 pounds each, and were finished in red and feature a full set of competition belts.

Although air conditioning was an option, power windows were not. In fact, there weren't even wind-up windows. Ferrari chose sliding windows to fit the car's functional and traditional themes, though roll-up windows were added later. Similarly Spartan, the pedals are bare metal and drilled. Set in the dashboard is a classic-looking Ferrari instrument panel fitted with a tachometer, speedometer, fuel gauge, and a dial for oil pressure. In contrast to the red seats and door panels, the rest of the interior is finished in flat black.

With previous Ferraris, you would have expected to hear about panel beaters pounding out aluminum F40 bodies on forms. By 1987, Ferrari had learned to lay-up bodies of carbon fiber, Kevlar, and resin. The single-piece front deck weighs in at 39.6 pounds, with the rear one a mere 48.5 pounds, including the wing. The doors, complete with hardware, are 3.3 pounds.

Ferrari's contemporary competition was Porsche's 959, and the pair had similar (high) performance. The 2,420-pound Ferrari clocked a 0–60 time of 3.8 seconds, topping out just over 201 miles per hour, about what the super Porsche could achieve. Where the Ferrari appeals very much to the heart, the Porsche goes for the brain.

There are any number of ducts on the F40 to add cool air to or relieve hot air from the supercar, which is a problem in high-horsepower supercars that need to be as adept at speed on a track as at a crawl on the street.

This is a U.S. version of the F40. Ferrari did an excellent job of reworking the Pininfarina body to accommodate the "safety" bumpers required by the U.S. government. Engineers had to deactivate the adjustable suspension on the U.S. F40s to meet the bumper-height rules.

Carbon fiber, Kevlar, and other advanced materials were also used in the F40's chassis. Things began conventionally enough with a steel tube frame, but it was reinforced with panels molded in plastic and glued in place. A few sections, such as the front well for the spare tire, looked like plastic sculptings. Naturally such critical areas as the engine and suspension mounting points were metal. Fitted inside the body just ahead of each rear wheel well was one 15.8-gallon fuel cell per side. Competition filler pipe and cap were available on request.

Ferrari claimed the "plastic car" was several hundred pounds lighter, but four or five times stiffer than a traditional metal/frame body design.

Both the front and rear suspensions of the F40 were laid out with unequal-length A-arms, coil springs, Koni shocks, and anti-roll bars. The change for Ferrari was to add adjustable ride height, the F40 settling automatically at high speeds—down 0.8 inch above 74 miles per hour—and having the option of adding an extra inch of ground clearance to get over such obstacles as driveway ramps. F40 tires are Z-rated Michelins, measuring 245/45ZR-17 at the front and 335/35AR-17 in back.

Tucked inside all that rubber are 13-inch-diameter disc brakes. To keep weight down, both the four-piston calipers and discs are aluminum, the latter with cast-iron braking surfaces set in the discs. No power assist here, and no ABS, thank you; that just was not in the tradition of these cars.

Ferrari also explained that the brake system was up to racing standards, ". . . and this means a system which can be used for competition purposes if necessary." It isn't surprising, then, to discover the rack-and-pinion steering is also unassisted.

Ferrari developed the 288 GTO Evoluzione's twin-turbo V-8 for the F40. Displacement was increased to 2,936 cc and bigger water-cooled IHI turbos were added, with the maximum pressure set at just over 15 psi blowing though a pair of air-to-air intercoolers. Weber-Marelli designed

Three types of seats were offered in the F40, the driver having to be fitted for the proper seat at the factory or by his dealer. Though the interior can be somewhat noisy, there are amenities, like optional air conditioning or roll-up windows.

sequential, phased electronic fuel injection for the F40, which would prove to be a particular benefit to U.S. Ferrari owners several years later.

This mechanical stuff was all very interesting, but most exciting is to see the V-8 set fore-aft under the louvered rear window. One look in the tail section and there is no doubt this car is a race car waiting to get down to business. And it has the power, with 478 horsepower at 7,000 rpm and 425 ft-lb of torque at 4,000.

Set in the F40's instrument pod is a classic gauge package: tachometer, speedometer, fuel gauge, and oil pressure. This is the end of the era of classic gauges for several automakers, as LED panels became more popular and reliable.

F40 owners had the choice of two different gearboxes, but it wasn't the usual question of manual or automatic. In the Ferrari, you could specify either a five-speed with synchromesh or, for those who wanted to feel they were in a real race car, the same gearbox without synchros.

One thing the F40 was designed for was four-wheel drive a la Porsche 959. Ferrari built a prototype with drive to all wheels, but said it preferred to keep the F40 in the more traditional style.

Not that owners of the Ferrari had to apologize to those with an original 959. Weighing in at around 2,420 pounds, the F40 got to 60 miles per hour in 3.8 seconds with a top speed of 201 miles per hour, the times all within a tick or two of the 959.

That should be enough for most of us . . . .

Where Porsche's 959 was a technological showcase, the F40 was more a display of Italian brio, speed, and beauty. The brain opted for the 959, while the heart went for the F40.

At the time the F40 was literally unveiled on that hot day in July 1987, it was promised there would be a U.S. version, though the process took three years. Building F40s at the rate of one to two per day, Ferrari was still at it three years later and, in that time, a great deal had been about certifying supercars for the United States and happily applied to the F40.

Externally, there was little difference for the U.S. edition. Small black strips above and below the grille act as impact surfaces for the 2.5-mile-per-hour bumper crash regulations. Ferrari deactivated the adjustable suspension on cars for the States rather than design a bumper that would be tall enough to be effective through its upper and lower heights. There was also a rear safety bumper, and like the front, it had added internal structure to meet the rules. Also outside were numerous small lighting changes, including a high-mounted rear brake light.

Inside, the only major change was a motorized "mouse" seat/shoulder belt to meet passive restraint regulations.

Thanks to that Weber-Marelli electronic fuel-injection system and the latest catalytic converters, Ferrari engineers were able to Americanize the twin-turbo V-8 without a major power loss, still claiming 478 horsepower and 425 ft-lb of torque.

Opposite page: You can almost see Bologna from the countryside near Ferrari's home in Maranello. The F40 is parked near the factory along one of the hillside roads that Ferrari uses to test its prototypes and production cars, one reason Ferraris tend to be so adept on public roads and racetracks.

In July 1987, Ferrari hinted it would cap F40 production at 400 cars, but the model proved so popular (and profitable) that it just kept building them, finally completing 1,315 cars . . . and angering many of the early owners who were looking for rarity in their supercar. Some had paid up to $1.5 million for their F40.

Ferrari also eventually got around to having a race version of the F40 built. It had Michelotto in Padova do the conversion, which was called the F40 LM. The interior was

Leonardo Fioravanti, who designed such great Ferraris as the Daytona and Boxer, led research and design for Pininfarina when it designed the F40's exterior. At the launch he explained how the F40 was wind tunnel developed and has a 0.34 coefficient of drag with minimal lift front and rear.

Ferrari's F40 production line was a slow-paced affair . . . and a long-running one. Owners criticized Ferrari for building too many F40s (1,315), diluting the pride (and profit) of ownership.

stripped still more and a digital dash installed, while the exterior was tuned to competition, replacing the fixed rear wing with one that could be adjusted for downforce.

Power was boosted to 720 horsepower with the potential for 900 in qualifying sessions, a trick that was common in the turbo days. Formula 1 driver Jean Alesi drove an F40 LM in its racing debut at the Laguna Seca's IMSA race in October 1989, and led the race until his tires let him down and he finished third. A pair of F40 LMs was campaigned in IMSA in 1990 and had four podium finishes, though never a win.

Racing F40s were successful in the mid-1990s in the European BPR Championship and in a Japanese series, with some victories against newer, more completely developed cars. Minimal development also hurt the F40 LMs' chances in endurance races, like the 24 Hours of Le Mans.

This lack of racing success shouldn't take away from the aura of the F40. At the time, it and the Porsche 959 were *the* supercars. Drive an F40 with its barely tamed race car demeanor—with mechanical sounds reverberating through every piece as you rap up through the gears—and you discover a delightful hard edge that is lost, for better or worse, in the exotic cars of the twenty-first century. ■

The F40 requires something of a festival of louvers to relieve hot air from the engine compartment. But doesn't it look cool? You can see how the car's rear window is shaped to flow air over the rear wing.

CHAPTER 10

At the famed Nardo high-speed track in southern Italy, this Jaguar supercar managed 219 miles per hour, close enough to earn the car its XJ220 moniker. Like Porsche's 959 and Ferrari's 288 GTO, the XJ220 was originally meant to be raced under the FIA's Group B rules, which were later rescinded.

220
MILES PER HOUR

JAGUAR XJ220 1988

"That was one of the scariest things I've ever done in a car."

"Really? Why?"

Davy Jones, ace Jaguar sports car driver (and future Le Mans winner), explained the dangers of holding the Jaguar XJ220 on the 8-mile, high-speed banking near Nardo, Italy, as we went for top speed. He mentioned the single-rail steel barrier and how, at high speed, we'd be long gone before anyone even knew we'd crashed.

Ah, the blissfulness of ignorance on my part. I had thoroughly enjoyed the ride, fitted with fire suit and helmet and strapped

Two great Jaguars, the D-Type (in the back) with the XJ220. Designer Keith Helfet gets credit for the supercar's sleek exterior. His goals were to create a shape that would contain and cool a 500-horsepower engine, be aerodynamically stable at 220 miles per hour, and look like a Jaguar.

into the long Jaguar. We'd seen 216–217 on the speedometer, subtracted for speedo error, added mile-per-hour for tire scrub, and been able to claim a top speed just one tick shy of the big cat's namesake number: 220 miles per hour. Close enough.

Appropriate, too, for while Jaguar's famous sports car, the XK120, was meant to go 120 miles per hour, its newest was aimed at 220.

What made the speed so deceptive was the nature of the XJ220. Where other supercars had a slightly hard edge or a sense of a muscle-taut sprinter just out of the starting blocks, the Jaguar did not.

That image began with the exterior shape, which was sleek and flowing compared to other exotics, an obvious 1990s extension of the 1950s Jaguar D-Type and 1960s XJ13 race cars. A member of the family.

Inside many high-speed exotic cars, there's a feeling of tuned-down race car with hard seats and minimal luxury. Not in the Jag, its dashboard broad and like a production car, leather everywhere, and seats looking downright overstuffed compared to those in a Ferrari or Lamborghini. Knowing the low-roof design of the XJ220 would cause a dark, enclosing bunker effect inside, the car had a glass roof so the interior was light and welcoming, not a bit threatening like some supercars.

Jaguar hand-built the XJ220s in a converted mill in Bloxham, not far from Banbury, England. After the XJ220 production run was finished, the factory was turned over to Aston Martin DB-7 production.

Quite simply, Jaguar's XJ220 was the limo of the supercar set.

Credit for the idea of the XJ220 goes to Jaguar's then-director of product engineering, Jim Randall, who wanted to build a Group B machine—a la Porsche's 959—based on the 1984 Jaguar race car. Specifications included V-12 power and four-wheel drive. There were no production intentions, and for three years a group of Jaguar employees, who called themselves "The Saturday Club," worked on the 220 during off-hours. Outside suppliers donated much of the materials needed.

Keith Helfet of Jaguar Design did the exterior design of the 220, which had to be street legal and cool a 500-plus-horsepower engine at a sustained 200 miles per hour. Manufacturing was kept in mind, just in case. . . .

Nick Hull created the interior, trying to capture the wraparound feeling of the D-Type race car, but with air conditioning, leather upholstery, power windows, and other driver amenities. What the XJ220 brief did not include were such driving niceties as power steering, cruise control, or automatic transmission. Back then they didn't seem right in an exotic car.

Shown to the public at the 1988 Birmingham Show, the 220 was so well received that production was approved. Jag had neither the time nor facilities to build the limited-production supercar, so the job went to JaguarSport—the joint project of Jaguar and Tom Walkinshaw Racing (TWR) meant to take Jag racing and do just this sort of low-volume, high-performance project.

Getting the XJ220 to production necessitated changes. Most significant was substituting the 3.5-liter turbo V-6 from the XJR-10 and 11 race cars for the V-12 in the show car, and using rear- instead of all-wheel drive.

If there is a technical downside to the XJ220, it was its engine. Originally it was to have V-12 power, but ended up with a 3.5-liter twin-turbo V-6. It was powerful enough, with 542 horsepower at 7,000 rpm and 475 ft-lb of torque at 4,500 rpm, but sounded as though it belonged in a super tractor, not a supercar.

One of the first aims was to trim weight from the 3,700-pound show car XJ220. TWR got the heft down to just over 3,000 pounds, a hunk gone when it shortened the car's overall length by 10 inches, 8 inches of it gone from the wheelbase—a move made possible when the V-12 went, in favor of the V-6.

The XJ220's structure was based on panels of aluminum honeycomb sandwiched between aluminum sheets. Exterior bodywork was done in aluminum by the famous firm of Abbey Panels in Coventry, England, while hidden inside was an integral steel roll cage.

The 220 body wasn't just pretty and safe, it was also aerodynamically efficient. The coefficient of drag was 0.36 and there were 600 pounds of downforce. At the front was a fixed lower splitter to get the air under the car, where it flowed through channels to the rear venturi outlets, aiding downforce. Air through the nose grille cooled the engine and air conditioning condenser, then vented out of the top of the nose. At the back was a full-width resin spoiler.

Davy Jones slides the big Jag through a handling course. The XJ220's handling was developed at England's Donington circuit and Germany's Nürburgring, where it held the production car lap record. High-speed testing was conducted at Nardo in Italy and MIRA and Millbrook in the UK.

Jaguar's XJ220 started as an after-hours "what if?" project headed by Jim Randall, the highly regarded then-director of product engineering for the automaker. A group of Jaguar employees called "the Saturday Club" donated their time for the car's early development.

While the XJ220 had plenty of speed and style, it fell victim to the world economy. Debuted in 1988 and approved for production the next year, the car was priced at $660,000, and required deposits of almost $100,000. Between order time and delivery time two years later, the exotic car market fizzled. Jaguar ended up in court with its supercar buyers.

The front and rear suspension designs were unequal-length upper and lower A-arms. Coil springs and Bilstein shocks were mounted inboard and operated through rocker arms. Bridgestone supplied the tires, Speedline the single-piece alloy wheels, and AP the non-ABS vented disc brakes.

Fuel was held in a racing fuel cell between the cockpit and engine compartment.

Looking almost diminutive in the back of the XJ220 was the 3.5-liter V-6 twin turbo with dual overhead cams, four valves, and some 25 psi of maximum boost. The dry sump V-6 looked like a race engine in street dress with an air conditioning compressor and alternator. Companion to the V-6 was a five-speed manual transaxle, which had a viscous limited-slip differential.

Here's how the XJ220's horsepower and torque stacked up to the Italian competition of the day:

Jaguar XJ220: 542 brake horsepower at 7,000 rpm and 475 ft-lb at 4,500 rpm

Lamborghini Diablo: 492 brake horsepower at 7,000 rpm and 429 ft-lb at 5,200 rpm

Ferrari F40: 478 brake horsepower at 7,000 rpm and 427 ft-lb at 4,000 rpm

And here are the results—using Jaguar's numbers—of the final performance tests against the F40 and Diablo:

	0–62 miles per hour	Top Speed
XJ220	3.85	212.3 mph (208 average)
Diablo	4.29	202.1 mph
F40	4.10	201.3 mph

High-speed XJ220 testing was done in Nardo, Italy, as well as at the MIRA and Millbrook testing facilities in England. Ride and handling work was completed at Donington Park Grand Prix Circuit in England and the Nürburgring in Germany, where driver John Nielson set a new production-car lap record with the Jaguar.

With the XJ220's pedigree, good looks, and performance it would be nice to say it led a loved, charmed life. That never happened, because the demise of the very thing that made it seem logical to build the car turned the XJ220 into a supercar orphan. The surging world economy (particularly in Japan) had fueled a dramatic rise in the demand and price of supercars in the late 1980s. When that world economy cooled dramatically in 1990, down went supercar values.

Jaguar approved the XJ220 in 1989 at a time when exotic car cars sales were storming along, and priced it at $660,000 with a deposit of $94,000 on a signed contract. The company promised no more than 350 of the supercars would be built and buyers happily stepped up . . . including speculators planning on making a few bucks. This speculative

Jaguar's designed the XJ220 to compete with the Lamborghini Diablo and Ferrari F40 on the performance scale. They succeeded; with 542 horsepower, the Jag out-powered the Italian pair. The English car bested the other two in top speed by 10–15 miles per hour.

There is none of the hard-edge almost-race-car feeling inside the XJ220 that you get in some supercars. The interior is pure Jaguar, from the comfy leather-covered seats to the instrumentation on the dashboard. To keep the interior from feeling low and dark, engineers sensibly gave the XJ220 a glass roof.

In the mid-1960s, Jaguar came close to reentering international competition with the mid-engine XJ13 race car. Powered by a 500-plus-horsepower V-12, the XJ13 was designed in 1964 but slow development put it behind the times, and Jag killed the project. The XJ13 was kept a secret until 1973. The car is now in Jaguar's museum in England.

Two great Jaguar shapes: D-Type and XJ220. While the D-Type has a long, honored history as a race car, the XJ220's competition aspirations as the XJ220C were limited, though it won its first race in the English BRDC GT championship.

disease, incidentally, affected the price of other exotic cars and valuable vintage cars around the world.

Bad timing on their part, as it turned out, because the exotic car market imploded in the two years between deposit time and when XJ220 production began in a converted old mill in Bloxham, not far from Banbury, England. Would-be buyers wanted out of their contracts on cars already worth less than the original agreed-upon value. Lawsuits ensued and dragged on until the spring of 1994, when the speculators were offered the chance to walk away from their contracts for one payment of $150,000.

There were also, of course, owners perfectly happy with their XJ220, but by the time the dust cleared and production ended after 280–290 cars, Jaguar had a small warehouse of unsold XJ220s.

What to do?

Eventually, a batch was sold to a dealer as the possibility of certifying them for the United States improved. You can now find them in the States, certified and ready for the road.

But that didn't help Jaguar, and in summer 1993 the company thought it had a solution to some of the XJ220 problems. Jaguar had built a racing version called the XJ220C, which won its maiden race, a BRDC (British Racing Drivers' Club) GT Challenge event. It was first thought an XJ220C had taken the Grand Touring Class in the 1993 24 Hours of Le Mans . . . until it was disqualified two weeks later.

Now the idea of racing returned, with a dozen XJ220s prepped by Walkinshaw for a U.S. series called Past Masters. The idea was to match the XJ220s and former driving greats in a series of events at small U.S. tracks where the races could be televised easily.

The first race was at Indianapolis Raceway Park and it was embarrassing—like watching Carl Lewis in a gunnysack race or Jeff Gordon in a goofy bumper car. Suited to 200-plus miles per hour on Le Mans' Mulsanne Straight, the Jaguars looked like well-dressed ambitious fat men being forced around the tight, narrow road circuits and, often, into each other. Thankfully, the series was a failure.

It was also a sad, lasting remembrance of the XJ220 in many enthusiasts' minds.

Speedometer and tach needles are about pegged to the right as we rocket around the Nardo track at just shy of 220 miles per hour. Driver Davy Jones—who later codrove to victory in the 24 Hours of Le Mans—commented that the hot lap was scary. Luckily the photographer was too busy (or too dim?) to realize this until Jones told him later.

The XJ220 deserves better. The cars have arguably the most elegant-yet-exciting styling of that era's supercars. And they drive the same way, nothing rough or rumbly, smooth controls and very nice fit and finish. It is a big car and it takes a while to get used to moving that amount of real estate around, but it isn't intimidating.

Given the Jaguar's elegance, the feeling of 0–60 in 4.9 seconds seems a bit out of character, but not so much as the engine sound. For all the XJ220's beauty and grace, the V-6 sounds like a fight in a country bar. Ugly.

But only to your ears . . . to your eyes there is all the leather-wrapped luxury and elegance you expect from Jaguar . . . even at 219 miles per hour. ■

CHAPTER 11

Porsche's 959 wasn't just styled to look like it's going 180 when standing still; it earned that look through rigorous wind tunnel work to optimize its aerodynamics. The shape has a low drag coefficient of 0.31, and Porsche claims it has zero lift.

199
MILES PER HOUR

PORSCHE 959 1988

By nature, Paul Frere is not a nervous man.
Yet he was fidgeting next to me, suggesting, "John, I think the traffic is building. . . ."

But I had the Porsche 959 at 280 kilometers per hour, creeping to the magic 300 (186.4 miles per hour) tick on the speedometer. The traffic wasn't *that* bad.

Frere, the world-famous race driver and automotive journalist, stirred and cleared his throat: "Ahem!" The speedo inched up 295 . . . 300, *bingo*. . . . Okay, Paul, time to slow.

These days Bentley four-door sedans top out at 195 miles per hour, but in 1989, the 959's 198.8-mile-per-hour terminal

Porsche designed the 959 for Group B competition, which covered rally and road racing. Rules demanded an automaker build 200 such machines, but put no limits on minimum weight or technology, and with that came a horsepower war. Also in the fight were Lancia, Ford, Ferrari, Jaguar, Peugeot, and Audi.

Porsche showed it was serious about the FIA's Group B racing class when it showed this white concept car at the 1983 Frankfurt Show and, appropriately, called it the Gruppe B. Its rather futuristic Porsche styling wowed us, but what we didn't appreciate was what would lurk beneath the sleek bodywork of the production 959.

velocity was a lofty goal for a supercar. Besides, the 959 wasn't just a car aimed at a top speed—another potent drivetrain stuffed in a lightweight chassis and body—but an integrated system of systems that felt more like a performance aircraft than an automobile.

First hint at the 959 appeared as the *Gruppe* B show car at the 1983 Frankfurt Motor Show. It was Porsche's response to the FIA's Group B regulations for rally and racing cars: no minimum weight, no caps on technology, and all the horsepower you please . . . no holds barred. Build 200 examples and you're in.

Porsche, Ferrari, and Jaguar began work on Group B cars meant for race circuits. Others went the rally route, creating all-wheel-drive, lightweight, 500-horsepower machines like the Audi Quattro, Ford RS200, Peugeot T16, and turbocharged/supercharged Lancia Delta S4.

They created amazing cars, the Group B Rally Car website figuring an S4 got to 62 miles per hour in 2.3 seconds on gravel, and Finnish driver Henri Toivonen could have put his sixth on the grid for the 1986 Portuguese Grand Prix. But it proved a fatal recipe that year when Toivonen and his American co-driver, Sergio Cresto, were killed on the Tour de Corse. Exit Group B.

With the end of the class, Ferrari's 288 GTO and Jaguar's XJ220 were orphaned as wonderful oddities, yet Porsche's 959 became a legend.

Engineering legend Helmuth Bott headed that department at Porsche as work began on the 959 early in 1983. At its heart would be all-wheel drive. It quickly became apparent the front-engine, rear-gearbox layouts of the 924, 944, and 928 were impractical for this drive layout. Ditto for development of a purpose-built mid-engine machine, so it was decided to adapt the traction system to the evergreen 911.

Audi made all-wheel drive lightweight and practical in high-performance road cars, its Quattro's World Rally Championship wins adding an official stamp of approval. It seemed every automaker now wanted in, and with rear-engine placement, routing power to the front wheels of the 911 was, in theory, relatively simple.

There was the usual drive to the rear wheels, with a central driveshaft carrying power to a front-wheel differential. Power had to be variable between front and rear wheels because of uneven traction possibilities. Usually a central differential did that job, but in the 959 that variation was handled by the Porsche-Steuer Kupplung—the electronically controlled PSK, 13 discs in an oil bath that could theoretically vary front/rear power distribution from 0/100 (all rear drive) to 50/50 (an even front/rear split).

When Porsche determined that it would lose money on every 959, it decided to not certify the car for the U.S. market. One attempt to have them imported as race cars failed. It took an act of Congress to create a new law that would allow the super Porsche (and other exotic cars) to be driven in the United States.

Although based on a steel platform, the rest of the 959 is done in more exotic materials. The doors and hood are made of aluminum, while the top, front fenders, rear quarters, and the huge engine cover are made of lightweight Kevlar.

JAY LENO ON THE *PORSCHE 959*

Seinfeld has one. They're pretty amazing, but it wasn't a car I lusted after." Porsche didn't sell the 959 in the United States, so it was a car Leno never saw, for which he never had a chance to develop lust.

Leno also explains: "They are 4-wheel drive and I prefer rear-wheel drive. To me, half the fun of owning these cars is sliding 'em around. I'm not out there trying to race, I'm just out there trying to enjoy myself and have fun. I go into a turn and I see a little gravel, I give it the gas and kick the ass end around and then bring it back. That's very entertaining and I enjoy that. Obviously with a 959 (and the added grip of 4-wheel drive) you're going to do all those things a lot higher speed."

In reality, the maximum split was 20 front/80 rear, the driver choosing, via a steering column lever, from four traction programs: dry or wet tarmac, snow, or off road, all of which were indicated by a light glowing in the right-hand dash dial, adding to the sense of systems.

The suspension was a race-derived unequal-length upper and lower A-arm design with coil springs and a pair of shocks per corner. Normal ride height was 4.7 inches, though a dash-mounted switch would raise it to 5.9 or 7 inches. Above 49.7 miles per hour, the onboard computer (less powerful than a good personal digital assistant [PDA] today) lowered the car to 5.9 or to 4.7 inches above 99.5 miles per hour, except on the 959S (Sport) models, which had nonadjustable suspensions.

Another switch offered three shock absorber levels: soft, medium, or hard, the computer reverting to the firmest above 99.5 miles per hour.

In true Porsche form, the brakes were ventilated, cross-drilled Brembo discs (12.7 inches front, 11.9 inches rear) with four-piston aluminum calipers. In true modern form, they had ABS back when many high-performance automakers scoffed at such systems.

Ah, there's that word again—system—and here are two more on the 959 that are just getting general use today: run-flat tires and tire-pressure monitoring.

The most predictable component in the 959 was its engine, a flat-six, though it is not the 911 powerplant. Based on Porsche's all-conquering Indy/935/936/956/962 race engine, it is air cooled with water-cooled heads containing chain-driven twin cams and

Although the 959 is more than 15 years old, its performance times hold up nicely today, with a 0 to 60 in 3.6 seconds and a top speed just under 200 miles per hour. The 959s now being certified for U.S. sale by Bruce Canepa improve on those numbers, cutting the 0-to-60 time to 3.2 seconds and topping out around 215 miles per hour.

four valves per cylinder. To eliminate turbo lag at low rpm, Porsche used two sequential turbos with intercoolers, the first providing boost to 4,300 rpm when the second chimed in, giving those in the 959 a nicely added oomph, and 450 horsepower at 6,500 rpm and 369 ft-lb of torque at 5,500 rpm...from just 2.8 liters.

Rare for a modern Porsche, the 959's engine is in plain view once the huge rear lid is raised, exhibiting a terrific scene with the vertical fan and turbo plumbing.

Somewhat unusual for its time is a six-speed manual gearbox. This wide range was considered necessary to reach the 198.8-mile-per-hour top speed and still allow for low-speed work, as it was assumed 20 years ago that four-wheel drive meant off-roading.

Arguably, the most enduring 959 attribute is the styling of its body. The 911 shape is hiding in there, but the only carryover piece is the taillight. The rest is blended into a beautiful flow of scoops, grilles, and aerodynamic detailing, some of which is still used, in forms, by Porsche today. To maintain its light weight, the 959 was based on a steel platform with the top, front fenders, rear quarters, and engine cover done in Kevlar; the doors and hood in aluminum.

Although many Porsche engines are visually lost down in the tail of the car, the 959's is proudly on display. While still a flat-six, the 2.8-liter engine has water-cooled cylinder heads, four valves per cylinder and—to reduce response lag—two sequential turbochargers with intercoolers. Horsepower came out to 450 at 6,500 rpm and torque to 369 ft-lb at 5,500.

More than good looking, the 959 shape has an impressive drag coefficient of 0.31 and a claimed zero lift, plus a solid stance on the road—planted to the pavement, looking as though it had all the traction you could ever need.

Interior changes were minimal, except for the tall center tunnel housing the front-wheel driveshaft and the instruments, which incorporated info lights for the drive and suspension systems. Ahead are enough dials to equip an airplane, showing turbo boost to 2.5 bar, a 345-kilometer-per-hour speedometer . . . the stuff guys love. Just as they like to read about 0–60 times of 3.6 seconds and the top speed just shy of 200 miles per hour.

Racing has always been an important part of Porsche, but the 959 had limited use. A pair finished 1-2 in the rugged Paris–Dakar Rally in 1986, the same year a track version—the 961—nailed down seventh overall and first in class at Le Mans. But that was about it.

Early on there was little doubt the 959 was headed for greatness . . . but not to the States.

Porsche planned to import the cars, but the numbers got upside down. It was costing the company a reported $500,000 to hand build the 959s at Weissach, some $155,000 above its price tag. To minimize loses, the automaker scaled back production, slicing out the United States and keeping the original total to 226, though there was such a clamor by buyers willing to pay as much as a reported $1 million for a 959 that Porsche assembled an additional 10–15 in the early 1990s.

American enthusiasts wanted 959s and the late Al Holbert, who headed Porsche racing in the United States, tried to help. He convinced the factory to build around 10 959S models as race cars, fitted with roll cages, sparse cloth interiors, 480-brake-horsepower engines, and the nonadjustable racing suspension. Holbert had to prove they were race cars, but at a test at Nazareth, Pennsylvania, the cars apparently appeared too docile, not enough like race cars for the feds, who had them shipped back to Germany.

A few 959s were imported under such legal exemptions as museum display, so famed collector Otis Chandler had one, but in the early 1990s the situation was too fuzzy. Others, like Ralph Lauren and Microsoft's Bill Gates and Paul Allen not only wanted 959s, but to freely drive them—which is where Bruce Canepa came in.

Yes, it looks like a 911, but the only piece retained from the stock car is the taillight. The remainder of the car was reworked into a beautiful flowing shape with just enough grille and scoops to make it look purposeful.

Once it had decided to use all-wheel drive for the 959, Porsche understood that its front-engine, rear-drive 924, 944, and 928 could not be easily modified for such a drive system. An all-new automobile was out of the question, so Porsche adapted all-wheel drive to the venerable rear-engine 911.

Representing 959 owners, Canepa had Warren Dean, a Washington, D.C., lawyer, develop an exemption law and get it to Congress. Under the rule, anyone could bring in a car if it is no longer produced, there had never been more than 500 made, and it met EPA emissions rules for the year it was made (1988 for the 959), plus an added 10 percent improvement. Department of Transportation (DOT) crash requirements would be waived, but annual mileage would be limited to 2,500.

President Bill Clinton signed the law in 1998, but it was two years before the final rule was finished, the feds being particularly fussy about that 2,500-mile proviso.

It had taken a decade, but now Canepa could import, convert, and sell 959s. The flat-six went through a development project to parallel Porsche's work, had Porsche continued with the 959. Knowing the engine and chassis had 600-brake-horsepower potential, Canepa's group reworked the electronics, replaced the KKK turbos with Garretts, and made other modifications so it pumps out 610 brake horsepower with 540 ft-lb of torque, dropping the 0–60 time to just 3.2 seconds and stretching top speed to 215 miles per hour. As in the 959S versions, Canepa's cars have nonadjustable suspensions, going with modern shocks and titanium springs.

And a price tag of $575,000 with, Canepa tells us, a line of potential owners. They would join an august group that already includes such men as Lauren, Chandler, Gates, Allen, and Jerry Seinfeld.

Legends with legends. ■

A 959 cockpit has a variety of systems controls so the driver can tailor his car to varying driving conditions. In addition to a lever that selects one of four traction programs, these switches allow the driver to firm or soften the shock absorbers and raise or lower the car's ride height.

Opposite page: Although originally intended to be raced, 959s led only civilian lives. Porsche did enter a pair of competition 959s on the ultrarugged Paris-Dakar Rally in 1986, and they nailed down a 1-2 finish. At Le Mans that year, a road racing version called the 961 won its class and finished seventh overall.

CHAPTER 12

Marcello Gandini, who designed the Countach (among several famous supercars), was hired to create the shape of its successor. Called Project 132, it was taken on by Chrysler when it bought Lamborghini. Chrysler Chairman Lee Iacocca didn't like the body proposed by Gandini, and the result was a shape that combines that design with changes made to it in Chrysler's U.S. studios.

205 MILES PER HOUR

LAMBORGHINI DIABLO 1990

Ferrari was providing the perfect aural background for Lamborghini. We were at a small race course near Milan, Italy, to test the then-new 6.0-liter Lamborghini Diablo. While driving the 550-horsepower Diablo on a nicely circuitous track, Ferrari was on another straightaway testing the software and durability of its Formula 1 car's launch system.

High revs off the line for the Ferrari, bumping up on the limiter, tires churning for grip time after time. That would inspire you.

So did the big Lamborghini. Like the Countach, there was no doubt when you drove the Diablo that it was long (175.9 inches), wide (80.3 inches minus mirrors), no lightweight

(3,700 pounds), and there was a lot of oomph (550 horsepower, 435 ft-lb of torque) just aft of your cranium.

A Diablo easily gets to 60 miles per hour in under 4 seconds and with enough track could trip the lights at 205 miles per hour.

It feels like it—a stormer—though with all-wheel drive you also sense security as you chase another Diablo, this one driven by a man who knows the track. You'd like to hang on a bit longer, but he's good and your guardian angel keeps whispering, "$250,000 . . . $250,000 . . . $250,000. . . ."

Given its druthers, Lamborghini wouldn't have kept building the Countach for 16 years, but for much of that time it was just trying to stay alive.

Ever-changing emissions laws and the two oil shocks of the 1970s were like grenades thrown into the laps of the builders of supercars. Ferrari had become part of the Fiat empire. Maserati went to De Tomaso and was out of the exotic-car business.

Can you see a hint of both the Lamborghini Countach and Diablo here? This is the Cizeta Moroder, another Marcello Gandini car designed between the two Lambos. The mid-mounted 64-valve V-16 engine produces 540 horsepower.

In 1973, Ferruccio Lamborghini unloaded 51 percent of his car company after the first oil crisis, dropped the remainder the next year, and went off to make wine. The new Swiss owners held out until 1978, when the company went bankrupt and into liquidation. A pair of wealthy French brothers, the Mimrans, bought the automaker and got it rolling successfully into the 1980s to the point where it needed additional capital.

Enter Chrysler, which purchased Lamborghini and brought with it money, expertise, and the attitude needed to convert this sometimes-sleepy automaker into an exotic-car power . . . and to design and develop the Diablo.

In 1994, Chrysler sold Lamborghini to Indonesian interests with "Tommy" Suharto at their core.

These were not the most stable of times for Lamborghini, which was pulled from the mire in 1998 when Audi AG bought it lock, stock, and assembly lines and began development of a successor to the Diablo.

Providing a historical foreground for a Diablo VT is the very first Lamborghini made, the 1963 350 GTV prototype. Actually it wasn't quite finished when presented at the 1963 Turin show, because the V-12 designed for the car by well-known engineer Giotto Bizzarrini wouldn't fit inside Franco Scaglione's beautiful bodywork.

The heart of the Diablo is its aluminum V-12 engine. With dual chain-driven camshafts on each cylinder head and fuel injection, the big engine began life in the Diablo at 5.7 liters, pumping out 485 horsepower and 428 ft-lb of torque. As in the Countach, the engine is in the car "backward" with the transmission sticking forward into the cockpit.

Lamborghini had been through several owners and some very trying financial times when Chrysler bought the automaker in 1987. The prototype for its replacement—called Project 132—was inherited by Chrysler and would be developed into the Diablo.

But let's run the tape back to the late 1980s when Chrysler still owned the Italian automaker and it was finally time to replace the aging Countach. It was sensible that the man who created the Countach shape, making it arguably the most influential supercar of its time, should get a shot at shaping its successor. So Marcello Gandini was hired to pen a car that was codenamed P132, but would become the Diablo.

Things get a little hazy here. Gandini also designed the exterior of a supercar called the Cizeta Moroder V16T and some stories have it that its design was originally meant to be a new Countach. The Cizeta was the gallant attempt by Claudio Zampolli to build a very exclusive exotic machine with a 560-horsepower transverse V-16 engine. This car also fell victim to the world financial crisis in the early 1990s, but that's another book.

Bob Lutz, then president of Chrysler, once told us the company signed Gandini to do the Diablo, but what it got was a variation on the Cizeta Moroder, and the Diablo's design was completed in Detroit. Retained were Gandini's forward-tilting rear wheel arches, an alloy wheel design with holes, the forward-sloping lower window, and who knows how much else.

Regardless of exact parentage, the Diablo is a stunner. Even bigger than the Countach, it is a gorgeous design with just the right amount of strength and glamour. The design is particularly delicious when seen from above. Yes, it is even more of a job to drive than the Countach, thanks to its size, but it is arguably a more beautiful shape.

During its 11-year lifetime (1990–2001), there were 13–15 Diablo models, depending on how you counted them, including two roadster versions. At times the design suffered a bit from the Countach's wing-and-vented-still disease, but it wasn't as contagious or deforming with the Diablo.

As the car's tenure continued, more carbon fiber body panels were integrated into the design. With Lamborghini now well under the wing of Audi and with the 6.0-liter version in 2000, we saw the closest thing to a Diablo redesign. It was relatively minor except that most of the body, which had been in aluminum, was formed in carbon fiber, save the aluminum doors and steel structural roof.

We do know that an American, Bill Dayton, drew up the original Diablo interior. Two almost-reclining seats bracket the wide center console needed to accommodate the forward-facing transmission. Like the exterior, the car's inside is broad, elegant, and uncluttered, with the emphasis on the instrument cluster and the meaty shift linkage. When the interior was reworked for the 6.0-liter version, it had a wide arcing instrument panel and plenty of carbon fiber on display, a welcome and appropriate change.

Lamborghini produced the Diablo at its factory in Sant'Agata, Italy, not far from Modena. The Diablo was made by fitting hand-formed aluminum body panels over a steel tube frame. The V-12 engines were also made by hand in the factory.

In 1993, Lamborghini introduced the 30th Anniversary model of the Diablo to celebrate the company's founding. The V-12 got a boost to 525 horsepower, and the factory claimed a 0–60 time under 4.0 seconds and a top speed of 206 miles per hour.

Tempting, eh? Step in, settle down in the leather-covered seats, pull down the Diablo doors, light the fire, and take off. The ambiance is about perfect, with none of the electronic detachment of modern paddle shifters.

Underneath, the Diablo is very much a continuation of the Countach. That new body shape hid a traditional steel space frame, upper and lower A-arm suspension, and disc brakes that thankfully grew over the years as horsepower increased. So did the electronic suspension content, as shocks with variable stiffness were added and then refined.

The true inner beauty of the Diablo is its V-12. Still classic Italian stuff, done in aluminum with twin chain-driven camshafts and fuel injection, it began as a 5.7 liter with 485 horsepower at 7,000 rpm and 428 ft-lb of torque at 5,200 rpm. There were versions that really pumped it out, like the 595-horsepower Jota.

Come 2000, the V-12 was stroked to 6.0 liters, taking the horsepower to 550, torque to 422 ft-lb.

Diablos were built for 11 years in a stunning variety of versions devised to spur sales. This included two- and four-wheel drive versions, plus roadsters. While there was some of the added wing-and-vented-sill disease that hit the Countach like an ugly stick, it wasn't as bad on the Diablo.

Always known for its wild color choices, Lamborghini settled on lavender metallic for the lightweight SE30 version of the Diablo. Deliveries of the 150 SE models built by Lamborghini began in mid-1994.

Several aerodynamic changes to the SE 30th Anniversary set it apart from other Diablos. The front spoiler was deeper with added air intakes, while new side sills directed air to oil coolers. The rear spoiler dipped at its ends, while the center was adjustable for downforce.

Another carryover from the Countach is the reversed drivetrain that poked the five-speed transmission forward into the cockpit. This odd layout proved helpful when Lamborghini opted to adapt all-wheel drive to the big supercar.

By Lamborghini's reckoning, there was never a Diablo that wouldn't hit at least 202 miles per hour, with estimates of a few special editions edging over 210.

If the Countach was always something of a rebellious prince, the Diablo became accepted royalty among exotic cars. The rough edges had been filed off and smoothed over. Thanks to Chrysler's money and big automaker attitude, the car matured into something powerful and sophisticated and, like a few monarchs, bigger than life.

Successful too, because in the end, the Diablo was a solid seller for Lamborghini, which built 2,884 examples.

It wears its crown with ease. ■

Among the many special editions of the Diablo was the 600-horsepower SE Jota, its production run limited to 15 cars, all finished in Electric Yellow. In addition to other body modifications, the Jotas had roof-top air intakes.

First shown at the 2001 Geneva Auto Show, the 6.0 Special Edition Diablo was only sold in two colors. Lamborghini built just 20 cars each in each color. In addition to the changes to the engine and exterior, the Diablo 6.0 had a redesigned interior with plenty of carbon fiber on display.

For 2000, the Diablo V-12 was stroked to 6.0 liters, with horsepower increasing to 550 and torque to 422 ft-lb. Driving the car was a thrill, with all that power under the hefty shift lever that sprouted directly from the forward-jutting gearbox and all-wheel drive to lay it down.

Opposite page: Once under the umbrella of Audi, the Diablo went through one major model change while the Murciélago was being developed. The visual changes were minor, but where the body panels had previously been mainly aluminum, they were now carbon fiber with aluminum doors and a steel roof.

CHAPTER 13

Neil Walling, who led advanced design for Chrysler at the beginning of the Viper project, told *Road & Track* the sports car's body shape "harkens back to cars of the early to mid-1960s."

163
MILES PER HOUR

DODGE VIPER 1991

Which Viper tale to tell . . . .

I could tell the one of the 1991 introduction program in Los Angeles, where we were set loose in the desert with the first-generation Vipers. There's no denying those early cars were a touch crude, nothing fancy, but good heavens, were they quick!

On lonely roads in the middle of nowhere. Stop, into first, hardly had to lean on the gas, dump the clutch, bam, and 60 miles per hour evaporated in 4.8 seconds. I could do it time after time with seemingly no wear on the car. Every so often I'd just keep working through the manly six-speed and 125–135 miles per hour would arrive in a flash.

When Carroll Shelby and Chrysler President Bob Lutz presented this Viper concept car at the 1989 Detroit Auto Show, everyone loved the idea, but there were skeptics who figured it would never happen. It did.

Or maybe it was the time at Chrysler's Arizona proving ground when the company set up a slalom course on a huge black asphalt area and suggested we should have a good time. We did, cranking the big Viper around cones and then playing the pedal connected to the V-10 so the back end would slide where we wanted it. Oversteer unbounded.

But the best was probably the Viper GTS coupe trip to Europe, belted in next to three-time Le Mans and Sebring winner Phil Hill as he rushed us around the tricky Nürburgring, deftly dancing the big machine through a series of S bends that blurred, up through the famous *kraussel* corner. Yup, that was the best.

Make no mistake, Vipers are meant for play. They've become much more civilized in their third generation, but you'll never mistake them for dual-purpose automobiles that are as happy to take you to the store as around a racetrack. You wouldn't reconcile buying a Viper to your wife by saying, "Gee, honey, we can drive it to the opera."

"Hop in and hold on, we're headed for Vegas and we're taking the back roads," would be more appropriate.

We were skeptical at the 1989 Detroit Auto Show when Chrysler—in the form of Carroll Shelby and Bob Lutz—presented an outrageous V-10 roadster concept car and suggested they might build it as a Dodge.

Sure, you bet, Carroll and Bob. What are you smoking? Ain't going to happen.

But it did and in late 1991 there we were, flashing across the California desert in the first production Vipers, big grins on our faces.

Lamborghini had been responsible for recreating Dodge's 8.0-liter pushrod cast-iron V-10 truck engine in aluminum, stuffing 400 horsepower and 450 ft-lb of torque under the Viper's long fiberglass hood.

That was the material used for the low, rounded body with the gun-sight grille, big side vents, and Targa hoop behind the cockpit, a shape perfect for the image. That body encased

Continued on page 156

At the time Chrysler created the Viper, it also owned Lamborghini, which worked on transforming the 8.0-liter Dodge cast-iron V-10 into an aluminum car engine with 400 horsepower and 450 ft-lb of torque. Today the V-10 displaces 8.3 liters, the horsepower is up to 510, the torque a bellowing 535 ft-lb.

JAY LENO ON THE *DODGE VIPER*

I have one of the early Vipers," Jay Leno explains. "It's an amazingly primitive car that I love to death. If you believe horsepower conquers all problems it's a great car. In 1992 when it came out there was nothing else like it, I mean 400 horsepower, what is that? And a V-10? It's a great car for weekend blasting around.

"I love the fact it came with a tonneau cover so you could have the passenger seat covered, which brought back memories of MGs and all that kind of stuff.

"People complain about the side pipes, the heat...well, a Viper burn scar is like the Heidelberg dueling scar, you wear it with honor. So you have a burn mark on your leg. Good for you.

"I like the first generation Viper more than the second. I don't like the new styling, I like the old Daytona coupe look. I realize that nose was the single most expensive piece to produce for any American car so they've gone to more of a Corvette look, but if you're going to copy Corvette I'll buy a Corvette.

"I also like the early Viper for what it wasn't. I like to get in and turn the radio on and off, press a button for a station. I was just in a new Mercedes S-Class with its version of I Drive and I don't want to type and drive at the same time. I don't need satellite radio telling me the name of the artist. I don't need all those visual things."

With its cut down windscreen, rotary switches, and simple white-face gauges, the Viper concept interior promised a welcome, vintage sports car simplicity. The deep-set leather-covered seats between the tall center console and door sills gave a cool, low-down feeling to the cockpit.

The original Viper soft top was a bit of a problem, which Dodge solved with the introduction of a removable hard top for 1996.

Dodge kicked off its Viper competition program with the GTS-R in two versions, one for amateur racing, another for international competition. The racing Vipers went on to be very successful, winning five European FIA championships, taking their class at the 24 Hours of Le Mans, and winning the 24 Hours of Daytona outright in 2000.

Chrysler has always kept the Viper simple. With 490 ft-lb of torque under your right foot, no traction or yaw control, the early Vipers were nothing if not fun on a tight slalom course.

The original Dodge Viper GTS coupes mix a delightful brew of brutal power and elegance, with the added civility of roll-up windows and a chance to stay out of the elements.

Continued from page 152

In 2002, Dodge gave us a look at the next generation Viper with the GTSR concept car. While that second iteration of the Viper was launched as a convertible, for the 2006 model year Dodge added the Viper SRT10 Coupe, which was very similar to the GTSR, though minus the side vents and with a taller, double-bubble roof.

a tubular steel frame that sat on upper and lower A-arm independent suspensions. The 13-inch disc brakes were inside alloy wheels with squat, chubby Michelin tires.

It was an uncomplicated, uncompromised driver's car. No ABS, no electronic aids—heck, you could hardly hear the radio. The small canvas top was of minimal worth in a hard rain (personal sopping-wet experience here) and threatened to blow off at high speed. You felt a bit crammed on either side of the wide center console, but the gauges were right there and so readable.

What are you here for, anyway? Grab that meaty shift lever and let's start rowing through the gears. For a fast drive down a lonely road on a day when it isn't raining hard, the Viper is pure, simple, go-like-hell fun. No excuse, no apologies.

We drooled over the GTS coupe that came along in 1996 with the second-generation Vipers. Now the big Dodge had a 415-horsepower, 488-ft-lb-of-torque update of the V-10. Times to 60 dipped into the mid-4-second area, the top speed rose to around 185, and the Viper proved more than just a drag racer, arcing around the skid pad to generate a respectable 0.97 g.

Lutz and Shelby knew that to be honestly accepted the Viper had to be raced successfully. Versions were created that made it easy to compete with the Dodge sports car on several levels, from amateur to pro racing. The Viper's most visible success came in Europe where it won the GT2 class of the FIA (Fédération Internationale de l'Automobile) GT Championship in 1997, 1998, 1999, 2001, and 2002. There were class wins in the 24 Hours of Le Mans from 1998 through 2000. Most impressive of the Viper's race accomplishments, however, was in Florida, where it took an overall win in the 2000 24 Hours of Daytona enduro.

Generation-three Vipers debuted in 2003 with a new body style that lost the original's roundness and huge one-piece (pain-to-make) nose for a more conventional hood and an arguably prettier shape. To many of us, it is a giant visual step forward for "the other great American sports car," though ironically its design came from Osamu Shikado, an immensely talented refugee from Toyota's design department.

Opened to 8.3 liters, the V-10 produces a ground-pounding 504 horsepower and 525 ft-lb of torque.

Available first as a roadster and later as a coupe, the newest SRT10s scramble to 60 in the low-4-second bracket. Top speed climbs to 190. Still something of a minimalist's car, ABS is the main electronic feature on the driving side.

Road & Track did a comparison test of the Corvette Z06 versus the Viper SRT10 Coupe. The 'Vette beat the Viper to 60 (3.9 against 4.2 seconds), but the run evened out through the quarter-mile, where the Chevy nipped the Dodge by a mere 0.1 second and 1.9 miles per hour—just half a sneeze. Where the Chevrolet's top speed was 198, the Viper's came in at 190.

R&T concluded, "The personalities of the 'Vette and the Viper couldn't be more different. Just as the Z06 has moved closer to the European ideal of sports-car performance, the Viper Coupe emphasizes its American muscle-car roots. And while the Viper is pricey at $83,995 compared to the bargain-of-the-century Corvette at $65,800, there will be far fewer Dodges on the road—perhaps somewhere in the neighborhood of 1,000. That exclusivity coupled with the fact that it takes real skill to drive a Viper Coupe hard means this isn't a car for everyone . . . just as it's meant to be." ■

The newest Viper, the SRT10, was designed by an ex-Toyota man, Osamu Shikado. It forsakes the one-piece hood—a bit of a production nightmare for Dodge—for a conventional hood over the 510-horsepower V-10.

CHAPTER 14

"You can cruise at over 200 miles per hour like you're on an ordinary road," says World Driving Champion Phil Hill when describing the experience of driving the Bugatti EB110. He ought to know, having just driven the car to 212 miles per hour while testing it for *Road & Track*, adding, "It's just an outstanding car." *Richard Baron*

212
MILES PER HOUR

BUGATTI EB110 1991

"You can cruise at over 200 miles per hour like you're on an ordinary road," world driving champion Phil Hill said of the Bugatti EB110. "It's amazing. The steering is lovely, and the gearbox delightful. It's just an outstanding car."

Hill had just clocked 212 miles per hour in the Bugatti at Volkswagen's Ehra-Lessien track in Germany for *Road & Track*. He added, "It's the most stable car I've ever driven here."

It was never a problem to get those who drove the EB110 to praise it. Some thought clutch effort a bit heavy, and the four IHI turbos on the 3.5-liter 60-valve (yes, 60) V-12 didn't

EB110s were assembled in a beautiful building in Campogalliano, on the outskirts of Modena, Italy. The huge sign behind this 1937 Bugatti Type 57S is still there 15 years later, though the factory is nothing more than an empty reminder of arguably the most spectacular failure in the supercar business.

Opposite page: Bugatti gave its EB110 a lavish send off when it debuted in 1991, parading the car from La Défense in Paris with a caravan of vintage Bugattis to the palace in Versailles. Throughout the car's short life there was much curiosity about who was really bankrolling the production of the supercar.

really get to singing until 4,500 rpm. That didn't stop *R&T* from getting an EB110 to 60 miles per hour in 4.4 seconds. As always, it was tougher to launch an all-wheel-drive car like the Bugatti off the line, but dumping the clutch at 7,500 rpm(!) worked, the car "not objecting one bit," according to Hill.

The clamor over the new Bugatti was enormous. It was the darling of the supercar set and future Grand Prix champion Michael Schumacher bought a yellow one. The EB110 had the famed Bugatti name, a carbon-fiber chassis built by Aerospatiale (of Concorde fame), and that marvelous V-12 penned by Paolo Stanzani (of Lamborghini fame), with its 650 horsepower at 8,000 and 472 ft-lb of torque at 4,200. There was a Lamborghini door-style body drawn by Marcello Gandini (of Countach, Miura, Carabo, etc. fame) and all this was painstakingly assembled in a brand-new factory in Campogalliano, near Modena, the hometown of Ferrari, Maserati, and Lamborghini.

What went wrong?

Romano Artioli bought the name Bugatti and its famous red oval badge in 1987, promising the EB110 in 1991, the car's name model number representing Ettore Bugatti 110 years after he was born. It made sense at the time, as the supercar world was booming.

If there was one small knock on the EB110, it was its non-too-spectacular interior, though it did feature excellent materials. In the end, only 125–145 EB110s were produced before the company filed for bankruptcy, caught up in a world recession that snuffed out many supercar ambitions.

The Porsche 959 captured everyone's attention, Ferrari's F40 was fresh, and prices flying high. But like Jaguar XJ220's, the EB110's timing went sour.

Those of us at the Bugatti's Paris debut on September 1991 were stunned by the opulence. Unveiled at La Grand Arche de la Défense, the car led a parade of vintage Bugattis to the palace in Versailles for a black-tie dinner. The apparent enormous expense of the day also raised the question of who was *really* bankrolling the venture, a curiosity that remains unanswered today.

Production began, deliveries started in December 1991, road tests rolled in, and everyone praised the car's performance. Perhaps the styling wasn't as exciting as it could be, the interior a bit pedestrian and the car a tad heavy, but build quality was excellent and no one

The EB110 had the right ingredients. Marcello Gandini, who penned the Carabo, Miura, Countach, and other great exotics, was hired to do the exterior design. Paolo Stanzani, who had worked at Lamborghini, was responsible for the powerful 60-valve V-12. And to get the power—611 horsepower in the SS version—to the ground, the car had all-wheel drive.

Richard Baron

was complaining loudly. A second model called the SS, a somewhat lighter version with 611 horsepower, was launched in 1992. Bugatti even bought well-known automaker and engineering firm Lotus, so everyone assumed that things must be wonderful.

But then it all fell apart. The world sank into recession and supercars suffered. In 1995 the company filed for bankruptcy and the magnificent factory closed after some 125–145 EB110s were made. Ten years later, the plant remained empty, the signage a sad reminder of what never happened.

But the famed Bugatti name is not one to just lie around unused. In 1998, Volkswagen bought the rights to Bugatti and its badge, and now we have the Veyron 16.4 being built in the marque's traditional home: Molsheim, France. ∎

CHAPTER 15

Last in the line of Vectors was the M12, which was basically the Vector styling wrapped around a Lamborghini V-12 chassis. At this point, Lamborghini owned Vector and while the M12 was not a Diablo clone, they shared many parts. One of the men who worked on the M12 exterior was Peter Stevens of McLaren F1 fame.

218
MILES PER HOUR

THE VECTOR 1991

It's easy to look back now and think we were suckers over the Vector when it was first shown, but that would be unfair.

You have to know how desperate Americans were for a truly American supercar in the early 1970s. Here it was, the country that built astounding technical devices like the SR71 Blackbird aircraft and put men on the moon, but its automobiles were technically mired in the 1950s. Italy had exotic Ferraris and Maseratis, Porsche 917s were eating up the sports car racing world, and Jaguar produced sports cars for which one would open a vein.

Bottom: This is the original 1978 Vector W2, and atop the car is Jerry Wiegert, the man who tried to make the project work. His aim was to create the great American mid-engine sports car, a world beater that reflected the technology used in the great jet fighter aircraft being developed in the United States.

Inset: Visually the Vector W2 was a treat, with its brushed aluminum body. It was only 45.5 inches high, and its 76.0-inch width was emphasized by great fender flares. Its tail topped by a tall wing, the car was very imposing and guaranteed to turn heads wherever it went.

What did Americans have? The Chevrolet Corvette. You certainly could get a big-block 'Vette through a quarter-mile in a hurry, but the car was really a testament to Zora Duntov's ability to assemble old Chevrolet parts in some semblance of performance order, and Bill Mitchell's design department's genius at wrapping it up in a delectable package.

The automotive performance world was falling apart in the early 1970s. Laws lowering automotive emissions and increasing safety in vehicles might have been long overdue, but the effect of their ham-fisted implementation in the 1970s was to toss a huge regulatory wet blanket over performance cars. Compression ratios fell, unleaded gas became the rule, heavy safety equipment was bolted on, and engineers who were once devising ways to make engines more powerful were now just trying to make them idle successfully. Emissions laws sliced the horsepower of the small-block Corvette from 250 to 205 in 1975. No wonder Americans were discouraged.

Plus, the United States suffered two gas shocks—in 1974 and 1979—when drivers lined up for blocks to pay more for suddenly scarce gasoline. This seemed wrong in the States, home of the free, land of cheap gas.

And then, in 1978, right into this rather depressing situation, drove the Vector W2. America's savior? . . .

We first saw a Vector at the Los Angeles Auto Expo in 1972. Designed by Gerald "Jerry" Wiegert, it had a rather amazing shape and a proposed price of just $7,500. Built in Lee Brown's body shop in Hollywood, the Vector show car had dramatic hard-edge styling with a low nose, huge glass area, and a kicked-up tail that caught our attention . . . that and its

Wiegert's desire to give the W2 a high-tech fighter look was best seen in the interior. There was flat screen instrumentation and rows of switches.

You could never say Wiegert wasn't tenacious, and he fought for years to get the Vector project off the ground. After about 15 years of fighting for funding, the company was bought by an Indonesian firm that tried to get Wiegert to step down, but he changed the locks on the factory and tied the place up in legal red tape for weeks.

In the W2's tail was a 6.0-liter Chevrolet V-8 with a pair of huge turbochargers. Horsepower was said to be 600, with torque at 580 ft-lb through a three-speed automatic transmission. There were claims of a 230-mile per hour top speed, but no one was ever allowed to test the W2 to verify this performance.

Opposite page: Like the Lamborghini Countach and many other supercars to follow, the Vector W2 had swing-up doors. Wiegert designed one tough-looking car. A price of $125,000 was suggested, and both interest and funding followed, but for years nothing but rumors came of it.

green paint, making the whole thing slightly reminiscent of the famous Alfa Romeo Carabo show car.

The color and shape earned it a place on a *Motor Trend* cover in 1973, though under the fiberglass was the tube space-frame of an old mid-engine Dolphin sports racer and no engine. It was guessed the weight could be kept down to 2,200 pounds, and the proposed engine was either a four-cam Porsche or one of the Wankel rotary engines that were becoming the rage. (This was the period in which Mercedes-Benz and General Motors were caught in their short-term infatuation with the compact powerplant.)

That Vector project died quietly away, but in 1978 Wiegert was back with a new mid-engine model, the W2, and it was sensational. The low (45.5 inches), wide (76 inches), brushed aluminum body with strong fender flares, a rear wing, and an imposing stance had great visual appeal. The chassis was just as intriguing with an upper and lower A-arm front suspension and a DeDion layout at the back.

Wiegert was pushing an all-American auto-aero-tech tie in the car, making comparisons with fighter aircraft, and the interior reflected that theme with rows of switches and circuit breakers and flat-screen instrumentation.

Out back the W2 had plenty of firepower. Turbochargers had come to the rescue of performance engine makers in this era of low horsepower, and Wiegert fitted his new car with two big ones mounted on a 6.0-liter Chevrolet V-8. Power was estimated to be around 600 horsepower and 580 ft-lb of torque. The transmission was a three-speed automatic, and there was talk of a top speed around 230 miles per hour and a price tag of $125,000.

American car fans had a little faith that they might finally have a native supercar. The W2 raised interest and funding, but disappeared into a mist of rumor, speculation, and waiting.

The Vector reappeared in the early 1990s as the W8 Twin Turbo, which made it to production in Vector's factory in Wilmington, a port city west of Los Angeles. In addition to a public offering that raised $20 million, Wiegert added funds when he sued Goodyear for using the name Vector on a line of tires and won.

The styling was a little softer now, but just as exciting, still with great flared fenders, a low snout, and a better-integrated tail spoiler. The suspension remained the same, as did the powertrain, though now claiming 625 horsepower and 630 ft-lb of torque. The 3,320-pound car was still aerospace oriented: aluminum monocoque structures off a central chrome-moly tube frame; the body finished in Kevlar, carbon fiber, and fiberglass; and the doors swinging up like a Lamborghini's. The inside-the-aircraft theme continued with toggle-covered flat panels and menus of information. All the switches and wiring were up to military spec.

The price now was just shy of $485,000, and after years of being asked, Wiegert finally allowed the car to be properly road tested. *Road & Track* got a W8 Twin Turbo to 60 miles

To go with the powerful styling and 600-horsepower drivetrain, the Vector W2 had a stout chassis. The front suspension featured upper and lower A-arms, while the rear was somewhat unusual for a mid-engine car with a DeDion layout.

In the early 1990s, after years of speculation, Vector was back with a car called the W8 Twin Turbo, which was tested by car magazines. *Road & Track* got one to 60 miles per hour in 4.2 seconds. The W8 was followed quickly by the Avtech WX3, and then Avtech S/C (seen here).

per hour in 4.2 seconds, which was quite respectable at the time, especially on a car hampered with gearing that gave it (at least theoretically) a top speed of 218 miles per hour. *R&T* staffer Doug Kott wrote, "Utter ferocity arrives as the tach's moving-tape display skitters past 4,000 rpm, the turbos hit full stride and what feels like the hand of God presses you back into the seat. Box the shifter handle into second, the electronically controlled wastegates exhale like Darth Vader with whooping cough, and the almighty process begins anew."

Great stuff, and cars were being delivered, with a reported 18–22 eventually built. But problems haunted the project, particularly when word got out that tennis star Andre Agassi returned his Vector because of all its problems.

Wiegert introduced a new model, the Avtech WX3, at the 1992 New York Auto Show. The chassis remained the same, but the styling was updated, still looking very exciting, particularly the back end, with the raised wing now better integrated into the body.

Funding continued to be short but got a boost in early 1993, when the company was bought by an Indonesian company, Megatech, which wanted Vector's founder, Wiegert, to step down as CEO but stay on as a designer. He resisted and was fired, but he refused to leave. Given a chance to quietly yield his spot in March, Wiegert instead used a weekend to change the locks on the factory doors, post armed guards, fire the staff, and take refuge in the buildings.

It was the stuff of daily news reports until Wiegert finally yielded and the new owners took control. The Indonesian company was owned by Tommy Suharto, son of the country's

There was even a 1993 Vector Avtech Roadster. The original W2 styling from the late 1970s is still in there, but rounder and somehow even more ferocious. There is no denying the visual appeal of the Vectors, which could get any car enthusiast's heart fluttering, but years of misfired promises had made us very wary.

ruler, and in January 1994 he also bought Lamborghini from Chrysler. (Suharto later went to prison for the murder of a judge.)

Vector moved to Lamborghini's Jacksonville, Florida, headquarters and tried one last model, the M12, which basically wrapped Vector styling around a Lamborghini V-12-powered platform. The M12 (for mid-engine and 12 cylinders) wasn't a Diablo clone, but was built on its own tube frame chassis with the V-12 turned around so the transmission sprouted out the back, rather than between the front seats as in the Countach and Diablo. The DeDion rear suspension was replaced by a more conventional upper and lower A-arm design. The styling had been through a wind tunnel and then refined by two men, Peter Stevens, who did the McLaren with Gordon Murray, and Michael Santoro.

Vector died with the M12, which was supposed to be built in Florida. If you look closely you can still see some of Wiegert's original wild styling—low nose, tall tail, huge air scoops—but the flamboyance was gone and, as always, the money dried up. Vector's owner at the time, Lamborghini, was going through another funding crisis.

The visual result was obviously an extension of Wiegert's original theme—forward leaning, tall tail, swing-up doors—with huge holes to feed cooling ducts, but something of the early Vector's halt-you-in-your-tracks visceral appeal was missing. Ditto inside, where the car had the expected look and rich materials, but not the earlier cars' tech appeal. Gone too, of course, was any semblance of aircraft heritage or the born-in-the-USA argument.

The M12 also lost a bit of performance, with a 0–60 time of 4.8 seconds, though *Road & Track*'s Kim Reynolds suggested that number didn't reflect the M12's true, quicker acceleration potential. Handling was reasonably good and there was talk of a 190-mile-per-hour top speed.

Vector figured it could sell 150 of its M12s per year at $184,000, built in a shop on a shuttered Florida navy base. Having seen the shop, it reminded me of one of the small English specialist companies like TVR or Marcos. Great stuff, with sparks flying from welders' work, drivetrains being readied, virgin body panels waiting for paint, even a racing version for IMSA being readied on the side.

And that's the last we ever heard from Vector. Things weren't healthy at Lamborghini at the time, leading to its sale to Audi in 1998, and Wiegert's dream evaporated.

Or so you might think. Apparently, Wiegert isn't one to give up . . . sign on to the Internet and check out www.vectorsupercars.com.

He's not letting go. ■

Opposite page: Vector M12s feature a more conventional supercar chassis, and thanks to the Lamborghini power could get to 60 miles per hour in 4.8 seconds, with gearing said to be good for 190 miles per hour. Also more conventional is the interior, now devoid of any aircraft influence.

SECTION III
THE MODERN SUPERCAR ERA
1992–PRESENT

190-250
MILES PER HOUR

CHAPTER 16

After winning the 24 Hours of Le Mans in 1995 and having four of the top five finishing cars, McLaren built a series of five special editions called F1 LM. Basically, they were the GTR race cars made somewhat streetable, but still with a fixed rear wing and straight-cut gears.

231
MILES PER HOUR

McLAREN F1 1992

Ever been to an IMAX movie, that great film system that spreads its vista of action around you? That's what it would be like to ride in a McLaren F1. With the car's unusual three-person cockpit, the driver is in the middle and you'd be sitting to his left or right and back enough to be looking over his shoulder. In most supercars, you're next to the driver as his companion. In the McLaren, you're a voyeur to the driving process.

Peek over his shoulder, over the competition-type safety harness, and take in a whiff of the Connelly leather upholstery. Down past the Nardi steering wheel, deeply recessed away from

The F1 was almost the second-generation street machine from McLaren. Having dominated the 1967 Can-Am season with his M6, the innovative driver/constructor Bruce McLaren considered using the M6 chassis to create a Grand Touring race car with hopes of winning Le Mans. A coupe version of the M6 was built for McLaren's evaluation as a street machine.

glare, is a trio of green-lit analog gauges. Deeper yet, down in the footwell, are three pedals cut from aluminum and finished almost to jewelry-store standards. No rubber pedal covers, but machined faces with "F1" inscribed on the nonslip surface.

Let's say you're on the right side, so you see the tall shift lever to the driver's right and then the broad panorama out the curved windscreen. Pull down the door. The other passenger does the same. The driver twists the key, then punches the starter button. To your immediate left, the 6.0-liter BMW Motorsport V-12 kicks on. Into gear, the driver nudges the car away.

Because of your odd placement to the driver, door, wheels, engine and such, things seem slightly out of place, but there's little time for judging that, because with the throttle down the car is accelerating at a 0–60-in-3.2-second rate and you're slammed back in the seat. That's when the IMAX effect kicks in, countryside flashing by on your right, trees and vehicles flitting past the windscreen, the driver working his magic to your left front, and the BMW growling away on your left.

Sensory inputs are off the scale.

I can't imagine what it's like at the F1's top speed of 231 miles per hour.

To say the McLaren F1 is special, even in the rarefied world of exotic cars, is to understate its significance. "Special" is too trivial a word. You can be special with knock-out styling, an outstanding chassis, or a tricked-up engine, and the F1 has all that. But it also has something else: genius in every square inch. That's a judgment that has held up since the F1 was debuted at the Monte Carlo Sporting Club on May 8, 1992, the Thursday before the Monaco Grand Prix.

Blame the genius part on Gordon Murray. While there were others important to the F1's creation—men like Mansour Ojjeh and Ron Dennis—the car is quite simply Murray's machine, his vision.

Other than the gray that streaks his long black hair, Murray looks little different today than when his first bit of public genius, the Brabham BT42-Ford, made its debut during

Built in the racing off-season of 1969–1970, the gullwing M6GT had a 5.7-liter Chevrolet V-8. McLaren was serious about the project, using the M6GT as personal transportation while it was considered as a production project. Any hope this might happen died with Bruce McLaren in a Can-Am car testing accident at the English Goodwood circuit in June 1970.

the 1973 Grand Prix season. He was only 26 then. Season after season, Murray's cars set the standard, usually in innovation, often in successes on the GP circuit.

All this changed in 1990 when Murray left the McLaren Grand Prix design team to help establish McLaren Cars. His title was technical director, his job to create the F1, a road-going McLaren.

"Over the years, you drive many sports cars," he points out, "and every time you get in one, you note the things you do and don't like. You build up a subconscious library of what you would and wouldn't do if you ever had a chance to build a production car."

Murray begins with packaging and an amazingly low weight target. From the outside, the F1 looks compact, and it is. As a comparison with sports car more commonly seen, at 168.8 inches long, the F1 is 5.8 inches shorter than a Corvette Z06, though the McLaren's 107.0-inch wheelbase is 1.3 inches greater than the Chevrolet's. The McLaren

One of Gordon Murray's aims was to design a light exotic car, and he succeeded, his creation weighing almost one-third less than a Corvette Z06. The F1 is also 5.8 inches shorter and 4.2 inches lower than the Chevrolet sports car. Then again, when new the F1 was some 15 times more expensive than a Z06 is today.

is 1.0 inch narrower and 4.2 inches lower than the 'Vette. Here's the stunner: a Z06 weighs in at around 3,130 pound, while the F1 is a mere 2,244.

Inside that compact package Murray fits three, not two, people. With a trio aboard, there's still room for 8 cubic feet of the supplied leather luggage, kept cool in storage compartments ahead of the rear wheel wells. Hold passenger count to two and it's 10 cubic feet, using a special bag that fits in the unoccupied seat. Add in underseat storage and various cubbyholes.

Typical of Murray and his creation, there's much more to passenger packaging, like that center driver's seat with its carefully determined sight lines and command view. Upholstered in a leather color that contrasts with the passenger seats' black color, the bucket is carbon composite and factory shaped to fit the owner's rear end. Steering wheel and pedals are also custom installed.

Climbing into the center seat is obviously not simple, but it's well short of the gymnastic routine

Designer Peter Stevens, working closely with Gordon Murray, gets the applause for the exterior design of the McLaren F1. What is most striking when you see the F1 is the fact it is so neat and compact.

you'd expect. Step over, swing your butt in, and drop down. To each side are small jet fighter–style control panels with buttons in carefully determined sizes, shapes, and places so they can be easily used without taking your eyes off the road.

On the right are heating, air conditioning, and vent controls; the right window lift; mirror adjustor; shift lever; and ignition switch and button. The left grouping has the hand-brake, that side's window lift, and the CD/stereo controls. But it's not just any system. Murray recalls, "I spoke to eight different stereo companies. Most of them walked out." Why? The average weight of the quality sound system he wanted for the F1 was quoted at 36 pounds, while Murray demanded his be less than 19 pounds . . . and he got it from Kenwood.

Wrapped around this package had to be exotic bodywork, but not just a designer's flight of fancy. McLaren brought on highly talented Peter Stevens for the shape, which had to satisfy wind tunnel instrumentation as much as the human eye.

They also had a problem Murray calls "the most difficult of all: that it had to be a McLaren and we hadn't done one yet. I didn't want anybody to say, 'I'm sorry, it's a bit like a Testarossa,' or, 'It's like a Bugatti.' We couldn't afford that. It had to have a character of its own that people would identify as McLaren."

Opposite page: Because he didn't want to clutter the exterior of the F1 with large spoilers, Murray devised an internal system for the car that keeps it stable at high speeds. Typical of a Murray design, the system is both elegant and lightweight.

Below: Riding in a McLaren F1 LM is a bit like living inside a video game. With the passenger's seat slightly aft of the driver, you look over the shoulder of the gamer.

Okay, I admit it's almost pure guy stuff, but the view of the McLaren F1 LM's carbon fiber instrument panel is like the printed instructions on a testosterone supplement. The large 9,000-rpm tachometer dominates, while to its right a 200-mile per hour-plus speedometer is more than just window dressing.

Like dihedral doors, which open up and forward, taking part of the roof and rocker panels with them to aid climbing into that central driver's seat. Or the rooftop air intake for the BMW V-12. Or the two front nostrils that take in cooling air for the aluminum radiators.

The center of the nose routes air under the car, along its flat bottom, and out a tail diffuser that generates downforce. This is part of a three-element tail aero system that includes two small fans—on the same theme as Murray's 1978 Brabham BT46B F1 fan car—and a short tail spoiler, called the Brake and Balance Foil. This strip flips up 30 degrees under hard braking to move the aerodynamic center of pressure rearward and

Gordon Murray said of the exterior shape of the F1, " . . . it had to be a McLaren and we hadn't done one yet. I didn't want anyone to say, 'I'm sorry, it's a bit like a Testarossa.'"

stabilize braking from high speeds. It also raises the coefficient of drag from 0.32 to 0.40. You were warned that this isn't your average exotic car.

Murray proves this again by using carbon composite for the exterior body and chassis, the latter in combination with aluminum honeycomb. Automobile engineers of most companies in the early 1990s when the F1 was being developed would have chuckled when they considered the cost of even a tiny piece done in this material, but Murray had the financial freedom to dive right in.

And he did. Using McLaren International's decade of experience with carbon composites, plus computer-aided design, he created a strong occupant cell with rollover protection built

What is it about swing-up doors that make them so fascinating on a supercar?

The F1's center driver's seat makes the McLaren one of the more difficult exotics to enter. You have to step in, swing over and settle into the seat . . . but it's well worth the effort. Drivers who raced the McLaren claim that the center spot was an advantage to them, particularly in long-distance events.

Gordon Murray wanted a large-displacement, nonturbocharged engine for the McLaren F1 and finally settled on a 6.1-liter, 48-valve V-12 built by BMW Motorsports. While the head and block are aluminum, many of the small elements are magnesium. The amazingly compact powerplant kicks out 627 horsepower at 7,400 rpm and 479 ft-lb of torque between 4,000 and 7,000 rpm.

into the A- and B-pillars. Immediate crush is handled by composite moldings in front and the large Inconel muffler at the back. Gasoline is carried in a centrally mounted fuel cell. The BMW test driver who walked away from a high-speed crash in the first F1 prototype can happily attest to the car's safety.

This carbon composite structure also gives Murray a very stiff chassis for the F1's suspension, which was developed with engineer Steve Randall. At first glance it is somewhat conventional, but attached in an unconventional manner. Up front are unequal-length A-arms attached through plain bearings to a subframe. This frame is then mounted to the carbon tub via four elastometric bushings that work at different angles—a McLaren-patented system Murray calls Ground Plane Shear Centre. While the arms are mounted to the subframe to give the geometry control needed for precise handling, the bushings damp

JAY LENO ON THE *McLAREN*

T he McLaren F1 is really sort of the greatest one of them all," Leno states, concurring with another well-known F1 owner, Ralph Lauren.

"It has 627 horsepower but weighs less than a Miata," Leno begins. In his garage Leno parks the F1 next to another car designed by famed engineer Gordon Murray. Called the Rocket, it has a cigar-shaped body, cycle fenders and a rear-mounted motorcycle engine, arguably the antithesis of the sleek-bodied F1 and yet Leno explains, "It's the same theory: you make it as light as possible. There's no power steering, no power brakes, no anything. The F1 is the most pure driving experience of any car."

Leno also likes the fact the car is such a small, integrated package, saying, "Everything is connected, everything is structural, everything is interrelated. Plus to me they did it the right way. They designed the chassis and engine and then built the body around it. I think the problem with the Bugatti Veyron and SLR Mercedes-Benz is they said, 'Here's what it's going to look like, make everything fit inside there.' Consequently there's a bit of a compromise. There are no compromises on the F1.

"I love the looks of the F1 because you don't know it's a brand-new car. A Countach looks period. A Ferrari Testarossa and the Miura look like an era. But the F1 could be a car from today or the '60s. Next to Ford's GT40, it's the purest design in terms of what a supercar looks like.

"From a packaging standpoint the F1 seats three people, you've got luggage space on both sides and yet it's smaller than a Corvette.

"And there's a great sense of theater involved with the McLaren. You open the door, it's an effort to get in, you put yourself in the center, you put in the key, you flip up the button...it's a bit like watching a pipe smoker go through all the machinations, tamping the thing, then you have the sterling silver lighter...

"Driving the F1 is an event.

"The downside is it's crazy expensive. There's a McLaren service center near here—that's the great thing about LA, no matter what you're interested in it's here—so I took it in for service and the guy said, 'We replaced the wiper blade.'

"I said there's no need to replace the wiper. It doesn't rain and if it does I don't take it out.

"He said, 'Well it's just a matter of course that we replace the blade.'

"I said, 'Okay, how much is the blade?'

"'$1,500.'

'Don't touch the blade the next time.'

"Anytime I drive the McLaren anywhere near its limit, or my limit, I think, 'Oh, geez, if I do anything here...if I crack the tub it's $300,000.' That's the problem."

That problem aside, Leno states, "It's a fascinating car and I think it's probably THE greatest sports car of the 20th century."

Although the shape needed for the racing McLaren GTR was fundamentally the same as the street machine, there were detail changes. Most prominent in this view was the addition of a tall rear spoiler for downforce, but you can also see vents atop the front fenders and altered aerodynamic detailing around the front wheels and along the bottom on the sills.

out noise and vibration. The combined Bilstein spring/shocks are mounted horizontally and operate through rocker arms off the upper A-arms.

Unwilling to accept even the smallest deflection caused by a softly mounted steering rack, it is an integral part of the cast front bulkhead. Incidentally, the rack-and-pinion steering has no power assist.

Basics of the rear suspension are again upper and lower A-arms, here mounted to the transaxle and engine.

In concert with the Brake and Balance Foil system mentioned earlier are the huge drilled Brembo brakes, 13 inches front, 12 inches rear. McLaren wanted carbon brakes, but at the time couldn't make them practical for street use. They did add a unique touch with intelligent brake cooling, electronics deciding when to open brake cooling ducts, which would otherwise effect aero, at high speeds.

McLaren's traditional GP tire supplier at the time, Goodyear, provided the F1's special skins, and OZ Racing created the magnesium alloy wheels.

Early chassis development work was done with a pair of steel-frame mules royally named Edward and Albert. While the carbon composite monocoque was still being engineered, these two prototypes gave McLaren several years of test service. Albert had a big-block Chevrolet V-8 for its horsepower, while Edward was fitted with what would become the F1 production engine, a BMW V-12.

Given Honda's Grand Prix ties with McLaren until 1993, it would seem natural for the Japanese company to supply the F1's engine. There was considerable discussion with Honda, but Murray wanted a normally aspirated powerplant and, as the projected displacement grew out of the 3.5- to 4.0-liter range, Honda's interest waned.

What most interested the engineer was a V-12 and plenty of horsepower, which BMW was able to offer in a 60-degree 6.1-liter 48-valve V-12 through its Motorsport division. This engine had little to do with V-12s found in 750i and 850i BMWs of the era and was purpose built for McLaren.

The head and block are aluminum, while many other castings—oil pump, cam covers, and the housing for the variable valve timing—are in magnesium alloy. It's a surprisingly compact powerplant, its height trimmed with dry-sump oiling. Topped by its carbon composite airbox, which shows its fabric skin pattern, with cam covers that declare "McLaren" and "BMW MPower," and with almost artistically twisted exhaust headers, the V-12 is a thing of mechanical beauty. And power, with 627 brake horsepower at 7,400 rpm and 479 ft-lb of torque between 4,000 and 7,000 rpm.

Remember the F1's long wheelbase measurement for its overall length? They get that minimal rear overhang thanks to a shockingly small transverse six-speed gearbox, which doesn't have to hang out the back. Between the engine and gearbox is a tiny aluminum flywheel and (another carryover from GP racing) a three-plate carbon-on-carbon clutch, a combination that provides minimal mass and inertia. And if you've ever fumbled your way through the muddled gear change in a mid-engine car, even some expensive exotics, you'll appreciate Murray designing a system that can get you down to racing gear-change times.

So is that all you got when you plunked down the $1 million for your McLaren F1? Nope. There are also Facom tools—a small titanium set for the car, a floor unit for your garage, and a car cover.

McLaren's F1 LM street machines kept the race spec engines but didn't have to use the air intake restrictors mandated by the race organizers. Horsepower jumped to 680, making these the most powerful F1s. Their straight-cut gears also make them the noisiest, requiring driver and passengers to use noise-canceling headphones.

McLaren had no plans to race the F1 and at first resisted pleas by owners to develop the supercar for competition. But when a trio of owners told Ron Dennis, who managed McLaren, that they would be racing their cars regardless, the company relented and developed the GTR racing version.

Like everything else in the F1, Gordon Murray wanted the transmission to be small and lightweight. The six-speed sits sideways behind the BMW V-12, helping shorten the F1's wheelbase. In addition to a small flywheel, the package has a three-plate carbon-on-carbon clutch to minimize mass and inertia.

When the McLaren F1 went on sale in 1992, it quickly snapped up all the acclaim expected of it . . . and all the sales, with customers more than happy to stand in line to pay $1 million for one of the 64 street F1s built.

But the story doesn't end there.

It was never intended that the F1 should be raced, but given its performance potential, several owners went to McLaren's Ron Dennis requesting a racing version. At first he refused, but when the owners then suggested they would do it on their own, he relented and the F1 GTR was created for 1995.

The main objective of the exercise was the BPR GT Championship and, more important, the 24 Hours of Le Mans. Regulations allowed some changes, but surprisingly few were made. Ride height was lowered, the suspension firmed, and brakes were upgraded to carbon discs inside larger wheels. An external rear wing was added for more downforce and the bodywork revised slightly for better high-speed aerodynamics and cooling.

Horsepower was reduced. Rules required an air restrictor that cut the BMW V-12 to 600 horsepower, so by the time you add the drag of the wing, the race car was actually slower than the street version.

There were the expected changes inside: the amenities gone, a roll cage added, race instrumentation, and such.

F1s won the BRP GT Championship in 1995, 1996, and 1997, with the car going through more development each year as the rules were revised to allow more deviation from stock. By 1997, there was a long-tail F1 that weighed just over 2,000 pounds, but as the rules got broader still, Porsche and Mercedes-Benz jumped in with cars that had little to do with production machines, and the series suffered.

Along the way, however, McLarens were amazing at Le Mans, where just finishing is a victory. In 1995, the cars finished first, third, fourth, and fifth. The next year they were fourth, fifth, sixth, eighth, and ninth, with a second and third in 1997 and fourth in 1998.

Pierre-Henri Raphael, now the *pilote official* for Bugatti, shared driving duties in the second-place car in 1997, when McLaren also won the GT class. Asked what was so special about the F1 GTR, he points out that the car's systems—engine, brakes, suspension, steering—were in good harmony, not as in some race cars where the engine power, handling, brakes, or gearbox might dominate.

He then points out that the greatest advantage was the central driving position. Unlike other race cars in which the driver has to allow for more race car space on the right or left side (depending on whether the car is left- or right-hand drive), that wasn't an issue with the McLaren. He says it was a great advantage, particularly in a long-distance race.

McLaren built a series of five special F1s in 1995 to commemorate its Le Mans victory. Called F1 LM, they were basically GTRs made streetable, still with the fixed rear wing

and straight-cut gears, but minus the air intake restrictors, so horsepower jumped to 680. Even rarer were the three F1 long-tail street machines built to homologate the revised bodywork for 1997, fitted with bodywork that extended both the nose and tail for aerodynamic efficiency.

One of the F1 LM owners is one of the world's great McLaren fans, in addition to being one of the world's great fashion designers. Ralph Lauren owns three F1s: two street machines and one of the Le Mans replicas built to celebrate the 1995 win. He has an extensive collection of great automobiles, but Lauren explains, "Once you drive the McLaren F1 it's over. It's like no other car I've ever driven . . . it's *Star Wars*. A hovercraft. I feel like I'm not touching the ground, like the road is down there and I'm up here. It's an experience I've never had before."

Which probably wraps up the opinion of anyone who has ever driven or ridden in a McLaren F1. ■

From behind you can see the rear aero system of the F1 LM. The high wing adds downforce by pushing the car down to the road. Under the car is a flat bottom that allows the air to flow smoothly beneath the car, while at the back a venturi system helps draw the air out in a manner that pulls the car to the road.

CHAPTER 17

Like its successor, the Enzo, Ferrari's F50 has numerous ties to the company's Formula 1 car. Unlike the Enzo, which was shaped to reflect the feeling of those open-wheel cars, the F50's Pininfarina-penned exterior looks more like a Group C sports racer.

202
MILES PER HOUR

FERRARI F50 1996

Ferrari's 1961 world driving champion, Phil Hill, was driving while I was happily belted into the passenger's seat as we set out to lap Ferrari's Fiorano test track for a story for *Road & Track*.

Unlike some supercars, this was a somewhat raucous ride. For one thing, we were out in the open, and the nature of the F50 was different from many of the others. This one was very much a race car for the street, one you could feel and hear all around you in the sounds that swirled forward from the V-12, and the vibrations and feedback that drummed up from the road. It accelerated in a slightly more brutal manner.

Carbon fiber, Kevlar, and Nomex were used for the F50 body, the hood was formed with heat-relieving vents to help cool the front radiator. Airflow is directed by the shape of the nose, while at the back the tall spoiler adds downforce. Coefficient of drag of the F50 comes in at 0.372.

When Phil was hard on the brakes I was hard forward in my belts as I rode down with the car. Then on to Fiorano's straight, aimed under a bridge and past the pits, where we wouldn't match the car's top speed of 202 miles per hour, but were well into three figures. The air over the car was at near-hurricane strength.

When you drive the F50, it tousles your hair, tingles your soul, and gives you a great sense of what it would be like to ride in a great sports racing or possibly a two-seat Grand Prix car.

Having a Formula 1 machine for the street is the stuff of many men's dreams. And since Ferrari has been fulfilling men's driving dreams for years, it only seems appropriate that the Italian company would base its 1996 supercar, the F50, on Grand Prix thinking.

That number, 50, not only coincided with the automaker's birthday, but also happened to be the natural numerical successor to the famous F40. And, like any proper successor, it was a significant step forward.

We begin with the part of the F50 that can't be like a GP car: the configuration and body. Pininfarina, the traditional designer of Ferrari exteriors, also did the two-seater F50, and needed to make it both exciting to look at and aerodynamically efficient. While one wouldn't call the F50 a beautiful car in the manner of Ferraris like the 250 GTO, Lusso, and Daytona, it is undeniably exciting . . . it stirs your soul. The basic shape—done in carbon fiber, Kevlar, and Nomex honeycomb—tells you it's a mid-engine design and appeals to your heart. And to your head, because you know Pininfarina wouldn't let this car out of the studio without proper wind tunnel development work.

As a result, the bonnet of the F50 has been shaped both to relieve heat from the front-mounted radiators and provide front downforce. The leading edge of the front bumper separates the air that flows over the car from the flow that is sent underneath and out the channels at the back of the car's underside, providing more "stickion" to the road.

At the back, the tall spoiler adds a proportional amount of downforce to match the front's push down on the road. Coefficient of drag is 0.372. In a clever concession to complaints that top-level Ferraris should be open cars, the F50 can be used as an open roadster Barchetta, or with a hardtop in place creating the Berlinetta version.

Whether the wind is in your hair or you are cozy under the hardtop, the interior is the same, mixing the new and the old at Ferrari by emphasizing the use of both leather and

Ferrari opted for a naturally aspirated 65-degree V-12 for the F50, an engine that shares fundamentals with the company's successful 333SP sports racing car. The 60-valve engine comes rated at 513 horsepower at 8,000 rpm and 347 ft-lb of torque at 6,500.

Carbon fiber is obvious in the interior, mixed with leather and, on the seats, a breathable cloth. The seats came in normal and large sizes and are adjustable, as are the pedals. Instrumentation is an electronic LCD display, reflecting racing ties, but the car also has climate control.

visible carbon fiber. The seats are grippy and come in two sizes, normal and larger. Based on shells of composite plastic, the seats are trimmed in leather and a breathable cloth. Naturally, the driver's seat moves for adjustment, but so do the pedals, all the better to suit the pilot's size.

At the driver's right is the gearshift, with a carbon fiber knob and the classic metal shift gate. Again following F1 practice, but breaking with Ferrari road car tradition, the instrument panel is an electronic LCD display lit by electroluminescent bulbs. Naturally, the main dials are the tachometer and speedometer, but also on the display are oil pressure and temperature, coolant temperature, and, of course, fuel level. Would-be racers like the FIA-standard roll bars and four-point seat harnesses, but the F50 also has such amenities as climate control and leather pouches for odds and ends, plus a courtesy light . . . which is not F1 practice.

Back in the Grand Prix frame of mind, the F50's chassis is based on a carbon fiber tub that weighs in at only 224 pounds but is quite stiff in torsion. Also like a race car, the Ferrari's fuel cell (not a tank, mind you, but a proper rubber compound cell) is located behind the driver-passenger compartment ahead of the engine and centralized away from as many accident impacts as possible.

Look at the front of the bare F50 tub and you will see steel plates where the suspension is attached. In back, the suspension is bolted to a piece that fits between the engine and gearbox, which are rigidly mounted to the tub, housing an oil tank, another F1 holdover. Both suspension designs are based on, in race car practice, upper and lower A-arms with

If you are a fan of modern Ferraris, this is your hero: Amedeo Felisa. Not only did Felisa engineer the F50, but he also has been responsible for the fact Ferraris in general have become as reliable as they are fast and beautiful. Felisa has been rewarded for his work and is now deputy general director of Ferrari.

Like the F40 and Enzo, the F50 was hand-built in Ferrari's factory in Maranello, Italy, on what looked like a race car production line. The pace of the F50 production was snail-like compared to the line on which the regular production Ferraris are made.

Showing its relationship to Formula 1, the F50 has a carbon fiber central tub, which weighs just 224 pounds but is quite stiff. Instead of a traditional fuel tank, the F50 has a racing-style fuel cell behind the cockpit.

push-rod-controlled shock absorbers. Those shocks, incidentally, are electronically controlled to vary the damping with the driving and road conditions.

Other chassis components include a rack-and-pinion steering system designed by TRW and cast in aluminum alloy. Going to its racing supplier for the brakes, Ferrari used Brembos with aluminum calipers gripping cast-iron discs that are cross drilled for better cooling. With diameters of 14 inches front and 13.2 inches rear, the disc brakes are large enough to haul the F50 down from all conditions without needing any sort of power boost. Because of this, and the nature of the Ferrari supercar, anti-lock is not part of the F50 braking system.

Other important elements of the F50 design are, of course, the wheels and tires. Those Speedline wheels do double duty, their star-shaped design adding to the aggressive visual image of the Ferrari, their function aiding the handling. Fitted to those wheels are another (at that time) Ferrari-F1 tie, Goodyear tires. The big "skins," measuring 245/35ZR-18 front and 355/30ZR-18 rear, were specially developed for the F50, and named after Ferrari's private test track, Fiorano.

While Ferrari likes to make a great deal about the ties between the F50 and Formula 1, the fact is the supercar also shares a great deal with Ferrari's 333SP world championship sports car. That's where you find much of the heritage of the F50's 4.7-liter V-12 engine. The heart of the engine is the block with its two banks of cylinders separated by 65 degrees. There's a seven main bearing crankshaft with titanium rods and aluminum pistons. The oiling system is by dry sump.

Atop each cylinder bank, two camshafts on each head open five valves per cylinder. By using five valves, they can be made smaller and more able to take high revs—over 10,000 rpm—without floating. Feeding fuel and air past those valves is a Bosch Motronic 2.7 engine management system looking after the electronic fuel injection and static ignition.

Another interesting feature of the F50 engine is the exhaust system, which uses two different exhaust system lengths. One length gives the sort of all-around low-end torque that is expected from even high-rev modern supercar engines. The second length is utilized automatically by the electronics and lessens back pressure in the exhaust system for more power at top speed and under full load.

All this is bolted together with an 11.3:1 compression ratio, giving the F50's V-12 engine 513 horsepower at 8,000 rpm. Torque is 347 ft-lb at 6,500 rpm. Getting all this to the wheels is a six-speed manual gearbox. Housed in a magnesium alloy case, the gearbox has an oil cooler and a limited-slip differential, but no traction control.

Ferrari named this car the F50 to honor the famous Italian specialist automaker's 50th anniversary. The F50 presents quite a contrast to the front-engine, 2.0-liter cars that marked the beginning of Ferrari's history.

Unlike the F40, which needed three years for U.S. certification, the first F50s were shipped to the States, in part to dive in before a new stricter emissions law.

After that, the factory worked away until 349 of the F50s had been built. And that was it. Critics felt Ferrari milked the F40 by building too many, more than 1,300. Ferrari didn't with the F50, but also hinted at another super Ferrari in the near future . . . which turned out to be the Enzo.

Ferrari also considered racing the F50 and built a trio of competition F50 GTs. Weight was cut to under 2,000 pounds and horsepower upped to 750 with a six-speed sequential gearbox. Reports had the F50 GT lapping Fiorano faster than the 333SP sports racer, but Ferrari decided to concentrate on Formula 1 and, after building only three F50 GTs, sold the cars and bagged the program.

Sad, because on those laps with Phil Hill around Fiorano, there was the sense that the F50 was more than just a street machine, that it was a thoroughbred just waiting to be let

Quite a view, right? That's World Driving Champion Phil Hill behind the wheel and Editor-at-Large Peter Egan riding as they do hot laps at Ferrari's Fiorano test track. Thanks to an easily removable hardtop, the F50 can run as an open Barchetta or closed Berlinetta.

Oppostie page: Ferrari seriously considered racing the F50, and built three competition versions. Weighing 2,000 pounds with a 750-horsepower V-12 matched to a six-speed sequential gearbox, the car was very quick around Ferrari's Fiorano test track. The automaker decided to scrap the program to concentrate on its Formula 1 program, a decision that resulted in multiple world championships.

loose. And it would be out of the gate in a hurry as *Road & Track* had timed the F50 to 60 miles per hour in just 3.6 seconds earlier in the day. Ferrari said the car was good for 202 miles per hour, though our expert witness figured the gearing for that acceleration might yield only 190. Oh, darn . . . only 190 miles per hour.

Just before the finish of the day, Phil took *R&T* Editor-at-Large Peter Egan for a ride in the F50. For the first few laps we led them around for photos, me in the trunk of another car as they drove up close for a car-to-car shot, the F50 just inches away as we twisted around Fiorano.

What a sight . . . I could have sold tickets. ■

CHAPTER 18

Paul Frere, renowned automotive journalist and race driver, with a Pagani Zonda on the Futa Pass, which was at one time part of Italy's famous Mille Miglia open road race circuit.

214
MILES PER HOUR

PAGANI ZONDA 1999

You see it before you hear it, the silver Pagani Zonda slipping through the Italian countryside at speed. Driven by noted automotive journalist and race driver Paul Frere, the rare supercar jinks left than right through a downhill set of esses, quite gracefully for its speed, the velocity not as apparent as you think. It flies by you like an elegant burst of energy and disappears.

Le Mans winner Frere figures the Zonda "provides excellent comfort by supercar standards, together with superb handling."

There is also a nasty side to the car, with 0–60 miles per hour in 3.5–4.0 seconds, depending on which version of the Zonda you have, but top velocity is on the uphill side of 200 miles per hour.

The first Zonda, the C12, was presented at the 1999 Geneva Auto Show. Given the nature of the exotic car business, especially for the very small, specialist firms, it's impressive that Pagani is still in existence.

Horace Pagani grew up in Argentina, but moved to Italy to fulfill his dream of working in the car business. After becoming an expert in fiberglass and carbon fiber work, he was able to create his own exotic car, the Zonda, which he builds near Modena, home of Ferrari and Maserati.

For most drivers, a dream car is one they wish to own, while Horace Pagani's dream was to build one. An Argentinean expatriate living in Italy, Pagani learned the fiberglass then carbon fiber trades, became an expert, and had the time and resources to design his car. And we mean the entire automobile, from its exterior shape to the mid-engine chassis to manufacturing in a factory he laid out.

His major outside supplier is Mercedes-Benz, which provides its latest AMG V-12, an excellent choice for its high horsepower, certified emissions controls, and quality. In his plant near Modena—the Italian supercar Garden of Eden—Pagani builds the entire car, which is basically carbon fiber. There are aluminum subframes front and rear to carry the suspension and drivetrain, but the rest is of the lightweight composite. Particularly slick looking are the few cars he has finished with the unpainted carbon fiber pattern as the exposed finish. That exterior shape is a bit quirky from some angles, but very cool looking and a celebration of details, particularly at the back end.

You can order your Zonda ($500,000–$600,000) as either a coupe or roadster. Horace Pagani says the chassis reinforcement needed to decapitate the Zonda costs a surprisingly low 44 pounds and the 11-pound carbon fiber top not only can be installed or removed in minutes, but also stays in place when traveling over 200 miles per hour. That's no simple trick.

Inside, the Pagani is again a bit quirky, as the air vents look a bit like factory ducts; it has huge toggle switches and a festival of carbon fiber, but it's fun. There are plenty of details to catch your eye and seats that sit as good as they look.

We first found the Zonda C12 at the 1999 Geneva Motor Show, and since then have seen five more iterations that are best described as "the same, only different." The body style remains unchanged, as does the chassis with its upper and lower aluminum A-arm suspensions, rack-and-pinion steering, and large disc brakes. Also unchanged is the light weight, because Horace Pagani takes full advantage of carbon fiber's properties to finish his cars in the 2,800–2,900-pound range and keep them impressively rigid.

What varies is the version of the Mercedes-Benz AMG V-12 out back, though you could plan on 7.0–7.3 liters, 550–600 horsepower, and an equivalent amount of torque in ft-lb from the aluminum twin-cam engine. Pagani opts for a six-speed manual transmission.

Horace Pagani drew the shape for the Zonda body, which is striking from any angle. But Pagani also designed what's underneath that carbon fiber exterior. At the car's core is a carbon fiber center structure with aluminum subframes front and back to accommodate the upper and lower A-arm suspensions and the V-12 drivetrain.

Pagani powers his supercars with a super engine, a Mercedes-Benz AMG-tuned V-12, backed by a six-speed manual gearbox. In the Zonda C12F you have to choose between the "normal" 602-horsepower version or the Clubsport with its 650 horsepower and a potential 0–60 time of 3.5 seconds. Top speed is around 214 miles per hour.

Interiors in the Zondas can be quite spectacular. There is plenty of carbon fiber showing in the roadster, nicely contrasting the leather seats and brushed aluminum center dash panel.

The most recent edition is the first Pagani truly meant for the United States: the C12F, the last letter in honor of Pagani's fellow Argentinean, the great race driver Juan Manuel Fangio. You have the choice of a 602-horsepower model or the Clubsport with its 650 horsepower and 0–60 potential of 3.5 seconds. And beyond that? Pagani claims 214 miles per hour.

Why would an exotic-car buyer be interested in the Pagani? It certainly is unique, with an estimated 60 built between 1999 and the beginning of 2006. Horace Pagani is a very likeable guy and there is a certain long-term honesty to his car. Every expert who drives it comes away impressed and, unlike some very-limited-production automakers, there is no sense of scam or scandal about the place. No salacious rumors about funding or the future.

Best of all, at speed the Pagani Zonda just flies by you like an elegant burst of energy and disappears. ■

Thanks to the clever use of carbon fiber, Pagani is able to keep the weight of his cars to less than 3,000 pounds. As these are personalized one-off cars, owners can virtually custom order their Zondas with various choices of engines, colors, and such.

CHAPTER 19

Aston Martin's DB7 Vantage V-12 was more than just a pretty face. Its original V-12 had 420 horsepower and 400 ft-lb of torque.

With a manual gearbox, it could dance to 60 miles per hour in under 5.0 seconds and keep right on dancing up to 185 miles per hour.

200
MILES PER HOUR

Mention the name Aston Martin to most Americans and they'll shoot right back with James Bond. And with good reason: 007 has driven Astons from *Goldfinger* (1964) to *Die Another Day* (2002), from the ejection seat–equipped, twin-cam-six DB5 to the rocket-armed V-12 Vanquish. From the days when Aston was a small, proud, stand-alone British specialist automaker to now, when it's a division of the Ford Motor Company.

And in reality, James Bond is all that most Americans know about Aston.

Aston Martin shipped bare V-8 chassis to Zagato, just outside Milan, Italy, where they were dressed with custom aluminum bodies. There were both coupe and convertible versions, and the carbureted V-8 was said to have 430 horsepower. Price was just over $150,000 for the coupe, the convertible some $20,000 more.

Unless he is one of the rare Aston Martin experts, an enthusiast may not know that the company dates from 1914, and is named for one of its founders, Lionel *Martin*, and the fact that he raced in the *Aston* Hill-Hillclimb. The company's most famous prewar car was called the Ulster and its first major tie to the United States came postwar, when Carroll Shelby co-drove a DBR1 to win the 24 Hours of Le Mans in 1959.

A pair of North Americans, Canadian George Minden and American Peter Sprague, owned Aston Martin from 1975 until the early 1980s. After being passed around between several investors, Ford bought 75 percent of Aston Martin in 1986, taking on the remainder of the stock in 1994.

What even enthusiasts have trouble recounting is the litany of Aston Martin models from the immediate post-Bond DB6 until Ford stepped in. Beginning in 1969, the small automaker built a series of powerful machines powered by a twin-cam V-8 designed by highly regarded Tadek Marek.

Starting life in a mid-engine Lola GT race car, the V-8 was used in Aston Martin's production motorcars for more than two decades, beginning with the 1969 DBSV8. Subsequent versions were simply called V8. After the car's only major redo, in 1989, the car was called the Virage, but later reverted to V8 once again. It can get a bit confusing.

Astons came in several variants—like the Volante convertibles—but the versions we like here in America are the higher-horsepower Vantage models. They were a touch brutish, but blessed with horsepower and speed.

There was also the Italian episode. One of the most beautiful racing GTs of the 1960s was the Aston Martin DB4GT, with a rounded body created by Zagato just outside Milan. Going back to that firm in 1986, Aston Martin had it create a new model, again bodied in Italy. Not as graceful as the original, perhaps, yet the new Aston Martin Zagato stood out in the exotic-car crowd and had its own Volante version.

It would be impossible to forget watching Formula 1 champion Phil Hill fly around England's Millbrook test track's high-speed banking in an Aston Martin Zagato, well into the 180-mile-per-hour range. Without open exhausts, I could hear the car displace the air at that speed. Being just feet away behind the fence on the outside of the banked circle had a frightening effect beyond what I could get with an unmuffled exhaust. It gave me the chills . . . very strange.

This is World Driving Champion Phil Hill in a 1988 Aston Martin Zagato at 185 miles per hour on the banking of the Milbrook test track in England. The V-8 sound was trailing the Aston, so when the car went by just feet away at speed, the prominent sound was of the car displacing the air. It was oddly scary.

This was the original Aston Martin V-8, which in various forms powered the English supercars for decades. This is its Virage form: 5.3 liters with four valves per cylinder and a glorious kick off the line.

While Ferrari and Lamborghini were converting to mid-engines for their fastest exotic cars in 1971, traditional Aston Martin would have none of that. Other than one famous mid-engine design called the Bulldog, it stayed faithful to the front-engine, rear-drive layout. The chassis stayed much the same throughout the cars' lifetimes: independent A-arms in front and a DeDion to the rear in machines never known for their lightness.

Even in its first production form, Marek's V-8 displaced 5.3 liters and, over the years, it produced an estimated 350 horsepower, depending upon the model. The normally aspirated Vantages had an estimated 435 horsepower. Why estimated? For years Aston Martin

Aston Martin has had a long history with the Italian coachbuilder Zagato. Aston's DB4GT Zagato from the early 1960s is a prized vintage race car. In the late 1980s, Aston went back to Zagato to create a series of 50 coupes that would be powered by the famous Aston V-8.

After Ford bought Aston Martin it had to come up with new products on a tight schedule and budget. So it developed the new DB7 on a Jaguar XJS platform, and to add sizzle to the steak had Ian Callum design the body. Then it added a convertible version plus a V-12 engine, creating one sublime automobile.

snobbishly refused to divulge horsepower and torque figures until emissions laws eventually required it. Torque was also impressive, probably in the area of 350 ft-lb.

Anyone familiar with driving U.S. V-8-powered muscle cars from the early 1970s would feel right at home in a V-8 Aston. They would recognize the easy torque and familiar boom of the engine.

Although critics harped that the British automaker was a bit too traditional—with the little tags that read "By Appointment to His Royal Highness" and all that—there was also something familiar about hustling all that horsepower around in a front-engine chassis. The big mid-engine Testarossa and Countach almost seemed to dare you to go fast. Do you have the courage and ability to do this? Not so in the Astons. This was particularly comforting when driving quickly on narrow, hedgerow-lined English roads.

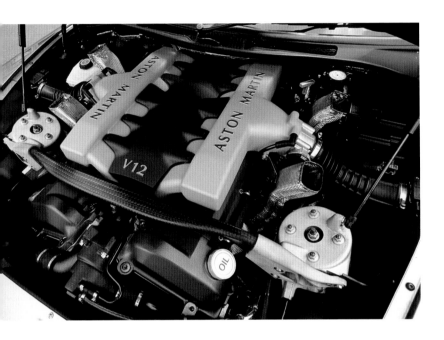

In its first iteration, the horsepower of the 6.0-liter Vanquish V-12 was pegged at 460 at 6,500 rpm, torque at 400 ft-lb. In 2004, Aston reworked the cylinder heads and the engine management controls to bump output to 520 horsepower and 425 ft-lb. Through it all, Aston has retained a six-speed manual transmission shifted via steering wheel paddles.

All the Astons but the Italian-bodied Zagatos were made in a factory in Newport Pagnell, about 50 miles north of London. It was unlike any exotic-car factory today, peopled by workers who were often the sons or grandsons of other Aston men. They even bought their tools in the same village shops. The engines were famous for being hand built by one man, each powerplant receiving a plate with the builder's name. Over in the panel-beating shop where the aluminum bodywork was formed, you couldn't hear yourself think for all the banging and hammering, the proud workers giving a suspicious eye to outsiders.

If the cars that came out of Newport Pagnell weren't exactly built to German standards, there was a sort of upper-class elegance to Astons in the tradition of tea at 4 P.M. and a gin and tonic before dinner that made that quality okay; heck, no exotic car is perfect.

And for all their weight, both physical and social, the Astons were fast, getting to 60 miles per hour in around 5.5 seconds with a top speed that often topped 180 miles per hour. Good times in the 1970s and 1980s.

The ultimate megahorsepower Aston Martin V-8 was the Virage Vantage. Marek's V-8 had been refined for the 1989 redo by Callaway Cars in Old Lyme, Connecticut. Fitted with a pair of big turbochargers, the 5.3-liter V-8 now had a claimed 550 horsepower and 550 ft-lb of torque. Top speed was 186 and 60 miles per hour came up in 4.6 seconds . . . and these were heavy cars. Then Aston coaxed another 50 horsepower from the Vantage for the 1998 V600.

After Ford bought Aston Martin, it developed a long-term plan to modernize the line. First evidence came with the 1996 DB7, based on an abandoned chassis from Ford cousin

Jaguar, powered by a 335-horsepower supercharged inline-six and graced with luscious bodywork from Ian Callum. The DB7 added the Volante name along with a V-12 engine in 1999. Aston Martin was setting to take on Ferrari, but it still needed a big gun.

Like a shot fired across Ferrari's bow, Aston Martin's Vanquish roared into the supercar wars in 2001, ready to take on the 550 Maranello. It was no accident that the new Aston's exterior measurements were close to those of the Ferrari, that its factory-claimed 5-second, 60-mile-per-hour time was just a blink under the Ferrari's or that each was priced (then) in the $225,000 range, but later glided up to the $250,000 bracket.

This twenty-first-century Anglo-Italian war aligned the Vanquish against the 550/575 Maranello and, as of 2006, Ferrari's 599 GTB. The DB7 Vantage, and now the DB9, take on the 360 Modena and its replacement, the F430. And, last, the new V-8 Vantage is meant to compete against the Maserati coupe and Spyder.

After its debut on the streets, the Vanquish had a famous debut on-screen, starring as James Bond's latest tricked-out car in the movie *Die Another Day*. Many Americans' first (and most lasting) exposure to Aston Martin was the DB5 that Bond (Sean Connery) drove in the movie *Goldfinger*.

While other exotic car companies have produced mid-engined cars, Aston remains true to the front-engine, rear-drive layout. The automaker only builds 300 Vanquishes each year, and the sticker price is $255,000, quite a jump from the $110,000 it charges for its smaller-but-similar-looking (and also quick) V-8 Vantage.

Aston Martin began its supercar project in March 1997, pulled the cover off the Project Vanquish show car at Detroit in January 1998 and, in 2001, began production of the big car.

Credit for the Vanquish shape also goes to Callum, now Jaguar's director of design and creator of such diverse automobiles as the DB7, the cute Ford Puma coupe, and Nissan's R390 Le Mans race car.

Callum gave the Vanquish a mixture of Aston Martin cues, such as the grille, a high-side/low-greenhouse profile, and an aggressive tail that seemed to tease, "Ta ta, old boy, you should have been faster." Callum is a master at giving a car its best stance, so he and the engineers placed proper-size wheels and tires in their wheelwells, then wrapped the bodywork around them to make the car appear broad-shouldered and well planted on the ground.

Callum calls it "an expressive, almost menacing Aston." No argument there.

But the Vanquish was more than just an aggressive face. Aston Martin built the Vanquish less like a car than an aircraft. Extruded aluminum is used for the basic body cage, combined with a carbon-fiber center tunnel, composite body sides, and carbon-fiber A-pillars.

Ahead of the front bulkhead is an aluminum, steel, and carbon-fiber subframe for the powertrain and suspension. This rig doubles as a crush structure for crashworthiness, in combination with another deformable composite structure that surrounds and contains the grille. Rear crash protection includes the aluminum side rails and composite trunk floor.

In contrast to the hand-hammered exterior panels of previous Aston Martins, the Vanquish's aluminum skins are heated and "super plastic formed," a la Ford GT. Aluminum and carbon fiber aside, the Vanquish weighs more than 4,000 pounds.

What makes all this aircraftlike is that the Vanquish was assembled with rivets and various adhesives, so the car is basically riveted and glued together. Classic welds? You would only find them fixing door skins to their frames.

A Ferrari 550 Maranello fighter should have no less than 12 cylinders, and the Vanquish uses the 6.0-liter V-12 that started life in the DB7 Vantage. Where the smaller car's powerplant had 420 brake horsepower at 6,000 rpm and 400 ft-lb of torque at 5,000 rpm, the Vanquish version is pumped to 460 brake horsepower at 6,500, while sharing the DB7's torque figure.

Magneti Marelli Holding S.p.A. makes the electro-hydraulic shift mechanism for Ferrari's steering-column-paddle-shifter gearboxes, and does the same for the Vanquish.

There is a certain scrumptiousness to British car interiors, and the Vanquish is no exception, with a decided handmade look. The seats almost look overstuffed when compared to those in Italian cars, and they are upholstered in fine leather.

For years, Aston Martin's most super cars had their engines built in England by one man, who then added a small plaque with his name, personalizing the process, as seen on this early Vanquish V-12. As Aston Martin production increased, engine sourcing switched to Cologne, Germany, probably sending shivers through the traditionalists at Aston.

Instead of humans fumbling gear changes, the Marelli's magic does those shifts in milliseconds. Unlike humans, it never blows a shift and offers a fully automatic mode.

Suspension engineers tuned the front and rear upper and lower A-arm designs to Aston Martin's estimation of the proper balance of ride and handling, with input from Lotus Engineering and former Grand Prix driver John Miles. Brakes are big ABS-controlled Brembos, vented all around and cross-drilled at the front, while a traction-control system is part of the package. Variable-assist rack-and-pinion steering guide the big Aston.

When settling into the leather-covered seats, you face a tight array of green-on-cream gauges. Interior materials are limited to leather and aluminum, with a few aluminum-like pieces made of plastic for safety reasons. In the dash center is a tall aluminum column with various large buttons: reverse, automatic mode, traction control on-off, etc, plus the red starter button. At the bottom is one of the car's few obvious ties to its Ford parent: the heating/air-conditioning/radio/satellite-navigation controls inherited from the Jaguar XJs.

Pull back on the paddles for neutral, punch the red button, and the V-12 whumps to life. Some drivers would object to the low roof and its slight bunker effect, with the carbon-fiber A-pillars seeming wider than one would like.

The specifications sheet of Aston's Vanquish mirrors that of most exotic cars: upper and lower A-arm suspensions with coil springs, tube shocks, and big vented disc brakes all around.

Those objections aside, the Vanquish delivers the sort of performance you would expect from an anti-Ferrari, *Road & Track* getting the Aston Martin to 60 in 4.7 seconds, the same as the day's 550 Maranello. The Vanquish missed the Maranello's top speed by a few miles per hour, but 190 should be enough for most drivers.

Handling is about as I expected for a car of the Vanquish's potential: firm-but-not-heavy steering that turns the car in nicely, with light understeer that allows one to plant the throttle with little concern about the rear end stepping out. When hustled down narrow Scottish roads, the Aston feels narrower and lighter than it really is. Many of those roads are also rather rough, but the ride of the Vanquish never becomes unsettled or jiggly.

Just as Ferrari upped the ante with the 575 Maranello, and now the 599 GTB, Aston followed up the standard Vanquish in 2004 with an S version. Visually there are minor changes, from a slightly larger grille to a reshaped trunk lid that trims aerodynamic lift and adds stability.

Most important, the V-12 came in for changes, mainly in the cylinder heads and engine mapping to increase the 6.0-liter V-12's output to 520 horsepower at 7,000 rpm, the torque up 25 ft-lb to 425. While the 0–60 time isn't particularly affected, the top speed is lifted to just over 200 miles per hour.

Knowing the added power needed added chassis support, Aston Martin made the firmer Sports Dynamics suspension standard on the S and beefed up the brakes with larger caliper pistons and added disc width.

They must have been quite busy at Aston Martin about the time the S was launched, because they put the DB9 into production in 2004 and the smaller V8 Vantage on the road in 2006.

Naturally, Aston Martin is a very different place today than it was when the V8s were made. Engines (V-8s and V-12s) now come from a dedicated factory in, of all places, Cologne, Germany . . . but then again, the classic British automaker has had a German CEO, Ulrich Betz, for a half decade.

Both DB9s and V8 Vantages are made in a factory in Gaydon, England, north of Newport Pagnell, but it's good to know that, at least for the time being, the Vanquish is built in the traditional factory. It is much more modern now, of course, but the line continues to run quite slowly and there are still sons and grandsons of original Aston Martin men working there. ■

First shown as a concept in 1998 and put into production in 2001, Aston Martin's Vanquish was a clear shot at Ferrari's 550/575 Maranello. The pair share many physical dimensions and generate similar speeds, with 0–60 times just under 5.0 seconds and top velocities a bit over 200 miles per hour.

CHAPTER 20

Latest "big" supercar from Lamborghini is the Murciélago LP640, the initials meaning "longitudinale posteriore" for the fore-aft engine position, and 640 to signify its higher horsepower rating. Lamborghini has already built some 2,000 Murciélagos since this model replaced the Diablo.

205
MILES PER HOUR

LAMBORGHINI MURCIÉLAGO 2001

Does Luc Donckerwolke work in the Batcave? The highly regarded Belgian is the man who clothed Lamborghini's Gallardo and Murciélago, but could be getting a check from Bruce Wayne.

Painted black, headed right at you, its side air intakes extended like tiny wings, the Murciélago would make a cool Batmobile. And a quick one, sending the Caped Crusader off to save the world at a 0–60 rate of 3.6 seconds. Here's hoping Gotham City's freeways are up to the Lamborghini's 205-mile-per-hour top speed.

It doesn't hurt, of course, that Murciélago means "bat" in Spanish.

Equipped with Lamborghini's VT (Viscous Traction) all-wheel drive system, the Murciélago has little trouble laying down all its horsepower. In the original model that meant 60 miles per hour popped up in 3.6 seconds; with the 6.5-liter V-12 that is shaved to 3.4 seconds. *Photo courtesy of Lamborghini*

In the late 1990s, Lamborghini went to Audi looking for an appropriate powerplant for a proposed new small car. That never happened, but in the process, talks began that led to the German automaker buying the Italian specialty house.

It's apparent now that the plan was a two-model range for starters, with the lion's share of time and treasure going to an all-new small car, the Gallardo. Not to be ignored was the big Lambo and, since there was already a basis in the Countach-Diablo line, why not start there?

The fundamentals are the same, but with the improvements needed after the Diablo's 11-year reign.

While the skeleton of the Murciélago remained a tubular steel frame, it was now reinforced with carbon-fiber/honeycomb structure pieces. A steel roof and carbon-fiber floorpan added significantly to the rigidity of the frame. The wheelbase was fractionally longer (0.6 inch)

Despite the width of the big Lambo and its door sills, it isn't difficult to slip over and into the driver's seat. You can sense how big the Murciélago is around you, but the touch and lightness of the controls make it feel like a smaller machine.

Inside the Lamborghini factory. This is a first-generation Murciélago. With the LP640, the dual exhaust pipes are joined into one outlet and the bumper is slightly reworked. If you want to show a little pride in your 6.5-liter V-12, there is an optional glass engine cover.

Lamborghini set the displacement of the Murciélago V-12 at 6.2 liters when the car was introduced in 2001. Horsepower for the twin-cam-head engine was 580 at 7,500 rpm, and torque measured 479 ft-lb at 5,400 rpm.

and the suspension and its electronics were upgraded, but the roots, including the dual rear springs, remained. At 14.4 inches front and 13.2 inches rear, the Murciélago's disc brakes are the same size as the Gallardo's.

Also retained is the unique Countach/Diablo drivetrain layout. The transmission still resides in the cockpit's broad center console, upgraded from five speeds to six and with the option of electronic paddle shifting. Aft of the gearbox is the engine, the power routed to all four wheels via Lamborghini's VT (viscous traction) system.

Engine specs carried over: a 60-degree aluminum V-12 with dual overhead cams and four valves per cylinder. The dry-sump engine is new, and it could be dropped almost 2 inches lower in the frame. Up top is variable valve timing and a system that varies the length of the intake system, all the better to broaden the torque curve and improve driving flexibility.

In 2001, when the Murciélago was first shown, its V-12 was certified at 6.2 liters with 580 horsepower at 7,500 rpm and 479 ft-lb of torque at 5,400. A half decade later, at the 2006 Geneva Auto Show, Lamborghini stepped up with the LP640, the initials signifying the engine's longitudinal position and the fact it now has 640 horsepower. The V-12 is opened to 6.5 liters, the intake side refined and torque increased to 487 ft-lb.

Donckerwolke's exterior shape for the Murciélago was the biggest leap forward from the Diablo, though it retained the crucial swing-up doors. Gone is the sexy, rounded-corner design

of the big Lamborghini, replaced by square corners and a look that is more serious and ground hugging. There is an obvious (too obvious?) styling link to the smaller Gallardo, but also an impressive aura about the Murciélago—this isn't a sissy car.

And it has those cool little bat wings, officially called the Variable Air-flow Cooling System (VACS). As the need to cool all that horsepower out back grows, the intakes swing out, upping the drag coefficient from 0.33 to 0.36, but snagging crucial cooling air. Also automatic is a small rear spoiler that rises to 50 degrees at 80 miles per hour, tilting another 20 degrees above 137 miles per hour.

Luc Donckerwolke, a Belgian designer, is the man who has penned the modern Lamborghinis. His distinctive style, with its crisp lines, has set the Murciélago and Gallardo apart from the Pininfarina-designed competition from Ferrari. In this Lamborghini-supplied artwork, you can see several of the design sketches for the Murciélago.

With the 2006 upgrade to LP640 spec, the body came in for some minor mods, mainly the front and rear bumper/spoiler designs, which tend to flare more and add a bit of sex appeal. A glass engine cover to display the V-12 went on the option list.

Road & Track turned off the traction control, ran the V-12's revs to 5,000, sidestepped the clutch to launch the 6.2-liter Murciélago, and said the car "explodes off the line." The explosion lasted 3.6 seconds to 60, so it figures the 6.5-liter version should drop that to 3.4. Patrick Hong wrote in *R&T*, "Did you ever stand at a railroad crossing and feel the ground shake as a train rushed past? Being in the Lamborghini produces the same sensation, except now the shaking is in your fingertips as you upshift through the gears."

After generating 0.9 g on an admittedly dusty skid pad, the big Lambo acquitted itself well on the slalom run. Hong concluded: "On the road, the new Lamborghini's ride is firm and borders on harsh for extended trips. The driver-selectable electronic damper settings can make only slight improvements to ride quality. However, the Murciélago is a sports car, not exactly intended for luxury cruises on the Interstate."

There is the option of a Murciélago Roadster. Lamborghini whacked off the top of the coupe and, for only 65 pounds of added weight, created possibly the most outrageous open road car in the world. It is a clever bit of engineering, reinforcing the frame where needed, then beefing up the door sills and A-pillars with added composite pieces. Bolted across the top of the engine bay is a steel buttressing frame or, for around $5,000 extra, you can have it in carbon fiber.

The Variable Air-flow Cooling System for the big V-12 in the back of the Murciélago is very slick. As the engine generates more horsepower and the resultant heat, these little wings flare out from the bodywork to gulp more cooling air. Fully deployed, they raise the car's coefficient of drag from 0.33 to 0.36. *Photo courtesy of Lamborghini*

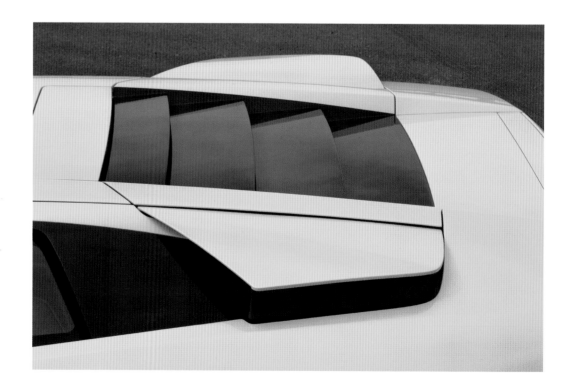

The top is a fold-and-stow and Lamborghini warns against driving more than 100 miles per hour with it in place, but other than protection against a sudden shower, what would be the point, anyway?

The 580-horsepower V-12 will still get you to 60 oh so quickly, just 3.8 seconds, only a whisper slower than the coupe.

That's the least you should expect for the $300,000–$340,000 check you would be writing for your Murciélago. ∎

At Detroit's 2006 Auto Show, Lamborghini uncovered a new concept, a modern interpretation of its classic mid-engine Miura, one of the original modern supercars. Although quite exciting, the new Miura looks a bit squared off, where the original was covered with sensuous curves.

CHAPTER 21

Phil Frank, working with Steve Saleen, gets the nod for the S7 body, which is as stunning as anything out of Italy. The low nose, dramatic air intakes along the sides, the arcing vents, the roof-top air intake, and that sweeping tail are all done in lightweight carbon fiber.

235
MILES PER HOUR

SALEEN S7 2001

I was at the 12 Hours of Sebring in Florida at sunset, down at the famous hairpin. Now was probably the best time to see this famous endurance event, the race cars showing some wear, a light coat of grit on their once-shiny finishes as they braked hard for this tight corner. The sound of their open exhausts rumbled around me as they dived for the hairpin and, in the dulling twilight, their disc brakes glowed bright orange.

Audis, Aston Martins, Ferraris, Porsches by the score, and a car that didn't come from any foreign land but the California costal city of Irvine: Saleen's S7.

It's not exotic Maranello, Italy, or Stuttgart, Germany, but Irvine, California, where a Saleen Twin Turbo V-8 is assembled. In the same facility where the company converts normal Mustangs into superquick Saleen S281 coupes and convertibles, the exotic mid-engine S7 is built on a line that resembles a race shop.

Saleen's S7 is not your average exotic car, but more like a race car tamed for the street. It takes a little effort to clamber in and nestle into those seats, but it's well worth the effort once there. You feel like you're belted into a race car.

Corvettes and Saleens have been upholding the honor of the U.S. racing community for years. The C6R 'Vettes are beautifully developed, highly specialized race versions of America's favorite production sports car. Saleen's race machines, on the other hand, are not that far removed from the S7 you can drive on the street.

Saleens are winners, having taken their class in the rough 12 Hours of Sebring, competed with honor at Le Mans, and captured driver's and manufacturer's GT championships in the United States, England, and Spain.

In fact, if you ever wanted to know what it's like to drive a race car on the streets, finagle your way into a Saleen S7. This is the real thing, now with a 750-horsepower twin-turbo V-8 that gobbles up 0–60 in 2.8 seconds and the quarter-mile in 10.7 seconds at 136 miles per hour. *Road & Track* discovered that from a standing start an S7 covers a mile in just 23.4 seconds, crossing the line at 205.7 miles per hour. Steve Saleen figures that if you don't lift and have enough road you'll redline at 235 miles per hour.

When you get into the S7 via Lamborghini-style flip-up doors, and if you have broad feet like me, you may have to remove your shoes to fit into the footwell. The procedure seems daunting, but isn't. Once in you are snug, but not squeezed into what is a very personal two-seater. The driver's seat is fixed, but the pedals can be manually reset fore-aft and the steering wheel tilt is adjustable.

The close-in proximity of your surroundings shouts race car, but the cockpit image says luxury, with fine leather, a proper center console, and watch-face gauges, all nicely finished and put together. The presence of amenities like air conditioning, power windows, and a sound system might lull you into luxury, but at the push of a button the V-8 startles awake behind you as a friendly-but-growling presence.

It's a heavy clutch—though not dauntingly so—and requires a balance between revs and take-up that at first has you feeling you've spun it too much . . . or stalled the engine. Once moving, the shift linkage is positive and you can feel there's big power just aft.

The route used to familiarize S7 owners with their new car is a course of lightly traveled roads and motorways, which quickly tempts the speedometer into three figures. As you pass between 90 and 100 miles per hour, you can feel the downforce a bit as the S7 settles in and steadies up still more. At 125 miles per hour the car is rock solid and the temptation to keep accelerating is sooooo great.

Despite being race car-based, the S7 is easy to maneuver in traffic, though you feel a bit down-there on the pavement looking up at not just trucks but even Toyota Corollas. Outward visibility to the sides and front is reasonably good, vision to the rear handled by a small video camera and dashboard-mounted screen.

The ride is what you'd expect from a race car-turned-road machine, very firm, though the reality of what you're driving seems to make you more understanding and amenable to the snug-down nature of the car. Sounds of the car hitting road imperfections bring you back down to earth.

Included on the drive is a twisty, up-down, left-right forested two-laner on which the S7 proves quite docile, feeling like it weighs about half its real-world ton-and-a-half. It seems that the faster you go, the narrower the car becomes. Turn-in with the light, quick electric-hydro assist steering is a breeze; just point and you are there.

You could drive on forever.

Flip-up doors and beautiful exterior and interior finish aside, under that body the Saleen S7 is race bred. The upper and lower A-arm suspension is adjustable, and many of the parts have the machined beauty of serious race cars.

While there are Ford roots in the Saleen V-8, it is a custom-made engine featuring many race parts. In a standard S7 you'll find 550 horsepower, but there's also the Twin Turbo version, which sends power to the stratosphere: 750 horsepower and 700 ft-lb of torque.

Okay, here are the physical facts: Curb weight: 2,950 pounds. Weight distribution: 40 percent front/60 percent rear. Wheelbase: 106.30 inches. Track: 68.82 inches front/ 67.32 inches rear. Width: 78.35 inches. Length: 187.95 inches. Height: 40.98 inches. Best of all, the Twin Turbo V-8 gets those dimensions to 60 miles per hour in 2.8 seconds.

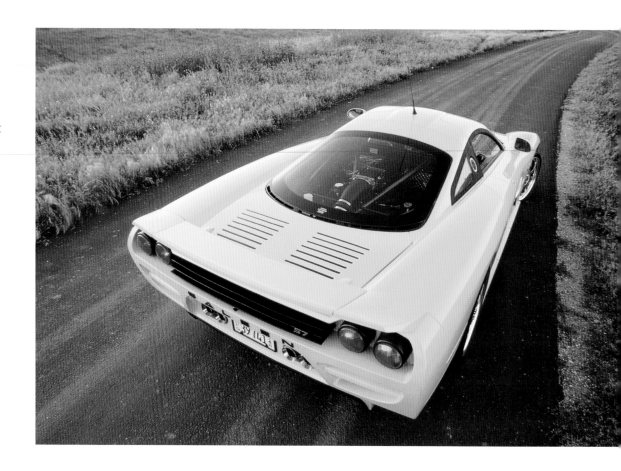

Its brakes glowing hot, a Saleen S7 dives for the hairpin during the 12 Hours of Sebring. Saleens have held up the racing honor of the United States throughout the world, taking their class at Sebring and winning GT championships in the United States, England, and Spain.

For the past 25 years, Steve Saleen has been successfully racing and building Ford-based cars.

Like Louis Ruf in Germany, Saleen isn't a tuner, but a manufacturer, right down to his own vehicle identification number (VIN) plates in each car. Most of the employees in Saleen's 120,000-square-foot factory in Irvine are making up to 400 changes to Mustangs, converting as many as 1,000 each year into Saleen versions.

Because these modifications are so extensive, Saleen had to become a manufacturer and do both crash testing and emissions certification of his cars. He does this with Ford's blessing, selling his cars through franchised Ford dealers, complete with warranty.

Saleen is so tight with Ford that his factory was the skunk works for the Ford GT project, and he is manufacturing the mid-engine exotics for Ford in a facility just outside Detroit.

The S7 is not, however, the Ford GT in different clothing, but its own animal, constructed race car-fashion in what looks like a competition shop, where each car's basic structure is welded up of chrome-moly tubing reinforced by aluminum honeycomb panels. The results are so sturdy that when you ask Saleen about meeting government crash standards,

he grins and quips that it's not difficult with a structure meant to protect a race driver who might leave Le Mans' Mulsanne Straight at more than 200 miles per hour.

Suspension layout is as expected of a race-bred car: upper and lower A-arms and dampers with coil-over springs; but what impresses is the quality of workmanship, like the CNC cut-from-a-billet aluminum front hubs or the fabricated suspension arms. And like any proper race car, the suspension is fully adjustable.

Vented Brembo non-ABS four-piston caliper brakes, measuring 15 inches front/14 inches rear, lurk inside wheels with squat Michelin Pilot Sport tires mounted to alloy wheels with race car single center nut mounting.

Ford parts are a few of the beginnings for the aluminum 16-valve V-8, but any comparison quickly fades when you see how the big engine is built. Saleen engineers have kept some Ford dimensions, like the bore centers so they can use the best aftermarket racing gaskets, but the aluminum block, heads, plus stainless-steel valves, and such are custom-made for Saleen, complete with special touches like beryllium exhaust valve seats. The dry-sump engine sits very low in the car, making it about the toughest to photograph in my experience, and it is fed fresh air from a scoop at the front edge of the roof.

Some car fans have trouble taking Saleen seriously, because the car doesn't come from Italy or Germany, which is about as silly and short-sighted as not taking a Corvette Z06 seriously. The design, the detailing, and the execution of the California-built cars are up to that of the imports. You can drool more over the S7's details by checking in at www.saleen.com.

The S7 I drove was the original with a mere 550 horsepower, but as of 2005 Saleen began fitting the big motor with a pair of turbochargers, sending horsepower sky high, straight to 750 at 6,300 rpm with torque an equally impressive 700 ft-lb at 4,800. And this in a car that weighs 2,950 pounds. No wonder it gets to 60 in 2.8 seconds.

Around all this is a very dramatic carbon fiber body, shaped by Phil Frank and Steve Saleen, and meant to yield the combination of sleekness and downforce needed in a high-speed GT. Aero effectiveness aside, it's a thrilling form that looks like it should cost the $550,000 Saleen charges. The shape has a high louver and scoop count, though they are all there for one purpose: to aim airflow in the proper direction, from the gaping nose to the airflow exhaust diffuser under the rear spoiler.

As I said, it's the real thing, makes you wonder what it would be like to make the right-turn hairpin at Sebring in a Saleen S7 and just keep going. . . ■

CHAPTER 22

When *Road & Track* tested the Enzo it generated a very impressive 1.01g on the skid pad and snaked through the 700-foot slalom at 73.0 miles per hour. The Enzo has a surprisingly comfortable ride for a car with such high handling potential.

218
MILES PER HOUR

FERRARI ENZO 2002

This is how you drive a Ferrari Enzo: Yes, the car is wide but so is the door, and when it swings up and forward the structural sill you step over to get in is surprisingly narrow. Settle in, belt up, step on the brake. Turn the key to the right. Pull both paddles that electro-hydraulically shift the six-speed transmission back to get neutral. Push the start button. Tug back on the right paddle for first, off the brake, and drive away.

As the revs wrap up on the redline at eight grand, pop back on the right-hand lever—don't even lift off the gas—and you're in second, though you'll be back at 8,000 in two quick breaths, with the V-12 singing its heart out behind you.

You pop into third gear at 75 miles per hour and sooner than you realize you are at criminal-offense speeds and back off. It's sooo easy, and there are three more gears between you and 218 miles per hour.

This does not mean that you can go to Ferrari's Italian test track, Fiorano, and start challenging Grand Prix legend Michael Schumacher's lap times. That's another matter altogether—like needing serious driving talent—but at least you can get up a head of steam in a heartbeat and even sound like you know what you're doing on downshifts without any of the old impediments.

In fact, the Enzo is so easy to drive your mother could do it . . . if she had the $1 million to buy one.

How I learned all this about the Enzo is another story. When the supercar was launched in 2002, Ferrari had no test examples, so *Road & Track* had to find an accommodating owner. Enter Richard Losee of Provo, Utah, an old friend of the magazine and an Enzo

Pininfarina designer Ken Okuyama has revealed that when an early design for the Enzo wasn't stirring enough souls, he penned the basic shape of the production car over a lunch hour. From this angle you can get a sense of the Formula-1-car-with-fenders design they attempted to achieve (and succeeded).

owner. He offered the car for testing as soon as he got it, but it needed pre-track miles, so would we come to Provo and help him drive it to Newport Beach, California—*R&T*'s home—to put 1,500 miles on it?

You bet. Four of us, world driving champion Phil Hill, Design Director Richard Baron, Road Test Editor Patrick Hong, and lucky me, went to Provo so we could drive the Enzo back. And it was "we" because the ever-generous Losee wanted all of us to drive the car.

You bet. Ain't life grand?

In Provo we found it a bit shocking to see an Enzo on the street for the first time, even for those of us who love the design. It would be like seeing a Martian, though an attractive one, at the grocery store. It *really* stands out in a crowded road.

You can read about the Enzo's creation in the sidebar story with its designer, Ken Okuyama, but there is also the aerodynamics story.

If you stood back, climbed a 6-foot ladder, and looked down on the Enzo, you could easily see that the shape was like a dramatic shrink-wrap around an F1 machine. The design, however, was meant to do more than just attract the eye.

Ah yes, that supercar staple, the flip-up doors. When you open the Enzo's, it's surprisingly how light they are, until you consider that much of the car is fashioned in carbon fiber. Thanks to the lightweight material, Ferrari was able to hold the Enzo's curb weight to under 2,800 pounds.

Open or closed, an Enzo will draw a crowd. When introduced, the body shape was controversial, but has since come to be admired by most supercar fans. It doesn't hurt, of course, that during the exotic Ferrari's production run, Michael Schumacher was nailing down win after win for the company's Formula 1 team.

Using the Enzo's launch control, the Enzo can be jet quick. *Road & Track* took the car to 60 miles per hour in 3.3 seconds, flitted past 100 miles per hour in 6.6 seconds, and completed a quarter-mile in 11.1 seconds at 133 miles per hour. Just as impressive, perhaps, is that the Ferrari supercar did many standing starts with nary a complaint.

Ferrari and Pininfarina wanted a 200-mile-per-hour-plus exotic car without the large external wings seen on earlier supercars, so the Enzo went through extensive wind tunnel aero work. You would find intakes and outlets at important points on the body, all meant to channel airflow precisely and contribute to aerodynamics and the cooling required for a 650-horsepower high-performance engine to propel an Enzo quickly to more than 200 miles per hour.

The nose design contains a hint of a Formula 1 car's wing, while inside that low nose are hidden flaps that open and close to aid cooling and downforce. The small rear wing rises at

37 miles per hour to aid and balance downforce, but retracts in steps as velocity increases to trim the car's shape for ultra high speed. Ferrari pointed out that the downforce increased from 758 pounds at 124 miles per hour to its max of 1,709 at 185, but lowered to 1,290 pounds to cut drag and get the Enzo to its top speed of 218 miles per hour.

An important part of the downforce package is hidden under the car, a flat bottom with a venturi under the rear bumper that helps suck the car down to the road. I followed the Enzo on a very dusty road and had a dramatic demonstration of how the system vacuums the air from beneath the car.

Up on that ladder you'd also be looking at a lot of carbon fiber, because all the body panels and the inner monocoque tub that is the structural heart of the Enzo are made of carbon fiber with appropriate aluminum honeycomb panels. This F1-like tub was computer designed for low weight and high strength. It weighs an amazingly low 202 pounds. This structure design is also critical to safety, as an Enzo owner found out in Malibu, California, when his car broke in half against a power pole at 125 miles per hour (or more), and he walked away with just a bloody lip.

The business end of the Enzo: a 65-degree aluminum V-12 that dynos to 650 horsepower at 7,800 rpm and 485 ft-lb of torque at 5,500. Thanks to its Bosch engine management system, the big engine will not only go into afterburner mode, but also will happily putter along in traffic when needed.

Aluminum subframes were included to attach the driveline and suspension to the tub.

Computers also aided in the design of the upper and lower A-arm suspensions with their pushrod-activated coil springs/shocks, which are located inboard horizontally. To stop its 200-mile-per-hour-plus supercar, Ferrari included 15-inch carbon-ceramic disc brakes. Around them are alloy wheels with Bridgestone Potenza RE050 Scuderia tires, the fronts being 245/35ZR-19s, the rears 345/35ZR-19s.

Carbon fiber is also a main ingredient in the Enzo's interior, looking as studly as it is structural. The red-faced tach and speedometer are hooded straight ahead, just past a very purposeful steering wheel. No sissy buttons on this wheel for radio volume or telephone activation, but big-time stuff, like shock absorber settings and traction control. The leather-covered carbon fiber shell seats hug the driver around the middle for lateral control, without squeezing inappropriately tight.

The most important thing in the interior is the big red start button that fires the 6.0-liter twin-cam 48-valve V-12. With a mighty 108.4 horsepower per liter, the 65-degree vee aluminum powerplant comes in at 650 horsepower at 7,800 rpm and 485 ft-lb of torque at 5,500. What makes the Enzo so eminently drivable in city traffic or on the open road is the Bosch Motronic ME7 engine control system and the fact that you have some 380 ft-lb of torque down around 3,000 rpm.

Inside the Enzo's nose are flaps that can open and close to aid cooling and downforce. To balance downforce at the rear of the car, a small wing will rise up, but then retract to trim the car's shape for its 200-plus-mile per hour top speed.

KEN OKUYAMA ON THE *FERRARI ENZO*

Some of us love it and others don't, but it's tough to find anyone with a neutral feeling about the exterior design of Ferrari's Enzo. And then its designer reveals that the basics of the supercar from Maranello were drawn in 15 minutes over a lunch hour.

Enzo lovers might say, "Eureka, a stroke of brilliance . . . 15 minutes of genius."

Detractors could mutter, "You bet, it looks like it was done in 15 minutes."

Here's how it happened:

Ken Okuyama, a well-known Japanese designer who worked at Pininfarina, left to teach at Pasadena's famed Art Center College of Design, and then returned to Pininfarina and penned the Enzo.

Okuyama smiles and begins, "Ferrari is such an emotional brand, so the decision-making process is always emotional."

Pininfarina had a proposed Enzo design ready to go, "Which was much more like a Group C Le Mans racer," Okuyama explains. "The design made sense but didn't give us the heartbeat we wanted." As they approached an afternoon meeting during the car's design approval process, Okuyama explains, "About an hour before the presentation, we said of the Group C design, 'This is not going to go. We need something else.'

"I made a sketch during lunchtime of the concept of a Formula 1 car underneath four fenders, an F1 two-seater in plain view with four fenders. That was the concept of the car. So the Enzo was sketched in 15 minutes during a lunch break.

"When we presented it after lunch we had a mixed reaction from people, but my boss, Sergio Pininfarina, said, 'We're going to turn this into a model.'

So you could putter your way to the store with little concern. When you want power and push the accelerator, the intake stacks will literally shorten to change the intake runner length and the V-12 will instantly respond.

It was difficult to resist doing this every quarter-mile or so when driving the Enzo. Hard to get into the touring mode as we drove from Provo to Newport Beach, because the Ferrari is so easy to drive and, as a result, so tempting. We could be at 100 miles per hour lickity-split. A bright red Ferrari Enzo was also the main object of attention to anyone else (this would include the police) on the road. We were the Martian in the grocery store.

Naturally, the Enzo drew a crowd whenever and wherever we stopped. Gassing up the Ferrari proved to be an adventure, the car causing so much commotion in one station that a young lady backed her Toyota into a phone pole in the confusion.

When sold new in the United States, the Enzo was government-certified with the worst fuel mileage in the country at 8 miles per gallon in city traffic and 12 miles per gallon on the highway. In fairness, that's about the same as a Dodge Ram pickup truck . . . but the

Continued on page 248

"We did, and when we had a final presentation, the Ferrari engineers—about 30 people—went against the F1 direction because it was complicated, not Ferrari."

Luca de Montezemolo, president of Ferrari, was at the meeting and asked, "Which do you like?" Everybody went for the Group C car.

But then Montezemolo said, "Okay, but there's no democracy," and endorsed the Enzo.

In the end only three men wanted the Enzo, but they were the most important: Montezemolo, Pininfarina, and Okuyama.

It proved to be a controversial decision and the initial press photos released of the Enzo did it no favors. "I almost broke into tears when I saw them," Okuyama admits. "That's not the car. I had to tell people to wait until the car came out."

How did Okuyama react to the controversy over the Enzo? "We're used to it. That's just the case for car designers."

Okuyama does comment, "The only thing I don't like about the Enzo is that the roof was meant to be black. It has to be black to see the silhouette of a Formula 1 car. And it was black until the last minute, when it was changed to body color."

He also reveals that, "We had two versions of the nose until the last minute, a sports car nose and a Formula 1 nose. We weren't sure if Ferrari was going to win the Formula 1 Constructors Championship that year, and if we'd lost the championship, a Formula 1 nose wouldn't have been right. But we won that year [1999] and chose the Formula 1 nose."

He adds, "I don't think we should take the same approach for all production Ferraris. They should be more elegant and easier for most people to swallow, but in the Enzo's case we really wanted to make a statement for decades."

They certainly did.

Arguably the most important thing in an Enzo's interior is the big red START button.

If you look at the bottom of the Enzo's backside, you can see the venturi that helps air escape from under the car and increase downforce. Follow an Enzo on a dirty road and you can see grit come from under the car as if it's being vacuumed up.

Opposite page: A picture is worth 1,000 words, and an Enzo is worth $652,830—at least it was when new. Expect to pay more than $1 million to buy one today. A $7,700 lump in the original U.S. purchase price went toward the government's "gas guzzler tax."

Continued from page 244

After taking criticism for building too many F40s, Ferrari decided to limit how many of any supercar it will make. In the Enzo's case, that was originally to be 399 units, but then Ferrari popped one more for Pope John Paul II. The Vatican auctioned that car for $1.2 million and gave the funds to charity.

Ferrari is much more fun. Those who bought Enzos new paid $7,700 as a "gas guzzler tax," a pittance compared to the car's $652,830 sticker price, which, by the way, included a three-piece set of fitted leather luggage.

Speeding ticket-free back in California, we were anxious to get the Enzo to the test track and see if its true numbers matched our on-the-road enthusiasm. In the 700-foot slalom, the car slithered through at 73 miles per hour, fastest ever for *R&T* with the steering and, in test driver Patrick Hong's words, "quick and smooth, as though responding telepathically." Around the skid pad, the Ferrari generated 1.01 g.

After a few runs getting the launch control down pat, acceleration tests began.

Off with ASR, put the car in race mode, left foot on the brake, right foot sets the throttle—about 2,100 rpm seems best—then step off the binders. Like Michael Schumacher blasting off a Grand Prix grid, the Enzo does an electronic launch, the driver's main responsibility being to limit wheelspin with the throttle. The needle arcs quickly toward the redline. Don't lift, pull on the upshift paddle and, in 150 milliseconds, you're in second . . . then third . . . then fourth. . . .

Get this right and the Enzo is at 60 miles per hour in 3.3 seconds, at 100 in 6.6 seconds, and through a quarter-mile in 11.1 seconds at 133 miles per hour . . . 0.5 second and 8 miles per hour faster than a McLaren F1. And with an estimated top speed of 218, it's nice to know the Ferrari also set a new *R&T* braking record by stopping from 80 miles per hour in 188 feet.

At this point in the testing, even the most understanding of owners would be suggesting we've got the numbers, how about dinner?

Not Richard Losee. He encouraged Patrick to try more acceleration runs. Who was the tester to offend the owner? The Enzo was kept at it all day and never so much as spit, coughed, or leaked one drop of oil. The next day Losee calmly filled the gas tank and drove back to Provo.

So much for temperamental exotic cars.

Stung by criticism that it built too many F40s and diluted the pleasure (and profitability) of owning the exotic car, Ferrari promised it would build 399 Enzos and no more.

They lied by one, but for a good cause. After the production run in 2002–2004, Ferrari assembled one last Enzo and gave it to Pope John Paul II. Apparently it didn't fit in the Vatican motor pool, and this last car was auctioned for $1.2 million, with the proceeds given to charity.

That price is Bugatti Veyron 16.4 money, but somehow, despite its value, an Enzo isn't as intimidating to drive as the German-engineered car and has a lighter, freer spirit.

It's also more enjoyable in a good-time-was-had-by-all sense. Like the time on our Provo-Newport Beach trip when I was driving the chase car behind the Enzo and we were doing about 70 miles per hour on a dry, straight, level, beautifully paved stretch of pavement way out in the desert. No one in sight. The Enzo's driver planted the gas and, from my perspective, the car quickly shrank from full-size to red nano-particle. I won't tell you who was driving or where it happened, but 185 miles per hour was seen.

Wow. Your mother wouldn't do that . . . would she? ∎

Computers were used to help design the upper and lower A-arm suspension of the Enzo. The coil spring/shock units are not on the suspension, but situated inboard, worked by pushrods and rocker arms. The Enzo brakes are 15.0-inch carbon-ceramics to assure repeated stops from high speed.

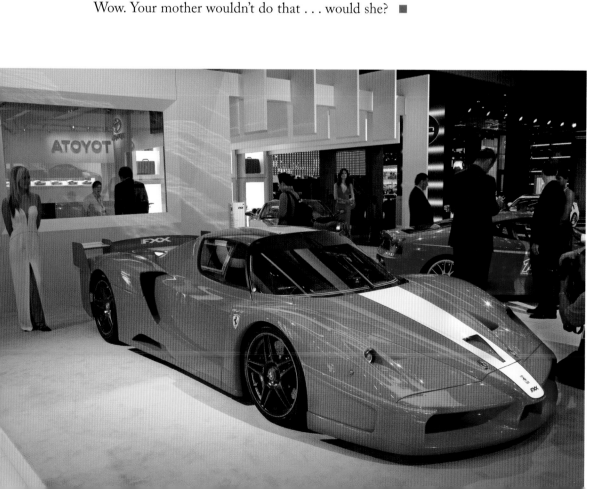

Ferrari evolved the Enzo into the FXX, which began deliveries in early 2006. The V-12 engine is enlarged to 6.2 liters, power punted from 650 to 800 horsepower. It's said that at $1.8 million, the FXX is the most expensive new car ever marketed. You had to be an established, accepted Ferrari owner to buy one of the 29 made.

CHAPTER 23

Ah, the joy and security of driving an all-wheel-drive high-performance car. Having the Gallardo's 520 horsepower spread between all four wheels is comforting, though you can switch off the yaw and traction control and set it a bit sideways if you like.

200
MILES PER HOUR

Talk about fun.

I was at Homestead Miami Raceway, a concrete oval with a road circuit carved inside, on a brilliant warm day with time on my hands. The baby blue Lamborghini Gallardo Spyder I needed to photograph was in use. I had time on my hands and there was a spare gray 192-mile-per-hour (the top-down top speed) Spyder just sitting around, looking lonely.

Couldn't have that.

So I dropped into the Spyder's seat, belted up, and punched the starter button. The exhaust note rattled noisily around me, amplified by the surrounding hard surfaces. Inspiring.

Pulled back on the right-hand paddle of the e-gear (electro-hydraulic) transmission into first. Very quickly I was out of the pits and turning into the left that led to the serpentine road course. Two more lefts led to a fun right-hander that dipped a bit with some camber advantage. Right foot to the floor . . . talk about fun!

Some drivers love their exotic cars to be rear-drive so they can kick the back end around, while some of us prefer the stability of all-wheel-drive machines like the Gallardo. Sure, you can force the small Lambo sideways by turning off the yaw and traction control, tucking the nose in and nailing the power. Some of us prefer the way you can hit the apex a touch later, floor the gas, and feel all four wheels send you on a high-speed mission to the next turn.

Enjoy the ride, because this is a machine that will get you to 60 miles per hour in less than one-thousand-one, one-thousand-two, one-thousand-three, one-thousand-four. Stop counting.

Stay with it and the Lambo will scramble on to just shy of 200 miles per hour.

You slip through the corners with little effort, and then on the front straight the exhaust sounds as wide open as the Spyder's top. The sound raps off the cement around you like Lynyrd Skynyrd's "Freebird" at 100 decibels. Keep talking about fun.

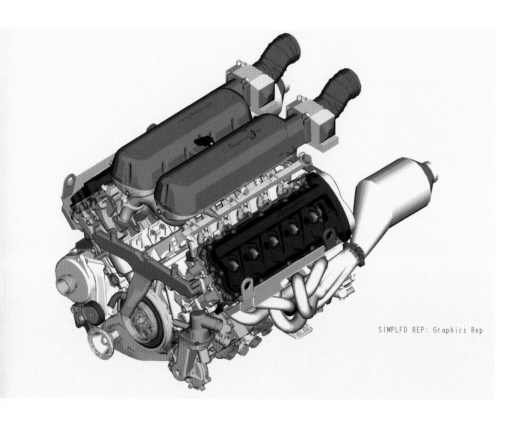

SIMPLFD REP: Graphics Rep

In this Lamborghini-supplied computer rendition of the Gallardo V-10, you can see the 90-degree layout of the cylinder banks. In its SE version, the 5.0-liter engine gives the driver 520 horsepower at 800 rpm, the torque a happy-driving 376 ft-lb at 4,500 rpm, much of that on tap from below 2,000 rpm. *Illustration courtesy Lamborghini*

When Audi bought Lamborghini in 1998, it decided on an initial two-model policy. At the top would be the Murciélago, a major redevelopment of the Diablo with its V-12. Second choice would be the Gallardo, an all-new car that would inherit nothing from previous small-production Lamborghinis or the various stillborn prototypes that were meant to fill that slot. This car's technical heritage would be in Germany.

There's no question that the exterior designs of the Gallardo and Murciélago came from the same studio. Their basic shapes are the same, their front ends differing mainly in headlamp detail. But where the 180.3-inch-long, 80.5-inch-wide Murciélago comes off a bit too big and wide, the Gallardo is a tight, more muscular design at 169.3 inches long and 74.8 inches across.

While having unique, strong, exciting designs with great-looking greenhouses and purposeful cooling vents and slots, the hard-edge Lamborghinis don't look particularly

sexy or, for that matter, Italian. This is an observation, not a complaint, as the square corner designs separate them from the machines made not far down the road and around a few corners in Ferrari's Scaglietti works.

Like Ferrari's F430, the Gallardo comes as a coupe or Spyder, one as exciting and elegant as the other. The Spyder's top is fully automatic—up or down in 20 seconds—and tucks neatly in a well behind the cockpit under a carbon-fiber engine/top cover. A pop-up rollover bar system protects the occupants in case they get upside down. Ouch. Also like the F430, and unlike many past Spyders from most automakers, the Gallardo looks quite good top up.

Lamborghini's parent company, Audi, has been a leader in the use of aluminum in modern cars, so it's logical to expect no less from the Gallardo. Inside it has an aluminum space frame assembled from extrusions and castings. Outside is aluminum bodywork—some thermoplastic—with only the doors done in steel for side impact crash reasons.

Climb in, sit down, belt up, close the door, start the Gallardo. We'd suggest you set the paddle-shift automatic in Sport mode. Nail the throttle, and the gearbox will spit quick shifts with every tug on the paddle. In less than four seconds you're at 60 miles per hour on your way to just shy of 200 miles per hour.

Nice playground, eh? Unlike its big brother, the Murciélago, the Gallardo has conventional doors. The dashboard and center controls are thoughtfully laid out and contain one of the few hints to the fact Audi owns Lamborghini: the climate controls. Equipped with the paddle-shifted "manual" transmission, this Spyder lacks a conventional shift lever.

Performance changes slightly with the Spyder's added 264 pounds, and while the Spyder will hit 196 with the top up, you're limited to 192 when it's folded. Better nail down your toupee.

Unlike its big brother, the Gallardo has conventional doors and entry isn't the least intimidating. The edgy severity of the Gallardo's exterior slides away when you're in the driver's seat, hooded gauges conveniently set ahead and atop the center console. Located there is a raft of controls on the rising surface, including two of the few direct visual ties to Audi: the climate control panel and the sound and navigational system.

To be a player in the $150,000–$200,000 exotic market you need an aluminum chassis. No problem for Lamborghini, as parent Audi has been a pioneer in such work. Under the slick aluminum bodywork, with some thermoplastic pieces like front and rear bumper covers and side sills, is an aluminum space frame made of extrusions and castings. Only the doors are steel, and that is for crash protection.

It's not surprising to find the Gallardo has upper and lower A-arm suspensions front and rear with coil springs and tube shocks. Brembo does the brakes: eight-piston caliper 14.4-inch discs front, four-piston 13.2-inch discs rear. All the anticipated electronics are onboard, like yaw and traction control that can be switched off and ABS that can't. Pirelli does the tires, P Zero Rossos sized at 235/35ZR-19 fore and 295/30ZR-19 aft.

Lamborghini's V-10 for the Gallardo is tricky. In theory, the best vee angle between cylinder banks would be 72 degrees, but engineers decided on 90 degrees, thus lowering the engine's height and center of gravity. To keep the cylinders' firing order sensible, there is a crankshaft with crankpins offset by 18 degrees. As expected, the 5.0-liter engine is all aluminum with twin cams and four valves per cylinder. Also keeping the V-10's profile low is the fact the engine has a dry sump, while behind it is a clutch with two plates so its overall diameter can be smaller.

Through its spinning alloy wheel you can see the Spyder's Brembo brakes, the fronts being vented and having eight-piston calipers. Around the alloy wheel is one of Pirelli's finest, a 235/35ZR-19 P Zero Rosso.

Adding to the aura of the V-10 is variable timing for the intake and exhaust valves and intake trumpets with a changeable length for optimum charge to the cylinders, aiding a wide, strong power band.

The newest version of the V-10 is the SE, which takes the original 500 horsepower to 520 at 8,000 rpm, with torque remaining at 376 ft-lb at 4,500 rpm, though 80 percent of that is waiting for you as of 1,500 rpm. Driven calmly in town, the V-10 has a light rasp to the exhaust, while at speed it literally roars.

Unlike the backward drivetrain in the Murciélago, the Gallardo has the V-10 in the north-south position with its nose to the north, the clutch back south, and the transmission hanging behind it.

Hanging on can be a traditional six-speed manual, or what Lamborghini calls e-gear. This option adds Magneti-Marelli's electro-hydraulic shifting to the gearbox with paddle shifting. As with other such transmissions, there are several modes: normal, sport, and winter. The latter is meant to give you max traction in snow. Normal and sport will upshift you automatically, normal at 7,800 rpm, sport at 8,200, and while normal pops shifts in 0.22 seconds, sport shortens them to 0.17.

It's a slick system, though in the automatic mode it feels a generation behind Ferrari's F430 in speed and smoothness.

Driven against the F430, the character of the company that owns Lamborghini comes through. There is a hard edge and firmness to the Gallardo that is so German that an experienced driver could peg it as such if he or she was blindfolded. Okay, that's not the best way to drive a car, but you get our point.

Not only does the convertible top of the Spyder rise or fall in a mere 20 seconds, but the soft lid comes with a pop-up rollover bar system that automatically deploys should the car get upside down. It is just one element of a safety system that includes airbags and yaw control suspension.

And this is not a bad thing. Ask Mercedes-Benz, which has made oceans of Euros with quite firm AMG models. The Gallardo is, however, rather German compared to the ride and handling characteristics of a Ferrari.

To give the Gallardo all-wheel drive, Lamborghini engineers include a front-mounted viscous coupling that splits power 30 percent front/70 percent rear under normal conditions. This split gives the Gallardo the feel of rear-wheel drive and added stability under most conditions, with the possibility of spinning more power to the front wheels if they need added traction.

Leave terms like svelte and sexy for Ferraris, because powerful and purposeful are two major words to describe the hard-edge design of the Gallardo. Like the Countach, the modern Lamborghinis are a bit more outrageous than their cross-town rivals, often sporting colors like orange and baby blue that you likely won't find on Ferrari's palette.

The city of Miami hovering in the background like a promised city of Oz, the Gallardo goes under wraps for a light seasonal rain shower. In less time than you can verbally spell L-A-M-B-O-R-G-H-I-N-I G-A-L-L-A-R-D-O S-P-Y-D-E-R the power top could be refolded neatly under its hard tonneau cover.

In *Road & Track*, journalist and race winner Paul Frere wrote that on the open road, ". . . the Gallardo remains an agile car and handles beautifully with hardly a trace of understeer."

On a race course, he wrote: "Essentially it handles like a rear-drive car, the cornering line easily adjusted by slightly lifting the accelerator pedal. Accelerate hard out of a bend taken near the limit and the rear end can be made to drive out. But a power slide is almost impossible to achieve because as soon as the rear wheels begin to spin, the viscous coupling intervenes by directing the excess torque to the front wheels. This, in turn, increases the

latter's slip angle with a stabilizing effect, without even invoking the stability control if indeed it has been left switched on."

Feeling firmly planted to the pavement is just one of the Gallardo's ace cards. Add that sub-4-second-to-60 time, a top speed that's a blink under 200, and styling that is at least distinctive and at best enough to steal your heart. And here's a cold, hard fact: Under its German owners, Lamborghini is building the highest-quality cars in its history. ■

CHAPTER 24

Looking low and delightfully nasty, Maserati's mid-engine MC12 marks the return of this historically important marque to the supercar set. The white-with-blue-trim paint scheme of the V-12-powered exotic is taken from the company's roots, being the colors used by "Lucky" Casner's America Camoradi Scuderia race team, which campaigned Maseratis.

205
MILES PER HOUR

Maserati's long white supercar snarls just a bit as it runs up on me, looking as though it might take a bite. The MC12 would love to be unleashed, to leap ahead and disappear, to let that 630 horsepower go and speed on to its 205-mile-per-hour top velocity. Considering it can slam to 60 miles per hour in just 3.7 seconds, that probably wouldn't take long, the driver blipping through its six-speed sequential gearbox.

Right now, however, it's picture time.

Automotive photographers spend a lot of time in the open trunks of cars looking back at exotic machines that are chasing them for a photo. It's called a car-to-car and the scene is spectacular.

Imagine Mario Andretti in his Formula 1–winning Lotus, its nose just inches away at speed. Phil Hill in a snarling Ferrari Testarossa 2 feet back. Brian Redman chasing your tailpipe in the 1970 Le Mans–winning Porsche 917.

Or Maserati's MC12 as we circulate around Ferrari's Fiorano test track. Okay, we aren't at its top speed, but that doesn't take away from the image as the supercar chomps at our heels.

It's encouraging to see Maser's famous trident symbol on the nose of a lightweight mid-engine machine meant to drub the likes of Saleen and Aston Martin on the world's race circuit.

It has the pedigree on two fronts. In racing, Maserati was a major Grand Prix threat until the late 1950s and a thorn in Ferrari's racing side until the early 1960s. The MC12's paint scheme—white with blue trim—echoes the U.S. racing colors used by "Lucky" Casner's America Camoradi Scuderia team.

Under its carbon-fiber bodywork is another pedigree: its basic tub inherited from corporate cousin Ferrari, the one used in the Enzo. Ditto with the 6.0-liter 65-degree V-12 and the paddle-shifted six-speed gearbox.

This is not, however, an Enzo clone.

For one thing, it's bigger. The MC12's wheelbase is longer and its overall length, width, and height of 202.5, 82.5, and 47.2 inches make it, respectively, 17.4, 2.4, and 2.2 inches larger than the taut Enzo.

Compared to the Enzo, the MC12 is 17.4 inches longer, 2.4 inches wider, and 2.2 inches taller than the Ferrari supercar. While they used the same type of 48-valve V-12, the Maserati's is tuned to 630 horsepower at 7,500 rpm and 481 ft-lb of torque at 5,500.

Maserati was a major force in racing, being a two-time Indianapolis 500 winner before World War II. In the 1950s and early 1960s, Maseratis often challenged Ferraris on the racetrack. One of its most famous sports racers was the "Birdcage" of the type seen here, its nickname inherited because its frame was constructed of many tiny tubes.

American Frank Stephenson guided the Giorgetto Giugiaro design of the MC12 though the wind tunnel and final development process, striving for beauty and downforce. It's a striking shape: the low, wide nose; the beautiful grilles over the outlets on the hood; louvers along the fender tops and the engine cover; the sweeping sculptural raised rear wing; plenty of front and rear overhang; and a long, unmistakable presence. Plus a few more pounds than the Enzo, which weighs in at 2,766 pounds versus the MC12's 2,943.

Beautiful and, unlike the Enzo, done as a removable-top Spyder.

Where the Enzo has the strong taste of carbon fiber and racing inside, the MC12 is more completely finished like a road car, though just as functional as the Ferrari. Here, carbon fiber is used more as visual trim, playing second fiddle to leather, a dash cover called BrighTex, and aluminum. Another major difference: the start button is blue.

Behind the cockpit is the V-12, which comes in at 630 horsepower at 7,500 rpm and 481 ft-lb of torque at 5,500, so it's slightly detuned from the Enzo's 650 at 7,800 and 485 ft-lb at 5,500. Other than that, the V-12 is as seen in the Ferrari, with twin cams working four vales per cylinder, plus dry-sump lubrication.

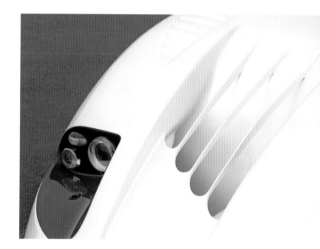

A U.S. tie to the visual design of the MC12 is Frank Stephenson, the man responsible for the exterior of the new Mini. Stephenson was design director at Maserati when the MC12 was shaped by another well-known creator of great automobiles, Giorgetto Giugiaro.

Maserati's MC12 is based on the same basic carbon fiber monocoque tub as the Enzo of corporation cousin Ferrari. While it is not a clone of the Enzo, the MC12 also has the same upper and lower A-arm suspensions with inboard springs and shocks operated by pushrods.

It's an Enzo ditto again with the upper and lower A-arm suspension and pushrod-actuated inboard springs and dampers. The Brembo disc brakes measure 15 inches in front and 13.2 inches in rear, with ABS and electronic brake force distribution.

Kim Wolfkill, an accomplished race driver who is *Road & Track*'s motorsports editor, had a chance to track test an MC12 and wrote, "An effortless handler at normal velocities, the MC12 comes alive as the pace climbs and cornering loads increase. Like any good race car, the big Maserati offers more feedback the harder the chassis is pushed, responding

Where the Enzo's interior is carbon fiber race car efficient, the MC12's is finished more like a road car. Leather and aluminum are the main themes, with carbon fiber a lesser element. While many supercars have a red START button, the Maserati's is blue. Unlike the coupe-only Enzo, the Maserati has a removable hardtop for semi-open-air driving.

with increased levels of grip control and steering feel. Any previous hint of corner-entry understeer disappears with increased chassis loads. Mid-turn behavior is always rock-solid and wagging the tail in anything but first- and second-gear turns requires a deliberate effort to back the car off the road. Once into triple digits, the downforce contributes further to the car's grip, adding an unusual element of faith to negotiating fast sweepers."

Maserati had to build 25 MC12s to meet racing regulations, but did 50 over the course of two years, all presold. Not to the United States, though a few were imported.

Although racing was the MC12's purpose, something got bollixed up and the car ended up too long and wide to meet the rules under which the 24 Hours of Le Mans are run. Maserati shortened the car's length so it could run in the American Le Mans series, but it couldn't make it narrower, so it had to run for no points. However, in the FIA's very competitive European GT series, the Vitaphone team won the 2005 GT1 Championship with MC12s.

It certainly looks like a winner seen down low in my photo session, though also like a caged animal at this speed. With my Canon's memory card full, I waved the test driver by as we entered the straightaway at Fiorano. He grinned, downshift one gear, and simply disappeared.

Zowie-e-e-e. ■

Built to be raced, the MC12 won the FIA's 2005 European GT series. Unfortunately it fell afoul of the regulations for the 24 Hours of Le Mans and couldn't race there. Modified to compete in the U.S. American Le Mans series, it couldn't run for points, but competed strongly against other GTs at tracks like Florida's Sebring (seen here).

CHAPTER 25

Road & Track hustled a Carrera GT to 60 miles per hour in 3.6 seconds. Tester Patrick Hong wrote, "Exiting the corner is when the driver has to be patient to unleash all of the V-10's might. Too eager on the throttle and the rear will step out."

205
MILES PER HOUR

PORSCHE CARREA GT 2004

Like a jet fighter just before takeoff, a Porsche on the Mulsanne Straight at Le Mans is an awesome sight. Especially at night when you are only 20 feet away, you can feel the car fly by. Could be a 917, a whistling Turbo, a 956, a 962, or a GT1, but the speed could be near or above 200 miles per hour . . . about as fast as your heart is beating after seeing it.

Porsche and the 24 Hours of Le Mans have been a dynamic duo for decades, so it's appropriate that the German automaker's supercar, the Carrera GT, has it roots there. Almost raced there. But our story begins in another French city: Paris.

Porsche figures its automobiles have won some 23,000 races since 1949, ranging from minor club events around the world to the most important competitions on the planet. After winning the 1998 24 Hours of Le Mans with a GT1 like the car seen here, Porsche considered building a new roadster race car, the design that became the Carrera GT.

Just about the last thing you want during the Paris Auto Show is a 6 A.M. unveiling (ugh!), but Porsche promised it would be worth the early wakeup call. This was in autumn 2000, and it was dark and rainy when we trudged to the glowing pyramid of the Louvre, much too early . . . but it proved well worth it.

There, in the home of great art, Porsche presented its own masterpiece: the Carrera GT. Masterpiece—is that a bit melodramatic?

Not really. Many automotive journalists and enthusiasts were still ticked off that Porsche had announced it would be building the Cayenne sport utility vehicle (SUV), and we needed an indication that the famous automaker from Zuffenhausen hadn't left its moral compass untended. The Carrera GT was proof Porsche hadn't lost its way.

Porsche figures that automobiles with its name have won some 23,000 races since 1949, so it came as no surprise to learn that the Carrera GT was originally meant to be a competition machine.

It was 1998 and the German automaker had just won the 24 Hours of Le Mans with the ground-hugging GT1. Since Dickie Attwood and Hans Hermann won the French classic with a 917 in 1970, race cars with the name Porsche have won 16 times. In the afterglow of that victory, the thought was to create a roadster successor that would continue the Porsche run. Corporate priorities would derail that plan, but instead of the concept ending up abandoned on a siding, it was rerouted to the production department.

Run down the specifications of the Carrera GT and it is easy to see that it was conceived as a race car.

Begin with low weight. It isn't unusual to find an exotic car with lightweight carbon fiber used anywhere from bodywork to some monocoque components. Porsche, on the other hand, uses carbon-fiber-reinforced-plastic (CFP) for the entire monocoque structure tub of the Carrera GT. Think of that tub as every bit of structure that surrounds you when you sit in the car: behind you, to your sides along the door sill, the entire area in front of you, and even the windshield surround above you.

Porsche surprised the public at the Paris Auto Show when it presented the Carrera GT. To critics who wondered if Porsche had lost its way with the Cayenne SUV, the supercar demonstrated it had not, proving to be not only beautiful and powerful, but a technical tour de force. Here it is at its production launch at the 2003 Geneva show.

Porsche's Carrera GT supercar was originally intended to be a race car, but when corporate priorities changed, the design was turned into one of the hottest supercars on the street. A testimony to lightweight design, the Porsche has a top speed of 205 miles per hour.

Weighing just 452 pounds, the Carrera GT's 5.7-liter V-10 has an odd spacing of 68 degrees between its cylinder banks. A very free-revving engine, the V-10 is rated at 605 horsepower at 8,000 rpm and 435 ft-lb of torque at 5,750 rpm. *Photo by Marc Urbano,* Road & Track

This is the basis for the Carrera GT: an impressive piece and extremely strong, the tub weighs only 220 pounds and is the first use of a single CFP chassis structure in a road car. Needless to say it is also a very expensive single piece, so if you are going to crash your GT, *don't break the tub!* The repair bill will match at least half the cost of your $440,000 Porsche.

Porsche doesn't stop there. Bolted to the vertical rear wall of the tub is another CFP structure Porsche calls the engine carrier. So the GT is basically a very strong, impressively stiff carbon fiber chassis from nose to tail. The CFP doesn't rust, isn't affected by other environmental stresses, and looks impressive, which is why Porsche lets the carbon fiber surface show through in several places in the car, like on the dashboard. Also made of carbon fiber are the doors front and rear deck lids, the doorsills, and the rear side panels, and if you look very closely at them you can see just a hint of the cloth's pattern. Ditto with the removable roof panels that weigh only 5.3 pounds. Adds to the image.

Almost taking away from the image, when you close the lightweight doors, you don't get the solid "thunk" you'd expect, but what's best described as a lighter-weight sound.

Light weight was also the point of the design of the Carrera GT's engine, but so too were power and an impressively low profile.

Tipping the scales at only 452 pounds, the V-10 is made of aluminum, with its coolant and oil passages integrated into the block. Keeping weight down means more than creating an engine that isn't heavy, it also means an engine with lower reciprocating mass inside the V-10 so it will rev freely—hence the three-ring aluminum pistons, the titanium connecting rods attached to the forged crankshaft, and a redline of 8,400 rpm.

Where a Porsche Turbo clutch weighs 15.4 pounds and has a diameter of 15.0 inches, the GT's ceramic composite clutch tips the scales at 7.7 pounds and measures 6.6 inches across. The small, lightweight design allows the engine to be mounted lower in the chassis and to rev more freely.

The longitudinally mounted V-10 has an unusual 68-degree vee angle separating its cylinder banks. There are four valves per cylinder, with the intake camshaft chain driven plus VarioCam, which is Porsche's own system of variable valve opening.

An aluminum intake manifold feeds each of the engine's banks, and just as the free-revving 5.7-liter V-10 hits 8,000 rpm it is producing 605 horsepower or 105.5 per liter. Torque tops out at 435 ft-lb at 5,750 rpm, though it already hits a nice plateau of power around 4,500 rpm as it continues to climb.

For a competition or high-performance car, it's important to get the drivetrain as low as possible to keep the center of gravity down. The first step in this process is traditional—designing the V-10 with a dry-sump oil system. So instead of the usual reservoir of oil

sloshing around in the crankcase below the engine, it is pumped to the engine for lubrication, then collected at the bottom of the V-10. Nine pumps then move the lubricant to an external reservoir, which in the Carrera GT's case is in the gearbox housing. Using the dry-sump design also means the engine is more efficiently lubricated under extreme driving conditions, such as high side load corners.

That is only one design feature of the Carrera drivetrain that keeps the height and weight low. Even with a dry-sump engine, a driveline's height is often kept higher than desirable by the flywheel and clutch diameter. Add still another Porsche patent for the Carrera GT, this one being the Ceramic Composite Clutch. Engineers managed to slim the flywheel and clutch dramatically. As an example, the 911 Turbo's clutch weighs 15.4 pounds and measures 15 inches in diameter, yet the Carrera GT's clutch weighs just 7.7 pounds and measures 6.6 inches. With clutch plates made of a ceramic composite said to be extremely durable, this design not only drops the engine to just 3.9 inches above the floor of the car, but the flywheel-clutch package's lower rotational mass allows the V-10 driveline to rev that much more freely.

Porsche opts for a traditional six-speed manual; it is quite compact and is located it transversely behind the engine. Its casing also houses the limited-slip differential and the V-10's starter motor.

Going back to its Le Mans roots for the Carrera GT's suspension, specifically to the 911 GT1, the GT has upper and lower aluminum A-arm suspension front and back; the shock absorber and spring units are actuated away from the A-arms via rockers and pushrods. This design not only aids in setting up the suspension, but also gets the weight of the shocks and springs away from the wheels. Steering is through an assisted rack and pinion mounted to the front bulkhead.

Porsche's ceramic composite disc brakes, which are only half the weight of conventional metal brakes, also aid in minimizing unsprung weight at the wheels. These are less susceptible to environmental effects and are said to be quite durable. With a diameter of 14.96 inches, the discs are cross-drilled and vented to get the heat and moisture out, and are stopped by six-piston calipers.

ABS and traction control are part of the design, and the latter can be disabled if you dare. Michelin supplies the GT's tires, Pilot Sport 2 265/35ZR-19s at the front, 335/30ZR-20s at the back, mounted on wheels not made of the expected aluminum alloy but of magnesium, again to keep weight down.

You can't see much of this because it is hidden under the wonderfully aggressive bodywork designed by American Grant Larson, who also drew the original Boxster. It's hard to say which angle is the most exciting from which to view the car. Some would argue the front end, with its typically large Porsche inlets and Bi-xenon head-lamps, their shape said to be inspired by the 917.

Then there's the side view with the huge front vents that duct air from the front radiators and brakes, leading it back to the nicely sculpted intakes for engine air. This side view is where you see the GT's different proportions, the best example being the fact that it is 3.5 inches shorter than a Ferrari Enzo, but rides on a wheelbase that is 3.2 inches longer. Only 0.7 inch lower than the Enzo, the GT's body is 4.5 inches narrower, though their tracks are only about 3 inches different.

Arguably the best view would require you to climb a 6-foot ladder located just off a rear corner of the car and look down on the GT, with its mesh intake manifold covers that run forward to just short of the steel-reinforced rollover protection hoops. There's the rear spoiler with the center section that rises at speed, huge taillights, and check out the huge exhaust outlets on either side of the license plate.

Naturally, the shape's aerodynamics was verified in a wind tunnel, where the airflow under the body was also refined to add downforce.

When you get into a Carrera GT, there's no mistaking it for a Porsche. The starter key is on the left, a remainder of racing tradition. There are five dials straight ahead, stylized but classic Porsche nonetheless. You are sitting in seats based on lightweight carbon fiber and Kevlar shells, finished in leather and offered in two different butt widths.

Continued on page 279

Porsche cut unsprung weight at the wheels with ceramic composite disc brakes of its own design, which weigh half as much as conventional discs. Drilled and vented, the discs are stopped by six-piston calipers.

JAY LENO ON THE *PORSHCE CARRERA GT*

I love it. I like the fact it's a modern car that pays homage to people who like to shift." And then his love of technical qualities comes out when Jay Leno adds, "I bought it primarily because of the clutch.

"The Countach and McLaren F1 are wonderful cars, but if you drive them the way you are suppose to, you burn the clutch up. In the McLaren the clutch is gone at 2500–3000 miles. With the Countach you pull up to the light and there's the kid with the hot-rodded VW Jetta or whatever. He's going to blow your doors off if you don't want to use the Countach clutch too hard. You can do maybe three or four burnouts and you're screwed.

"With the Porsche you've got that little 6-inch ceramic clutch, it takes a tremendous amount of force and you can do burnouts all day long.

"When we were at Talladega [the high-speed NASCAR track where he was involved in high-speed record runs], we dropped the Carrera GT clutch at least 50 times just trying to launch it. It didn't complain, didn't bitch and moan, didn't smell. It was pretty amazing, so I like the fact a lot of effort was put into something you don't necessarily see.

"When I watch these shooter tune-up shows it's always Porsches and Corvettes because they're the strongest. People work on them themselves, they beat the hell out of 'em. I never see a Lamborghini or Ferrari at one of these tuner things because the cars can't take the abuse the Germans and the Corvettes can. So that's what I like about the Carrera, you can really drive it hard."

The Carrera GT does have its downside, so to speak: "It's really low. You can't pull into any sort of driveway. I have the factory lift kit in it, but can't take the Porsche home because it won't fit in the driveway. If you're getting gas you're going, 'I know I'm out of gas, but I can't go to that station because there's a lip on the driveway.'"

Not that it's the sort of problem you should have every day: "I met a guy who was complaining about his Carrera GT. He used it every day in San Francisco traffic. Well, you don't drink champagne every day unless you go crazy. These are weekend things..."

Opposite page: Porsche builds two vehicles in its new Leipzig factory, the Cayenne SUV and the Carrera GT. This is not a manufacturing facility for the sports car, but an assembly line. Components like the tub, engine, suspension, and such are built off-site and brought together to create finished cars in Leipzig.

Seeing the Porsche V-10 just off the assembly line is a good way to appreciate its compact size. The transverse six-speed manual transmission is tucked low behind the engine in a housing that also has the starter motor and limited-slip differential.

About halfway down the assembly line, you can see the bones of a Carrera GT. At its center is a monocoque structure made of carbon fiber-reinforced plastic, a cell that surrounds the driver and passenger. Weighing only 220 pounds, it has the engine carrier mounted behind it and front suspension and crash structure ahead.

Porsche divides the Carrera GT cockpit with a center console that locates the shift knob conveniently to the right of the steering wheel. The seats are molded in carbon fiber, and then richly upholstered in leather. *Photo by Marc Urbano,* Road & Track

At the front suspension, each coil spring/shock absorber unit is mounted on the monocoque, away from the wheel, operating through a rocker arm and pushrods. This design not only makes it easier to set up the suspension, but also keeps weight away from the wheels. *Drawing courtesy Porsche North America*

This cutaway shows the technical details of the Carrera GT. The 605-horsepower V-10 is mounted behind the cockpit. *Drawing courtesy Porsche North America*

Continued from page 273

A rising center console nicely divides the cockpit in this driver-oriented layout and while the wood inlay knob shifter looks as though it's situated a bit high, its location turns out to be about perfect for driving, being just to the right of the steering wheel. All this is beautifully finished with leather, metal, carbon fiber, or paint surfaces.

You can order your Carrera fairly stripped or add from a list of no-cost options, like air conditioning or a navigation and Bose sound system. In any event, you get such genteel equipment as power windows, remote central locking, and a set of luggage made to fit the car's storage areas and done in the same leather as the interior. Would you expect anything less?

Despite those amenities, Porsche's weight-saving work keeps the Carrera GT's weight to just 3,042 pounds. The light weight, combined with V-10 power, enabled *Road & Track* to get a Carrera GT to 60 miles per hour in 3.6 seconds, which is what you expect from an exotic in this class. Top speed is 205 miles per hour. On the skid pad, the Porsche managed just 0.1 shy of the magic 1-g level, which is impressive. Test driver Patrick Hong said, "Exiting the corner is when the driver has to be patient to unleash all of the V-10's might. Too eager on the throttle and the rear will step out. Even then, the onset of oversteer is so progressive that it will never catch you by surprise."

Porsche will tell you that without the profitable Cayenne SUV, developing models like the Carrera GT wouldn't fit in the profit plan. Appreciate the Cayenne or not, it's somewhat ironic that not only is the pair of Porsches the only products of a new factory in Leipzig (part of the former East Germany), but also the the 521-horsepower Cayenne Turbo S is Porsche's second-most-powerful vehicle after the Carrera GT.

The Leipzig factory has a sole, snail-slow Carrera GT line next to the Cayenne's, which you can actually see move.

Not so through the eight stations in which the GTs are slowly assembled. And "assembled" is the key word, as nothing for the car is actually manufactured here; it's put together from parts built elsewhere and shipped in. The assembly line is a great way to see the building blocks of the GT, beginning with the carbon fiber main section that has the tubing of the forward crash system jutting out front.

Along the stations, you see the engine with its carbon fiber carrier added, as well as the suspension systems, the carbon ceramic brakes, the interior, and, finally, the exterior body panels. After being finished, each Carrera GT is test driven on a 1.1-mile circuit that is part of the 2.3-mile, FIA-approved, Formula 1–quality racetrack Porsche built next to the Leipzig factory.

Watching a Carrera GT whip though a replica of Laguna Seca's Corkscrew turn and approach the slow right-hander that leads onto the back straightaway, it's impossible to not wonder what the mid-engine Porsche would look like, numbers on its sides, wide-open exhausts howling away in pure competition form.

After all, that's what it was meant to be in the first place. ∎

No argument, this is the coolest view of the Carrera GT, showing off the hoops at the back of the cockpit, the flowing covers over the air intakes, the mesh over the engine, the built-in spoiler, those taillights, the dual exhausts that look ready to spit power, the muscles in the rear fender shapes . . .

CHAPTER 26

Mercedes' long-nose, short-cockpit, flip-up door SLR is enchanting enough on the outside to distract from all the technology hidden inside. At the nose is a carbon fiber unit that acts as a crash barrier. Back of it is an aluminum structure for the drivetrain. That is bolted to the main body structure, which is really a carbon fiber cell. The body, doors, and hood are also made of carbon fiber.

MERCEDES-BENZ SLR 2004

207
MILES PER HOUR

With a nose that long, Mercedes-Benz's SLR must be packing big stuff—and it is. How about 617 supercharged horsepower at 6,500 rpm and—now get this—575 ft-lb of torque between 3,250 and 5,000 rpm? There's little doubt about those numbers when you flip the little cover atop the shift lever and depress the start button. The blown V-8 is not too loud and not too quiet; it's just right because it's a little bit rumbly.

Because you sit a bit low in the cockpit, you're very aware of the car's size—mostly that nose—but the SLR feels smaller as you drive it. You keep pushing it faster into corners—nice turn-in, a little understeer, great stability—until you dip into the electronic stability program (ESP) control system. Great fun.

There are three choices in the five-speed transmission: comfort and sport automatic modes and manual, which is shifted off the gearshift or steering wheel and has its own three modes: sport, SuperSport, and race. That should be choices, right?

Take sport, drop it into drive and pause for a second to listen to that little rumble again. Then *go*, the rear's chirping a bit, traction control intervening (an amber light winking), and in 3.8 seconds the speedo needle has said goodbye to 60 miles per hour and continues arcing right.

Without any drama, you're past 120 miles per hour and notice that sound again, now a powerful brew of V-8 and supercharger whine. Somewhere out there is 207 miles per hour, though not on the road in South Africa where I was taken to drive the SLR.

But the roads did twist and turn, so the fun didn't slacken.

You punch the start button in the Mercedes-Benz SLR and opt for the Sport mode in the transmission. Slam home the throttle, there's a light chirp from the rear wheels, and in 3.8 seconds the speedo needle has winged past 60. Given enough space and courage, there's a top speed of 207 miles per hour waiting out there for you.

As the supercar era progressed, Mercedes couldn't resist. We got our first peek at Mercedes' interpretation of the genre in 1999 when Mercedes unveiled its Vision SLR concept vehicle. Turns out it looked like the production SLR launched at the 2003 Frankfurt Motor Show, a few inches smaller in all directions and somewhat lighter on horsepower at "only" 410.

In 1999, Mercedes announced it had signed an agreement in which McLaren Cars would develop and build the SLR. The Formula 1 team, which races with Mercedes engines, finished its advanced McLaren Technical Centre in May 2004 and, shortly thereafter, began hand building SLRs.

Mercedes is responsible for the styling, which hints at both the McLaren-Mercedes F1 cars and a very special car from Mercedes' past. Called the Uhlenhaut coupe, this historical

Granddaddy of the modern SLR sports car is this gullwing version of Mercedes' long-loved SLR sports racing machine. A win in the 1955 Mille Miglia in an open SLR by driver Stirling Moss is one of the great epic races in history. Mercedes built this one-off for its legendary race engineer, Rudi Uhlenhaut.

One of the more sumptuous-yet-efficient interiors in the supercar ranks. The center console continues the rearward line off the SLR's nose, which itself is meant to mimic that of a Formula 1 car. The seats are based on carbon fiber shells, and you see a bit of that material in the interior, though the main theme is an elegant one of leather and aluminum.

This is it, the mother and father of engine compartments! In there resides a 5.4-liter V-8 that was hand-built at AMG by one man. He chose the block, added the single-cam, four-valves-per-cylinder head, and bolted on the Lysholm-type supercharger that huffs up to 13 psi past one intercooler per bank. He created the 617 horsepower and 575 ft-lb of torque. Good for him.

It is argued that the proportions of the Mercedes-Benz SLR make it controversial and sensational. That long nose allows the automaker to fit the complete engine, including the entire exhaust system, ahead of the firewall. That exhaust empties behind the front wheels, and the gills along the front fender sides were needed to cool the system.

JAY LENO ON THE *MERCEDES-BENZ SLR*

If there's any problem with the SLR," Jay Leno contends, "It's that the SLR is too much Mercedes and not enough McLaren.

"It's 3,800 pounds. My ass is big, but not so big it needs an electric seat to move it two inches one way or the other. I'm the only one who drives it so I can set the seat—pull up the lever, slide back on the rails—and that's where it will stay for the rest of its natural life. So I don't know why the SLR has all that. Every time I take one of my cars out I always check tire pressure, so I don't need the in-dash tire monitor.

"I was reading that around the Nürburgring the SLR is, I believe, just a half second slower than the Porsche Carrera GT, and I realized you have to be pretty good to push the SLR around. To me the Carrera GT is a much easier car to drive fast. I feel more attuned to it, maybe because it's stick shift and all that.

"The Mercedes engine seems to be fairly bulletproof. It's got tremendous torque, but I just don't happen to care for paddle shifters. I know you can shift the transmission yourself, but it's like playing chess with Hal the computer. Okay, you can set the computer to let you win, but in the end you're not going to beat it, and there's less involvement.

"That being said, the nice thing about the SLR is that like any Mercedes you can drive it anywhere. It has normal road clearance and it never scrapes. It has a trunk and the build quality is unbelievable. The stitching is excellent and I'd almost venture to guess every screw head is facing the same direction. That part of it is fantastic."

machine is a hardtop gullwing version of the legendary SLR race car, a one-off built in 1955 for Mercedes' equally legendary race engineer, Rudolph "Rudi" Uhlenhaut.

The modern design result is a bit controversial. Long-hood, short-deck proportions are a good thing, but the SLR exaggerates that theme. From some angles it looks so F1, so Mercedes, so powerful. From other angles it looks like it has a big nose.

Inside, beneath the forward-hinged gullwing doors, is a most delicious interior: carbon fiber shell seats with just enough leather-covered upholstery; a strong thick-rim steering wheel through which you view the prominent blue-rimmed speedometer and tach; and an elegant, silver-trimmed center stack with simple controls that get the job done.

Just as it hooked up with McLaren to win in Formula 1, Mercedes-Benz joined with the English firm to make the SLR. Designers of the SLR emphasized this Grand Prix relationship in the nose of the supercar, with the power bulge that runs from the pointed star rearward along the hood.

What you see is mainly leather and aluminum, with just a bit of carbon fiber, just enough to remind you what's underneath. That is the carbon fiber body shell that makes up everything aft of the cowl. This is a complex structure that caused Mercedes and McLaren to develop new carbon fiber construction techniques to make it practical. Ahead of this shell is a cast-aluminum structure to hold the drivetrain, while in front of that is another carbon fiber unit, this one for crash protection. The body, flip-up doors, and hood are also done in carbon fiber, and Mercedes figures this use of the lightweight material puts the SLR, at 3,890 pounds, about 30 percent down on an equivalent steel automobile.

Suspensions are upper and lower A-arms with coil springs and tube shocks, while Mercedes' electro-hydraulic brake system is very high tech with fiber-reinforced ceramic discs plus ABS and brake assist. Don't forget the high-performance driver's guardian angel, ESP that electronically controls the throttle, traction control, and brakes to stabilize an overly ambitious drive.

Then there's the engine and that sound again, a sort of comforting rumble of power. Built in AMG's factory outside of Stuttgart, Germany, each SLR V-8 is hand made and marked with the name of the man who assembled it. The 90-degree, 5.4-liter aluminum V-8 has a single camshaft per head opening four valves for each cylinder, but what gets your attention is bolted between those cylinder banks.

A Lysholm-type supercharger spun to as much as 23,000 rpm, driving the charge past one water-cooled intercooler for each side of the engine at up to 13 psi, that's where it gets that 617 horsepower and 575 ft-lb of torque.

Mercedes packages the engine and its exhaust systems ahead of the passenger compartment so that exhaust doesn't hang down and interrupt airflow under the car. By twisting and turning the system, it packs the catalytic converters and mufflers in the front fenders. It wasn't an easy design, and it explains those huge heat-relieving gills and the top vents on the fenders, as well as why the side-firing exhaust outlets cause an unusual sound when you drive with the side windows down.

This packaging allows Mercedes to concentrate on the SLR's aero shape. Now the underneath can be flat and sealed, save for a few cooling vents leading back to a six-channel diffuser at the tail. Upper surfaces with the F1-style front end get the same attention to keep air flowing smoothly above or below the car. The only moving spoiler is at the tip of the tail. You can set it at a 30-degree angle by pushing a button; it pops up to 10 degrees on its own when the SLR is driven fast. If

you hit the brakes quickly, the spoiler will angle up to 65 degrees, the higher drag helping to stabilize braking.

Mercedes said that McLaren would build 500 SLRs per year for seven years and, in February 2006, announced it had finished the 1,000th car. Going price? Some $450,000 delivered. At the SLR's launch there were hints we'd see changes in the car, more than just the original black and sliver paint jobs. More power?

For those who can't wait, some of the better German tuner companies will do it now. Like Brabus, with its $800,000 version that jacks horsepower up to 660 with an open exhaust.

Whoa, that engine will rumble. ■

Mercedes uncovered the production SLR at the 2003 Frankfurt Auto Show, but we'd already seen most of the car in 1999. Back then, the automaker had showed the Vision SLR, which already had the oh-so-long hood and the flip-up doors leading to a compact cockpit. Seen here with the Vision SLR is its namesake, a 1955 Mercedes SLR race car.

CHAPTER 27

Ford was looking for a symbol it could use to celebrate its 100th anniversary in 2003 and figured a modern interpretation of the Ford GT would do the trick. Just a concept car at the Detroit Show in January 2002, the GT was engineered and a trio of cars was ready at the anniversary ceremony in June 2003.

190
MILES PER HOUR

FORD GT 2005

To understand the excitement generated by Ford's GT, it's crucial to understand how important Ford's original GT40 was to U.S. pride. American automobiles couldn't make it big on the international racing scene after World War II. Briggs Cunningham came very close to winning the 24 Hours of Le Mans in the early 1950s, but Americans just couldn't seem to get a major victory outside the United States.

American drivers had succeeded big time in Europe—Phil Hill, Dan Gurney, Richie Ginther, Carroll Shelby, Masten Gregory, and others—but not American cars.

J Mays, who runs Ford's design efforts, explains that attempts to create a modern interpretation of the GT40 just didn't work, and they reverted to the original shape. Designer Doug Gaffka further explains, "The bottom line is, if you're doing a Ford GT, it had better look like a Ford GT."

Ford adapted the supercharged 4.6-liter aluminum V-8 from the SVT Mustang Cobra for the GT. Displacement was upped to 5.4 liters for the 32-valve engine, which has a water-to-air intercooler and two fuel injectors per cylinder. Horsepower and torque both measure 500, about the same power as the 7.0-liter race V-8s from the 1960s.

After the first few years of Ford's GT40 program at Le Mans, things didn't look much better. Losing again in 1965, Henry Ford II basically told the men in charge of that racing program (including Carroll Shelby) that if they didn't win in 1966 they would be looking for new jobs.

There was no budget limit, and Ford went on to finish 1-2-3 with the GT40 Mk II in 1966, winning once more with the Mk IV in 1967, a truly all-American victory with Dan Gurney and A. J. Foyt driving. When the FIA cut back engine sizes for 1968, effectively turning the Mk IVs into museum pieces, wily John Wyer resurrected the small-block GT40s and one of his machines—chassis 1075—won in both 1968 and 1969.

Some have argued that the GT40s were an Anglo-American effort; they were correct up to a point, but the program was covered with Detroit money and the Mk IV was all-American.

So when Ford unveiled a GT40 concept car at the January 2002 Detroit Show, Americans felt great pride in the famous old design's resurrection.

The following month, Ford held a "skunk works" meeting at Steven Saleen's factory in Irvine, California, where Saleen converts standard Mustangs into high-performance road

Ford's goal for the GT was to beat Ferrari's 360 Modena, which was a worthy target . . . and a historical one, as Ford and Ferrari were great race rivals. It can outrun the 360 to 60, and both have top speeds around 190 miles per hour.

cars. Engineers had to determine the feasibility of producing the GT. Could it be done economically? Did it make any sense?

After the California meeting determined that the mid-engine sports car could be built, Ford executives gave it the green light, but with the condition that three GTs must be ready for the celebration of Ford's 100th anniversary in June 2003. It was, to say the least, a crash program made possible because so much of the work—from exterior shape to chassis design to crash simulations—could be done with computers.

Although Steve Saleen created his own mid-engine exotic car (the California-built S7), and his company assembles the Ford GTs in a factory near Detroit, the two supercars share few roots.

One exception: Neil Hannemann, chief engineer of the S7, was deputized to Ford to be chief program engineer of the GT. He so impressed everyone that his next job was executive director of engineering for McLaren Cars in England.

The new Ford GT also had little in common with the original GT40, though they both are powered by Ford V-8s mounted behind the cockpit and have their obvious exterior design similarities.

Henry Ford II was determined to beat Ferrari at the racing game. This obsession resulted in the Ford GT40. After a disastrous first few years, they succeeded in beating the Italian automaker, winning the 24 Hours of Le Mans from 1966 through 1969.

Ford also got historical inside the GT, bringing back the original GT40's grommet vent cooling holes in the seats and the basic shape of the dashboard. These days the seats have carbon fiber shells, and there are modern climate control switches on the center console.

JAY LENO ON THE *FORD GT*

That's an emotional thing for me because when I was a kid we were a Ford family. When I got my dad to buy the 7 liter . . . . We had Falcons and my dad had a '64 Galaxy, so we went in to buy the '66 and I said, 'Dad, can I pick the engine?' My mother was saying, 'Oh, let the boy pick the engine. What difference does it make what engine is in the car?'

"So I met with the salesman, Tom Lawrence, and I pulled him aside and said, 'We want to get the Galaxy with the 7-liter option, the C6 automatic, and the glass-pack mufflers.' So we wait about four weeks and the car comes in and my father and I go to pick it up. He starts it and it goes: 'Hunga, hunga.' My father says, 'The muffler, there's a hole in the goddamn muffler. This is a brand new car and there's a hole in the muffler.' The salesman says, 'Mr. Leno, you didn't order mufflers. You wanted the glass packs.'

"And then, when we leave, my dad pulls out of the dealership, steps on the gas, the car fishtails with all that power. My dad says, 'Jesus Christ, what did I buy?'

"I remember a year later I found, in a drawer in a bedroom closet, a ticket he got for going 110 on a trip to Indiana."

"I was one of those kids who didn't care about the Super Bowl, but I remember seeing Ford win Le Mans. Americans have this wonderful sense of being underdogs. Especially in the '60s: we were the most powerful country in the world, we won World War II, we produced 15 million automobiles a year, and yet we beat a little Italian company and somehow we see ourselves as the underdog fighting. It makes no logical sense. But I remember the GT40s coming in 1-2-3 (in 1966), and I really believed there was a connection between that car and the Ford Falcon my mom drove and the 7-liter my dad had."

"Plus, I always think it's the most perfect shape for a sports car. You know, when a Jaguar XKE goes by, people who know nothing about cars—even in New York City where they don't care about cars—people say, 'Hey look at that. That's something, isn't it?' and the GT40 is almost the perfect-looking sports car. There's something about the shape of it. To me, watching a GT40 is like giving a bath to a beautiful woman. There are all these curves and places. You don't get that with a Countach. You get it with the Ford GT, the XK120, especially the Miura, any of these cars."

"The Ford GT was a car I just had to have when I heard they were going to build it. You know, it's only 13 percent bigger than the original and, hey, if I was only 13 percent bigger than I was in '66 I'd be thrilled."

Some critics argue that the Ford GT copies too much from the past, but it is hard to argue about the soul-stirring look of the supercar as it speeds toward you. The sight of the original GT40s winning on racetracks around the world brought a sense of pride to American race fans in the 1960s.

In explaining the retro look of the GT, J Mays, who runs Ford's design efforts, pointed out that they tried to do a modern interpretation of the GT40, but it never looked quite right. Doug Gaffka, who led Ford's Living Legends Studio, explains, "The bottom line is, if you're doing a Ford GT, it had better look like a Ford GT."

The new mid-engine supercar's exterior, designed by good guy Camilo Pardo, is 18 inches longer and 4 inches taller than the original, which was called GT40 because it measured 40 inches tall. Ford was not tempted to call the new version the GT44 and had to abandon the idea of using GT40 when the man who now owns that name wanted too much money for its use, so the automaker simply settled on Ford GT.

A short front overhang might be popular today, but keeping the original car's proportions meant the GT had to have a long nose, which proved handy for hiding the necessary crash bumper structure. Out back the flip-up tail spoiler was complemented by a small "floating" bumper that looks appropriate. Ford put the GT in a wind tunnel to tame the aero, particularly high-speed lift, and came away giving it a modern venturi tunnel underbody.

It may be a modern interpretation of a classic shape, but the GT is quite dramatic and exciting, not as soft, sweeping, and sophisticated as a Pininfarina Ferrari, perhaps, but appealing more to your muscles and your gut.

There is another modern interpretation of the GT40 inside, from the basic layout of the instruments to the seats with grommet vent holes. What catches your eye first is a center tunnel of brushed magnesium that houses the fuel tank. On each side of it are leather-covered carbon fiber-shell seats. There are nicely styled climate control knobs on the console, a row of modern-looking toggle switches on the instrument panel, and that most important of all controls, a big red start button for the supercharged V-8.

Plus, of course, there is equipment never dreamed of in a GT40, such as a CD-audio system, air conditioning, power windows, and a rear window defroster.

To get the GT's dramatic lines, particularly the doors that cut deeply into the roof like the GT40, Ford opted for aluminum exterior panels that are super-plastic formed, heated to almost 950 degrees Fahrenheit, and then formed over a die with high air pressure.

Aluminum is also used for the space frame, a collection of extrusions, castings, and stamped panels that Ford claims is stiffer than the competition, the Ferrari 360 Modena and Lamborghini Gallardo.

Like many modern supercars, Ford's GT has a heart and soul of aluminum. In addition to the V-8 engine, the chassis is assembled from aluminum—extrusions, castings, and stamped panels. Around all this is aluminum bodywork with panels that are superplastic formed, heated to near 950 degrees, and formed over dies with high air pressure.

Aluminum is found again in the unequal-length suspension control arms, which are matched with coil-over shocks and front and rear anti-roll bars. Steering is rack and pinion. The brakes are vented, cross-drilled, four-piston caliper Brembos with ABS, and the tires are Goodyear Eagle F1 Supercars measuring 235/45ZR-18 front and 315/40ZR-19 rear.

Ford already had a 4.6-liter supercharged 390-brake-horsepower twin-cam aluminum V-8 for the SVT Mustang Cobra, and that provided the base for the GT engine. In the mid-engine car, the V-8 is at 5.4 liters with four valves per cylinder, a screw-type supercharger, a water-to-air intercooler, two injectors for each cylinder, and 500 horsepower and 500 ft-lb of torque. As a gauge of technical progress, that fully emissions-certified engine has about the same power as the race-ready 7.0-liter V-8s in the 1960s GT40s.

Behind the low-mounted dry-sump engine is a newly designed Ricardo six-speed manual transmission with a twin-disc clutch and limited-slip differential.

Ford made the time goal, unveiling a trio of GTs—one each in red, white, and blue—at the company's centennial in June 2003. The number one production car was auctioned off that August to former Microsoft executive and Ferrari collector Jon Shirley, who paid $500,000 for the honor, though all the money above the car's retail price of just under $150,000 was donated to charity.

When getting into a Ford GT it is important to remember that, as with the original GT40, you have to duck under the dramatic door cut-ins as the door is closed.

When I drove a GT40 race car years ago I thought it would feel confined inside, but I was amazed at the wonderful, wide-open view through the windshield. Same goes for the new GT as you settle back into the seats, which have a vintage reclined feel about them. You can tell this is a car that was well thought out, as everything has a natural feel to it and there is no hunting for switches or buttons. Dead ahead is the tachometer, right where it belongs. The supercharged V-8 rumbles right behind your head, more of a strong presence than a noise problem.

Since the GT's main rival was the Ferrari 360 Modena, just as Ferrari was Ford's big foe at Le Mans, it was important to beat that car to 60 miles per hour. And it does, the Ford getting there in 3.8 seconds, 0.5 quicker than the Ferrari, with both their top speeds being 190 miles per hour.

As important as the numbers, the Ford GT's power is wonderfully linear, building so strongly through each gear. The V-8 proves both powerful and flexible, just as happy to pull away from low revs in a high gear as it is to spin right up to its redline.

Even on a track, you can feel that this is a car with few vices for the average driver. There is the expected precise turn-in and enough sense of initial understeer to keep you comfortable in the car, in which the chassis seems nicely matched to the power, neither

Aluminum is used for the unequal-length control arms in the suspension. The Italian firm Brembo adds the vented cross-drilled brakes.

overwhelming the other. And the brakes are willing to pull you down from speed repeatedly with no fade.

Getting out of the car, you again have to remember to mind your head, and you find yourself sneaking away while ducking too long to be clear of the door, the way people do when walking under spinning helicopter blades.

Ford has been holding production of the GT to around 4,000 units, building some nine per day, which isn't enough for each of its dealers to get one. And some dealers who did get one wouldn't sell it, so soon after GT deliveries began their prices climbed to as much as $250,000 when resold.

There are those of us who winced when we saw the GT40 concept at Detroit, dismayed that its design so closely copied the original. Couldn't Ford have come up with something new? Now, having driven the Ford GT and seen it on the streets, it's time to eat a little crow. ∎

At the front of the GT, Ford was able to use the long overhang to build in crushability for crash tests. At the back, it created a floating bumper that does the trick and looks appropriate. In the wind tunnel, the fast Ford was detailed for aerodynamics, which included an underbody venturi tunnel.

CHAPTER 28

It's okay to go ga-ga over the F430 Spyder's Pininfarina styling, but under all that beauty is a highly advanced chassis based on an aluminum space frame with a race car–like suspension.

196
MILES PER HOUR

FERRARI F430 2005

Unless you're in the spy business, deception usually isn't a quality meant to be praised. And yet the best way to describe a Ferrari F430 is to call it deceptive.

Here are the objective facts: without much fuss you can paddle-shift an F430 from 0–60 miles per hour in 3.5 seconds and to 100 in 8.1. Top speed winds out to about a needle's width shy of 200 miles per hour. Guess what? That about matches the performance of Ferrari's F50 supercar.

The brakes will haul you down from those triple-digit speeds almost as quickly as any other car in this book and do it repeatedly without fade. Handling limits of the Ferrari are so high you would have to be a little nuts to explore them on anything other than a racetrack.

So, what's deceptive about the F430?

It's almost shockingly easy and comfortable to drive . . . a pussycat until you bury the throttle and bring out its ticked-off tiger tendencies.

This deception has been a while in coming.

The F430 is the latest of what you might call Ferrari's little cars. The series began with the 308GTB/GTS in 1975, when the automaker stripped the Dino name off its smallest two-seat mid-engine car and gave it a V-8, along with typically sleek Pininfarina styling. The early cars—308, 328 (1985), and 348 (1989)—were nice enough for their eras, suffering early on from ever-changing emissions and safety rules, on which Ferrari seemed to have trouble getting a grip. All that was eventually smoothed over, but the cars still had a bit of

Pininfarina dipped into Ferrari heritage for the exterior design of the F430. The dual intakes in front are reminiscent of Ferrari's successful Grand Prix and sports racing cars in 1961 and 1962, including the car Phil Hill drove to victory in the 1962 24 Hours of Le Mans. The rear fender brake cooling ducts resemble those on the 250 LM racing GT.

the era's exotic car hangover. They were enjoyable enough to drive, but if the clutch wasn't a bit fussy, the brakes tended to fade under hard use or the build quality wasn't up to the car's price.

And then along came the Acura NSX. Called a Honda in markets outside the United States, the mid-engine, aluminum-frame Japanese sports car really brought it all together: power, excellent handling, exciting styling, and typically high-quality Japanese fit and finish.

Ferrari took notice—or more correctly, perhaps, was put on notice—that things had to change.

And they did. When the F355 was put on sale in 1994 it was dramatically better than its predecessor, the 348, and was the first Ferrari fitted with an F1 paddle shifter. Come the F355's replacement, the 1999 360 Modena, and it was another step forward, now with an aluminum space frame like the NSX. The F430 was the next logical step.

It began with the exterior design, a collaboration between Ferrari's traditional design house, Pininfarina, and American Frank Stephenson (who gets credit in a past life for the new Mini).

Ferrari dipped into its heritage for design cues, starting at the car's nose with wide, somewhat-oval intakes reminiscent of those on Ferrari sports cars from the Phil Hill era, like the 330 TRI-LM in which he won the 1962 24 Hours of Le Mans. When driving an F430 and looking in the outside rearview mirrors you would see another heritage hint: engine compartment intakes that looked to be right off the 250 LM race car from the mid-1960s.

Although best known for its V-12 engines, Ferrari has a rich history of V-8s that stretches back to the mid-1950s. The F430's lightweight V-8 has 90 degrees between its cylinder banks, 32 valves, and a very flexible 483 horsepower and 343 ft-lb of torque with at least 80 percent available as of 3,500 rpm.

On the F430's steering wheel is the *manettino*. Like the controls on the wheel of Michael Schumacher's Formula 1 Ferrari, it will alter the running mode of the car. The lever's five settings reset such things as shock stiffness, quickness of gearshifts, and the limits of yaw and traction control intervention.

It isn't all nostalgia. Hidden on the F430's underside is a modern venturi system that feeds airflow from nose to tail and helps suck the car to the pavement, dramatically adding downforce.

Out back are taillights rather like those on the Enzo, while on the back deck is a glass engine cover meant to display the car's 4.3-liter V-8 with its crackle-red paint intake manifolds. Hmm . . . delicious.

This is the business center of an F430, dominated by a tachometer. Keeping an eye on that tach, you can paddle-shift an F430 to 60 miles per hour in just 3.5 seconds, and with enough room and correct conditions, you could see that right-hand gauge wrap itself to the right, up to just short of 200 miles per hour.

Although it begins with the same engine block as the Maserati Quattroporte, the F430's V-8 is otherwise unique. Compact and lightweight, the 90-degree engine has a dry-sump oiling system that allows it to sit low in the car. Atop each cylinder bank are twin camshafts per head and four valves per cylinder with variable cam timing.

One of the classic measures of a powerful engine is how much horsepower it produces for each liter of displacement. The traditional goal of excellence has been 100 horsepower per liter, but the F430's V-8 manages 112.1 or 483 brake horsepower from its 4.3 liters. Torque is just as impressive, 343 ft-lb at 5,250 rpm with 80 percent of that on tap as of 3,500 rpm.

You can back the V-8 with a traditional six-speed lever-shifted manual, but the majority of F430 owners opt for the paddle-shifter version of the gearbox. Instead of messing with clutch and shift lever, just flip levers ahead of the steering wheel to shift— upshift with the right-hand lever, downshift with the left.

Pininfarina puts a great deal of time in designing the interior of Ferraris, and it shows. Those leather-covered seats have strong side bolstering, but they are also a pleasure in long cruises. You'll notice there is no shift lever, as this is an F430 with the paddle shifter manual gearbox.

While you lose the involvement of the manual shifter, this system is quicker with Michael Schumacher–like gear changes in as little as 150 milliseconds, revving the engine like a pro to match rpm as you go down a gear. It's not as quick as the Bugatti Veyron with its twin clutches, but it's faster than you are.

There is a pure button-activated drive mode and, unlike earlier Ferraris, this one is quite good with shifts that don't always feel as though you should shift yourself right over to a transmission repair shop. Mind you, it's not as smooth as a real torque converter automatic, but livable for normal driving. Reverse is engaged through a button on the center console.

As cool as the pinball flipper automatic shifting is the *manettino*. Very Formula 1–like, it is a small switch on the lower right of the steering wheel, across from the red start button. Its five settings—snow, low traction, sport, race, and CST—relate to rear-wheel traction and just how good a driver you think you are. They vary how quickly the F1 gearbox shifts, stiffness of the shocks, control of the clutch-pack limited-slip differential, and how much the F430's electronics will step in to save you via traction and yaw control. Bravest setting is CST, which shuts off all the save-your-backside electronic systems.

All this is inside an aluminum space frame with extrusions and castings for pick-up points. This would include the upper and lower A-arm suspensions with their electronically variable-stiffness shock absorbers, coil springs, and anti-roll bars. On hubs at their ends are arguably one of the more exotic options in Ferrari's order book, carbon ceramic brakes that are vented and drilled and smack an extra $14,300 on the price tag.

Ah yes, price tags, like $175,000 for the F430 coupe or $199,000 if you'd like the Spyder edition with its slick automatic folding canvas top . . . and minus the carbon ceramic brakes.

But what a treat, snapping through gears as you press the F430 up a mountain road, exhaust rapping off the hard mountain sides until the revs are high enough for the electronic exhaust bypass valve to open. Then the Ferrari literally roars. At the 8,500-rpm redline, "flip, bam, thank you ma'am" into the next gear. Belted snugly in the leather-covered seats, the tight instrument pod with its colorful tachometer ahead, or easily trundling through traffic, the Ferrari as tame as a pussycat, wonderfully deceptive. ■

You just know that any Ferrari will stop from its highest speeds repeatedly and with no fade, thanks to high-tech disc brakes. But you can also step up a level above that with special order carbon ceramic brakes that are vented and drilled and put an extra $14,300 on the car's price tag.

Ferrari is rightfully proud of its Grand Prix racing history. It has not only the longest history in the sport, but remains the only team with the technical expertise to create not only its own chassis, but also its engines. And Ferrari commemorates that proud history with a number plate in every F430.

Okay, you're not about to ride on the back deck of a Ferrari F430 at speed, but this is what it would look like—V-8 humming under glass, the world streaking by this latest (and greatest) example of the "little" Ferrari.

CHAPTER 29

Beautiful, but not subtle. To meet race car needs, the CLK DTM gets Arnold Schwarzenegger-style fender flares and a tall rear tail, while under the back is a diffuser that helps draw air out from under the car. Low in the front is a broad spoiler to add downforce and also gulp in plenty of cooling air for the supercharged V-8.

200
MILES PER HOUR

MERCEDES-BENZ CLK DTM AMG 2005

Fire up the supercharged V-8 of a Mercedes-Benz CLK DTM AMG, click into first gear, and floor it. A short paddle snap slaps you into second gear, and the Deutsche Tourenwagen Masters (DTM) is simply going like a bat out of hell! Speed limits are quickly behind you and, bang, into third gear. By Mercedes' reckoning, you're at 60 miles per hour in about 3.8 seconds, and the top speed is electronically limited (ha!) to 200 miles per hour. Thanks, Mercedes.

The brakes are as willing to force you forward into the belts as acceleration is to smack you back in the seat. Miles of rising or falling curves in the German countryside make it obvious

Don't be looking for a great deal of body roll from the CLK DTM, which is equipped with a very firm race car-like suspension. There's an adjustable coil spring suspension at each corner, and the rubber bushings, which calm noise and vibration, are replaced with uniball joints.

that the limits of handling, even with ESP, would be best tested during a few rented laps of the Nürburgring, not public roads.

Temptation, get thee behind me.

There are very sound reasons why race cars make lousy street machines. And equally good reasons why "normal" automobiles seasoned with racing equipment can be more fun than the law allows . . . literally.

Any number of such exotic machines are built by automakers in Europe to homologate them for certain racing series. Rules demand that for a car to compete in events such as the German DTM series, the automaker must build a certain number, usually a hundred or so, for the street. The more extreme the needs for the series—superchargers, ultrawide tires, carbon fiber bodywork—the more extreme the street machine.

We offer the Mercedes-Benz CLK DTM AMG as a prime example.

Don't expect subtlety. The normally handsome and svelte Mercedes CLK body has been lowered, gaping up front through huge air vents, with muscles flexing via Arnold Schwarzenegger fender flares, a carbon fiber spoiler perched in its tail, an aero diffuser under its rump, and a pair of oval tailpipes poking out like rude comments.

AMG has one man hand-build each DTM V-8. The aluminum powerplant is supercharged and produces 582 horsepower at 6,100 rpm and a glorious 590 ft-lb of torque from 3,500 rpm. The transmission that handles all that power is the five-speed paddle-shifted manual "automatic," also fitted in Mercedes SLR supercar.

Six-caliper vented disk brakes lurk inside 19-inch alloy wheels rimmed with squat 225/35R-29 tires. This is the sort of serious stopping power needed for a car that will snap you to 60 miles per hour in some 3.8 seconds and has the potential for a near-200-mile per hour top speed.

Each CLK DTM AMG 24-valve aluminum V-8 is hand built by one man at AMG, and certified at 582 brake horsepower at 6,100 rpm and a glorious 590 ft-lb of torque from 3,500. Transmitting the power is the same five-speed paddle-shifted manual automatic used in Mercedes' SLR supercar. The front disc brakes sport six calipers and the rears four, and they lurk inside alloy wheels, 19s in front with Dunlop 225/35R-19s, 20s at the back with 285/30R-20s.

The cars are built by HWA GmbH, which also developed and ran Mercedes' factory DTM cars to the 2003 championship. So it was familiar with the CLK DTM AMG's adjustable coil spring suspension, the uni-ball joints instead of rubber bushings, the multi-disc limited-slip diff, and so on. Both the ASR and ESP electronic systems have had their upper thresholds upped.

In order to qualify a car for the DTM series, an automaker must built a series of street versions of its proposed racer, complete with the same bodywork, wide tires, supercharged engines, and other parts that will be needed for competition. This rule leads to such extreme road machines as Mercedes-Benz' CLK DTM AMG.

Nothing subtle here. High-side racing shell seat you drop into, then buckle up a full racing belt system. The suede-covered steering wheel has excellent grip and various race car-like switches, though their functions are fairly mundane. There are even sound and navigational systems. Plenty of carbon fiber panels add to the race car feeling in the CLK DTM.

The difference between getting into a CLK versus the CLK DTM AMG: slipping onto the plush leather seats of the CLK then clicking the shoulder harness, versus climbing over and dropping into the high-sided carbon fiber shell seats (also leather covered) of the DTM, snapping home the crotch strap and wide shoulder harnesses, then pulling them tight.

Instead of reaching out to a smooth, color-coordinated steering wheel, you grip a small wheel with a rough back-side-of-the-hide surface.

Thanks to a thick structure-stiffening bar spanning the cockpit behind the seats at windowsill height, there is a sense of roll cage. This image is heightened by the absence of back seats, the rear cavity lined with a carbon fiber insert that has a carpet floor. Carbon fiber is also used on the door panels and to cover much of the center console, but there are indications of civility.

The expected climate and information controls a la normal CLK are there, complete with a navigational system, and the instrument cluster also looks familiar. Shifting is via levers on the back of the steering wheel, but there is a toggle switch to set the tranny on drive. Four buttons on the wheel look so businesslike, you may wonder if they command brake balance, roll bar stiffness, or even pit lane speed. Then you discover they scroll through the speedo-screen trip info center, and their biggest benefit is changing the volume of the sound system.

Unlike many race cars for the street, the CLK DTM AMG's ride won't back out your fillings, though you wouldn't want to sip a hot, brimming latte when under way. Then again, there quite naturally are no carbon fiber cup holders. *Nicht* Starbucks.

All 100 of Mercedes-Benz CLK DTM AMGs built were quickly snapped up at around $250,000, and they probably aren't cheaper on the used-car market. The CLK DTM AMG wasn't certified for the United States, so owning one in the States would involve legalities, but guess what quickly began showing up at exotic-car shows around the country?

Yup, CLK DTM AMGs, sitting squat and ready, race cars for U.S. streets.

Where there's a will—and a hefty check—there's a way. ■

And the CLKs make sensational-looking race cars. Here Mercedes-Benz team driver Bernd Schneider leads the field of Mercedes, Audi, and Opel DTM race cars at Holland's Zandvoort circuit. Though resembling their street brethren, the race cars are even more sophisticated and very, very expensive. *Photo courtesty of Mercedes-Benz*

CHAPTER 30

Driving quickly can be great fun, whether rocketing down a straightaway or trying a twisting road. But it needs to be done with common sense, with good automobiles on roads that are suitable, and with safety equipment in place. And with the driver putting respect for others first and his joy in going quickly second.

217
MILES PER HOUR

RUF Rt 12 2005

It was 11 p.m. on a dry, clear night when Hans-Peter Lieb greeted me at Alois Ruf's dealership in Pfaffenhausen, Germany, and said, "Why not now?"

Why not?

I strapped into the vestigial back seat of a 650-horsepower Ruf Rt 12 in what seemed a vain attempt to record what was about to happen. It wasn't really a back seat, just two deep dimples behind driver and passenger, but there were seatbelts, so I pretzeled myself in place and belted up.

Soon we were making a left on the "To Munich" on-ramp of Autobahn A96 and accelerating. Traffic was almost nonexistent,

Nothing of quality is cheap, and that includes a Ruf. The standard rear-drive version with 530 horsepower runs $234,100. If you prefer the 3.8-liter, 650-horsepower edition the tab jumps to $287,000. All-wheel drive is another $15,000. For an added $14,000, Ruf will integrate a rollcage into the interior.

just a few slow lights in the right lane. HP, as he's known, slipped to the left and went hammer down. My digital Canon was poised to record the event.

Did you see *Apollo 13* or another authentic depiction of what it's like to take off on the tip of a rocket? As the power overtakes the vehicle and it shudders and quivers, surging ahead? Little hard vibrations, some vertical, a few lateral, shake you about. You're pinned back. The sound of power wraps around you. Needles in gauges leap to the right.

That's about what it was like.

This wasn't a grocery run—this was serious stuff, yet HP handled it with ease. He had been there before. The digital readout climbed as we thundered beside the guardrail that became a double silver stripe. We were a freight train, then a jet airline well past takeoff speed. We were at 214 miles per hour and the Ruf was alive around us.

"Did you get the picture?" HP asked, noting the tach redlined at 7,200 rpm in sixth.

Hell, I didn't know. I had my trusty Canon aimed over his right shoulder, ISO cranked up to 1600, shooting away at the speedo, hoping for the best.

Turns out, we got it. Shazam!

That wasn't the first time I had been over 200 miles per hour in a Ruf, because Alois "Louis" Ruf has a history of building fast cars. I was riding with Phil Hill on a "World's Fastest Cars" story for *Road & Track* when he nailed down 212 miles per hour at Volkswagen's amazing Ehra-Lessien track (imagine a Daytona speedway built by the Germans). As we whistled along, a side wind caught and kicked us a lane to the right.

Hill was unperturbed because Rufs aren't just fast, but stable and dependable. World beaters.

But what's a Ruf?

It looks like a Porsche, sounds like a Porsche, and many of its parts started life in a Porsche factory, but legally it isn't a Porsche. Let me explain.

Ruf's shops are on the Mindelheimer Stasse in Pfaffenhausen in a southern region of Germany called Allgäu. The family has been there since before World War II. After the conflict the family built buses, ran a gas station, and provided a training ground for young Alois.

In the mid-1970s, he turned to tuning super Porsches. If you know about the tuning industry in Germany, you know it is peopled by some charlatans and some geniuses. The former build bizarre supercars with grenade motors and often-ungainly bodywork; the latter create truly great automobiles. This second group includes such firms as Alpina, which tweaks excellent BMWs, and AMG before it was swallowed up by Mercedes-Benz and found its initials on R-Class minivans. And it includes Alois Ruf, possibly to the chagrin of some Porsche executives.

For the past three decades, Ruf has been taking Porsches apart and making them even better, or being a step ahead of Zuffenhausen, like when he built five- and six-speed transmissions for his cars before the factory got around to it. Making a great thing greater.

Ruf so completely strips a car and rebuilds it that since 1981 he has had a Manufacturers' Certification from the German Federal Vehicle Offices. So his cars may look like Porsches, but they have their own Ruf serial numbers and chassis plates. Since the late 1980s, Ruf automobiles have also held their own manufacturer's emissions and safety certificates from the U.S. government—no easy task.

I first met Louis on the initial *Road & Track* World's Fastest Cars event, which he won. He brought a car we nicknamed the "Yellow Bird," officially a 1987 Ruf CTR that managed 211 miles per hour at a time when most supercars had trouble cracking 190. Where other automakers in the contest had spoilers and ducts to hold their cars to the ground and cool them, Ruf stuck a twin-turbo flat-six in a stripped Porsche narrow body and whistled by them all. The 469-horsepower CTR was a winner.

Through it all, the smiling, self-effacing Louis Ruf didn't say much.

His cars spoke for him, winning the next fastest cars' competition at 212 miles per hour with a lightweight 415-horsepower BTR painted the same blue as German autobahn signs.

His customers chimed in, too, telling us how their megahorsepower Rufs were tractable at low speeds, never fussy in any weather, and quite reliable.

Aha, the proof we were quick: the speedometer of the Ruf Rt 12 hovers at 343 kilometers per hour or 213 miles per hour. The tachometer rests on the 7,200-rpm redline. This high-speed run was made on the Autobahn on a dry day around midnight when the traffic was very light.

Ratchet forward to November 2004 and the Essen Motor Show, one of Europe's premier displays of speed machines. Ruf launched the Rt 12: Ruf Turbo model number 12.

All those Porsche parts that have gone into Ruf's garages have been carefully modified or replaced, the results rebuilt with the sort of individual care no mass automaker can afford. The flat-six is at 3.6 liters with all that you'd expect from a 997 Porsche: water-cooled aluminum block and heads, two camshafts per head, 24 valves, dry-sump lubrication, and those critical twin turbos and intercoolers, though many are now Ruf pieces and all of it blueprinted and carefully reassembled.

On Ruf's dyno that combo comes to 530 horsepower and 553 ft-lb of torque, though there are options. A $7,320 kick-up takes you to 560 horsepower and 583 ft-lb of torque, while an added $35,760 gets you 3.8 liters, 650 horsepower, and 642 ft-lb of torque.

Standard is rear drive, though all-wheel drive is an option. The transmission is a six-speed with your choice of gears.

Ruf tunes the suspension to match the greater horsepower, keeping Porsche's various electronic stability management systems. Their own 15-inch vented, cross-drilled disc brakes go inside Ruf design alloy wheels with Pirelli tires, 255/35ZR-19s at the front, 345/25ZR-20s out back.

As expected, you get unique bodywork; the standard Porsche shell now features Ruf's own front grille and spoiler, rear fenders with flares, and intercooler intakes that lead to outlet vents in the rear bumpers. And a new fixed rear spoiler.

Most famous of Ruf's cars is this 1987 CTR nicknamed *Yellow Bird*. In *Road & Track's* World's Fastest Car competition that year, the 469-horspower Ruf shot to 211 miles per hour, winning against tough competition from Ferrari and Porsche. In 2005, Ruf took the car to a new *R&T* test, and the then-18-year-old car rocketed to 185.8 miles per hour in a standing mile.

They take care of you inside, too, with Ruf's own electrically adjustable, leather-covered seats. Unique instruments in the Porsche five-pod style are seen through Ruf's three-spoke steering wheel. And all the little touches are there: shift knob, aluminum pedals, and stainless-steel door sills.

But it isn't just the bits and pieces that matter. What makes the difference is that Ruf's men so carefully put them together in a manner that no mass manufacturer, even one as careful as Porsche, could hope to do.

And the result is mightily impressive, as we found out on a crisp November day in Pfaffenhausen.

On the 100th anniversary of the turbocharger, it's good to know that it is very much alive and powerful as ever, and the Rt 12 is the proof.

Through the years, Ruf has managed to take Porsches—for which he has the greatest respect—and make them even better. As an example, this 1992 BTR had 360 horsepower from its single-turbo engine, an increase of 40 horsepower over Porsche's offering at the time. That same year, he offered his cars with an electronic clutch system, which eliminates the normal foot clutch.

Alois Ruf has been building super Porsches in Pfaffenhausen, Germany, since the mid-1970s. His first modification was to create a 3.3-liter Turbo model. He went on to produce his own five-speed transmission when Porsche stayed with four speeds.

Ruf takes care of more than just the engine and suspension in his cars, outfitting the interior with his own leather-upholstered, electrically adjustable (and quite comfortable) seats. Note the side bolstering for holding you in place during hard cornering. The steering wheels, pedals, and shift knobs are also unique.

Like so many of today's supercars, you can drive this Ruf like a Kia Rio. Just move the gearshift from well-defined slot to well-defined slot—who cares if you're at a mere 1,000 rpm—and the Ruf is a pussycat. A grocery cart. A candidate for the car pool.

And wouldn't the boys love it when Dad nails the gas.

Up to around 3,800 rpm from a mild in-town cruise, the Ruf is catching its breath, quick though not stunning. But, oh my goodness, what happens next is epic.

Boost goes skyward and so does horsepower. First gear is rather short for clutch-saving purposes, so you run up on the rev limiter, but with a wrist slip you're into second, the turbos are spinning like hell, and the Rt 12 goes into afterburner mode.

Because the suspension is kept reasonably pliable for dental purposes, you can feel the Ruf torque a touch to the right as road signs blur in your periphery. Then into third, and before you can mumble, "Dr. Ferdinand Porsche knew what he was doing," the digital speedo has tumbled over to 200 kilometers per hour (120 miles per hour). Then common sense rears its ugly head, especially if you are on two-lane public roads. Ugh! I hate that part.

Is a Ruf Rt 12 really as quick as it feels?

Road & Track declared it the fastest car it had ever tested as of early 2006, after launching a two-wheel-drive Rt 12 to 60 miles per hour in a mere 3.2 seconds. But get this: its very

Ruf so completely modifies Porsches that they are no longer Porsches, but officially called Rufs, complete with new serial numbers and chassis plates. In 1981 he earned a Manufacturer's Certificate from the German Federal Vehicle Office, and he has also passed all necessary safety and emissions tests of the U.S. government.

So the driver can enjoy all the power of the Rt 12, it is fitted with a six-speed transmission. The customer can specify what gearing he would like. The shift linkage is firm and positive. As an option, the buyer can specify all-wheel drive, which helps tame the power by splitting it front/rear.

You can't up the horsepower of a car like the Rt 12 without making appropriate changes throughout the car. The suspension is firmed without making it rock hard, and there's an option to hydraulically lift the front end 2 inches to keep from ripping the front spoiler. Ruf adds his own 19-inch wheels and then fits them with Pirelli low-aspect-ratio tires.

capable young assistant road test editor, Shaun Bailey, nailed down a 3.3 on his first try. He stayed with it and finished the quarter-mile in 11 seconds at 133.9 miles per hour, quicker than an Enzo, Carrera GT, or McLaren F1.

Is a Ruf Rt 12 really expensive?

Hey, speed and hand-built quality aren't cheap. Go with the standard rear-drive Rt 12 at 530 brake horsepower and you're looking at a tab of $234,100. Opt for the full-pop 3.8-liter

650-horsepower motor and the total runs to $287,000. Want all-wheel drive? That's another $15,000, while $14,000 handles the roll cage, which is so neatly integrated into the body shell you have to look to find it.

Oh, and there's the option for around $14,000 of a hydraulic adjustment that raises the front of the car 2 inches to make it easier to get in and out of driveways. Sound expensive to clear dips and rises? Ruf points out that replacing the lower front spoiler three times covers the 14 grand. This is not a cheap game to play.

It's that Ruf craftsmanship that costs . . . but also pays when you put the pedal down. It might be pressed lightly to get from point to point, such as going for tea. Or it might be way down as you pop through the gears on your way to 214 miles per hour.

Just be careful.

The *Road & Track* crew got its Rt 12 to 217 miles per hour on the same Autobahn that HP and I used, and kidded me about the fact that we were 3 miles per hour slower. I grinned and replied, "Ah, you say you went 217, but where's the proof? I have a photo." ■

Road & Track declared the Rt 12 to be its 0–60-mile per hour champion in early 2006 after blasting a two-wheel-drive version to that speed in a mere 3.2 seconds. The car was easy to use; Assistant Road Test Editor Shaun Bailey got a 3.3-second run on his first attempt.

CHAPTER 31

If you're working at it, just 2.5 seconds after launch you have the Bugatti Veyron at 60 miles per hour. Another 7.3 clicks of the clock and you've brushed past 125 miles per hour and within 10 more seconds (quick, take a breath) you're approaching 190 miles per hour. Stick with it under the right conditions and the 16-cylinder engine will propel the 4,163-pound car to 250 miles per hour. Proven.

250
MILES PER HOUR

BUGATTI VEYRON 16.4 2005

It was a recipe for disaster.

Heavy rain had fallen in the night and there was little chance the roads that curlicued through the tall hills of Alsace in western France would dry soon. Being autumn, the showers had laid down a heavy layer of gold and amber leaves, slippery as a greased anaconda.

Under us was 1001 horsepower and, even with all-wheel drive, there's only so much we could do to hedge on the coefficient of friction. But Ditmar Hilbig had the pedal down and the Bugatti Veyron 16.4 slipped through the turns with remarkable speed and stability, given the slimy conditions.

He guided the Veyron into a hairpin paved with autumn leaves, and it remained stable and unperturbed. The left-hand wheels were on a drying surface, the rights on slippery leaves, but the Bugatti never quivered. He aimed the Veyron 16.4 through tight esses where the camber danced right-left-right, and the car never equivocated, but stayed straight and true.

Magic.

It was difficult to tell if he was trying to impress or warn. He was driving on the outbound leg of this orientation drive, and I was to be in command on the way back. We were, after all, in a $1.2 million car . . . possibly worth more considering it was Veyron chassis number four. Ditmar's baby.

It's been a long time coming. Few cars have been as anticipated or through such a "when will they finish?" gestation period as the Veyron 16.4.

It is the fourth Bugatti created by Volkswagen since the German automaker acquired the famous name in 1998.

Ettore Bugatti created the Type 53 in 1931, making it the first major race car with drive to all wheels. The 5.0-liter engine and rudimentary AWD system made the car difficult to drive in circuit races, but it was a hillclimb winner. The late René Dreyfus, seen here with the Type 53, drove the car to a record at the La Turbie hillclimb in 1934.

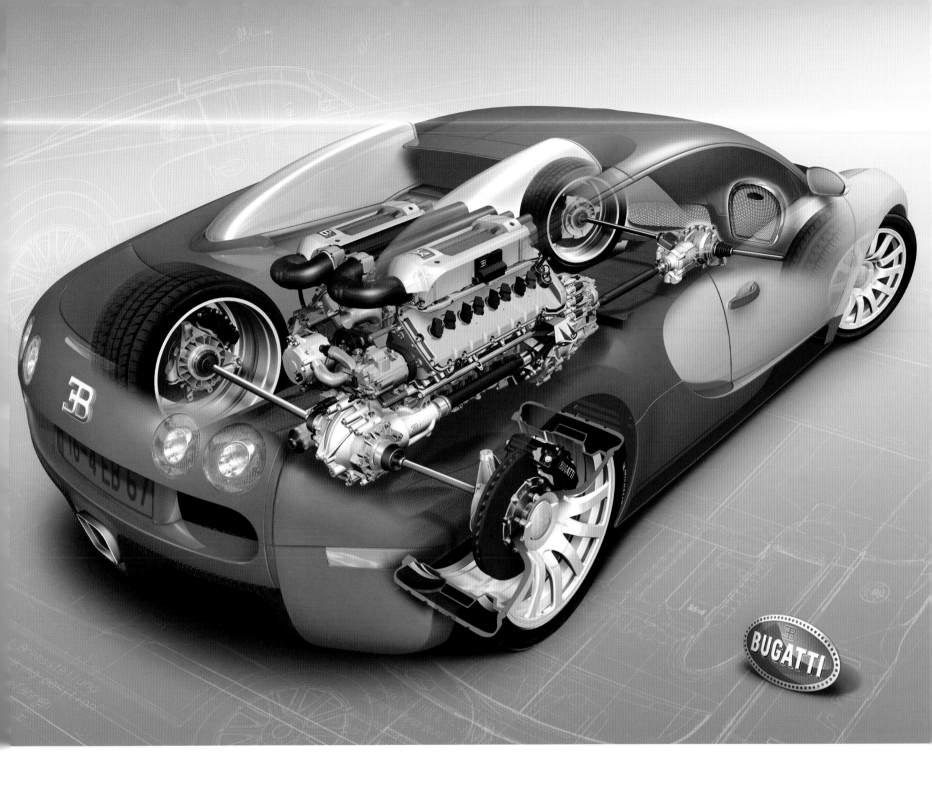

First came a trio of potential Bugattis, all shaped by Giorgetto Giugiaro's Italdesign. It began with the front-engine EB118 two-door coupe (1998 Paris Auto Show), followed by the EB218 four-door sedan (1999 Geneva Auto Show), then the mid-engine W18/3 Chiron supercar (1999 Frankfurt Motor Show) built on the chassis of an Italian Lamborghini Diablo VT, another VW-owned automaker.

All three show cars had 18-cylinder engines with the W-layout championed by VW and Dr. Ferdinand Piech, grandson of Dr. Ferdinand Porsche and the godfather of such other renowned machines as the all-conquering Porsche 917 race cars—an engineering genius if not a subtle man.

In this cutaway, it's easy to see the layout of the Veyron. The big W-16 engine with its four turbochargers, the rear differential for the back axle, then the driveshaft that sends power forward to the front-drive axle. Notice the width of the Michelin tires and the big ceramic disc brakes. *Courtesy of Bugatti*

Where a Ferrari might look like a lithe animal or athlete, the Bugatti Veyron reminds one more of a knight in armor. Behind the car is the stairway to Chateau St. Jean, part of the traditional Ettore Bugatti property in Molsheim in eastern France. Volkswagen has carefully restored the property and now uses it for meetings.

It was under Piech's reign at Volkswagen that the company bought Bugatti, Lamborghini, and Bentley as its luxury brands. It then began the design and engineering of a Bugatti that would trump the supercar competition from the likes of Ferrari, VW's own Lamborghini, Porsche (on whose board Piech sits), plus the out-of-production-but-legendary benchmark McLaren F1.

Piech is a man who gets what he wants, and the Bugatti supercar is a prime example. The VW-designed car was first shown to the public with an 18-cylinder engine at the Tokyo Auto Show in late 1999, and in its definitive 16-cylinder form at the Paris Auto Show in autumn 2000.

Heart of the Veyron 16.4 is its W-16, which is surprisingly light and compact. This last quality comes with the engine's layout, essentially a pair of dual overhead cam V-8s with only 15 degrees in their V angles set side by side and matched to a common crankcase.

Bugatti's Veyron has three driving modes. Normal has a ride height of 4.9 inches, and the spoilers are tucked in. Handling deploys the rear spoiler and drops the ride height. Turn a special key, and you can go to High Speed. As the spoiler retracts, the car hunkers down still more, and air diffuser flaps close to lower aerodynamic drag.

Like complexity? You'd love the W-18 engine developed for the Bugatti Chiron concept car. Basically made up of three Volkswagen narrow-angle V-6s, the W 18 has 72 valves and a displacement of 6.3 liters. With direct fuel injection, the engine creates 547 horsepower at 6,800 rpm and 479 ft-lb of torque at 4,000 rpm.

This 64-valve 8.0-liter engine is assembled in Germany with such lightweight components as titanium connecting rods. With four intercooled turbochargers and direct fuel injection, the 16 cylinders produce 1001 horsepower at 6,000 rpm and 922 ft-lb of torque between 2,200 and 5,500 rpm.

It's a magnificent engine and looks the part . . . what you can see of it. It's possible to look down on the top of the W-16 sitting behind the Veyron's cockpit, set like a huge

Continued on page 330

A technical *tour de force*, the Bugatti Veyron features not just a 1,001-horsepower engine with seven-speed transmission, but also advanced ceramic disc brakes with six-piston calipers inside alloy wheels fitted with the widest production tires in the world, made by Michelin. The price of all that sophistication? A cool $1.2 million.

Inside the Veyron are comfortable, deep-set individual seats with a tall center console. Ahead is the hooded instrument binnacle with the speedometer reading to 420 kilometers per hour (261 miles per hour) and a horsepower meter reading up to 1,001. Note the nicely finished pedals and the low roof, the latter creating a slight "bunker" effect.

Continued from page 327

diamond. The inside cam covers and intake manifolds are exposed to the elements, one of the concessions made to dissipate heat generated in making the 1001 horsepower. But you must virtually disassemble the car to see any more of the W-16.

As technically interesting as this impressive powerplant is its transmission, a seven-speed gearbox with automatic shifting and a pair of clutches. Built in England by Riccardo, it is like a super-sized VW DSG transmission in that as one clutch disengages a gear, the second clutch immediately engages the next, making for extraordinarily smooth and quick gear changes. Although you can drive the Veyron in a conventional automatic mode, the manual shifting via paddles is usually too entertaining to pass up.

Even though the Veyron weighs a healthy 4,163 pounds, Bugatti logically figured that all-wheel drive was needed to get the power down with any sense of stability.

By Bugatti's figuring, 0–62 miles per hour comes up in 2.5 seconds; you're past 125 miles per hour in around 7.3 seconds. By the time you've counted "17 Mississippi," you're quickly approaching 190 miles per hour. The Bugatti's proven top speed, 250 miles per hour, makes this the fastest car in the world . . . which is what Piech wanted.

Suspension is the expected upper and lower A-arms with conventional springs and shocks, though the system has hydraulics that will raise and lower the car, depending on speed, and are part of the high-speed handling and aerodynamic package.

There are three modes.

Normal: ride height is 4.9 inches front and rear, rear spoiler is down, front diffuser flaps open to let air under the car, and the drag coefficient is 0.393.

JAY LENO ON THE *BUGATTI VEYRON*

Bugatti says about the Veyron, 'Your wife could use this to go to the market.' Why? Why would I give my wife the Veyron to go the market? Why would you even think of going to market? 'Oh, I've got the Veyron. I think I'll go to the market.' It doesn't make any sense to me.

"I got to drive it at Pebble Beach, and it's very impressive. Technically, it's amazing. It does suffer from that thing about not being able to see the motor, which for me is important. I mean, that seven-speed double-clutch transmission is brilliant but . . . .

"Bugatti was more artist than engineer, and this Veyron is more engineer than artist. There's no sense of involvement with the car, nothing sort of rumbles, and you get in and press a button and you put it in 'D' and you go. It's a bit like being in a jet plane. The real fun part is the takeoff and landing, not the actual driving."

"I do appreciate the Veyron," Leno explains, calling the engineering of the car, "A brilliant job, but physics are physics and it weighs 4,300 pounds. I always think of that movie, *The Incredible Lightness of Being* and I like that phrase. That's what I like about Lotus Elans.

"The dashboard is a little too 'bling, bling' for me. I come from the school of the airplane cockpit look. I like to see the oil temperature and everything. I find the gauges too small, but that might be more age than anything else. To me, knowing the oil or transmission temperature is more interesting than listening to the radio."

"Plus, I don't quite understand the car's purpose. It's not quite a GT, it's not quite a sports car . . . it does all those things well and it is fast. My great fear is that it's one of those cars that will bring prying eyes to the sport: '1,000 horsepower in this day and age! Can we afford . . . .' All of a sudden General Motors says we have to pull back on this and everybody decides. It just shines the light. That's the trouble. The articles I've seen in the mainstream press ask, '1,001 horsepower? Is this what we need now?'

"You know, the F1 McLaren obviously made a huge splash, but it made its huge splash among people who already knew about cars. It didn't really make waves among people who don't know, and that's what I like. The idea that some idiot would go in and say, 'Hey, give me one of those Veyron things. Those are really fast, right?' And then they hit a tree and the next thing there are calls for horsepower limits.

"That being said, it's a wonderful achievement. It's amazing."

Bugatti was famous for the use of engine-turned metal surfaces, and it does the same with the Veyron. From the top of the center console: the clock; vents; climate and sound system controls; and the shift lever for the amazing seven-speed, twin-clutch automatic transmission, which can be used in full automatic or shifted manually.

Giorgetto Giugiaro and his son, Fabrizio, with the Bugatti 18/3 Chiron show car, unveiled at the 1999 Frankfurt Auto Show. Built on the chassis of a Lamborghini VT—another Volkswagen-owned company—the Chiron was named for famous race driver Louis Chiron and was one of the prototypes for the production Veyron.

Handling (when manually deployed or above 135 miles per hour): ride height drops to 3.15 inches front and 3.74 inches rear, the rear spoiler rises and can take an angle of 15–27 degrees for added downforce, diffuser flaps stay open, and the drag coefficient is 0.417. This is the maximum downforce setting.

High speed: ride height lowers to 2.56 inches front and 2.75 inches rear, the rear spoiler retracts but maintains a 2-degree down angle, the diffuser flaps close, and drag drops to 0.355.

Incidentally, to get to that high-speed setting you have to stop, turn a second key, and run through a checklist of very good ideas, like making certain tire pressures are correct.

With the Veyron 16.4's acceleration and top speed, brakes have to be of a high order. Bugatti specified massive, high-tech carbon-ceramic brakes, the front discs measuring 15.7 inches and stopped by eight-piston, four-pad calipers, while the 15-inch rears have six-piston, two-pad calipers. Better yet, at high speed a good stab at the brake pedal also tilts the rear wing forward up to 55 degrees to increase rear downforce and aero drag.

There is no engine cover over the Veyron engine, in part to help dissipate heat. The 16-cylinder engine is made up of two 15-degree twin-cam V-8s set side-by-side in a common crankcase. With four turbochargers and intercooling, the sturdy engine is rated at 1,001 horsepower at 6,000 rpm and 922 ft-lb of torque between 2,200 and 5,500 rpm.

Inside the modern Bugatti factory are four bays in which the Veyrons are assembled from large modules shipped in from outside suppliers. Here you can see the car's safety cell interior and the fact that when the body panels are removed the Veyron looks less like a conventional automobile than an aircraft.

Tires threatened to be a problem. Bugatti needed them to hold together at 250 miles per hour, stay put at 1.3 g on a skid pad, and be run-flats, eliminating the need to stow a spare. A tough set of standards. Michelin came through with Pilot Sport PS2 PAX skins for the Veyron, claimed to be the widest production tires in the world, the rear treads taping 14.4 inches across, the wheels at 20 inches front, 21 inches rear.

That's the technical background, but what is it like to be around the Bugatti on its home ground in France, and then drive it?

Seeing the Bugatti outdoors, away from the auto show circuit, you understand why you don't find a lot of people head-over-heels in love with the Veyron's styling, though everyone comes away mightily impressed. While the Veyron isn't a beautiful car in the manner of a Bugatti Type 57 or Ferrari 250GTO, it is imposing and oh so interesting. Where the body of a high-performance Ferrari might remind one of an athlete, the Veyron is a knight in armor—Carl Lewis versus Ivanhoe.

Go ahead. Climb in and you will have little doubt you are about to drive big stuff. You feel it around you, rather like a presence. Being a big machine, it surrounds and envelops you, so there is a certain bunker feeling to being in the cockpit: low windscreen, high sides, the A-pillars a bit obstructive. The overall sense is imposing but not threatening.

The controls are elegant, as is the interior in the manner in which nicely finished metal elements—the Bugatti-esque engine-turned-center console, the rimmed gauges, the door controls panel—contrast with high-quality leather. It's a look, an ambiance that isn't especially warm and enticing in the manner of a Jaguar or a Bentley, but it gets your attention and admiration.

Starting the engine isn't so much like starting a car as something more imposing (there's that word again), like an unlimited hydroplane or a Spitfire (oops, Messerschmitt). Varoooom.

For all that drama, what happens next is quite civilized. Snick, away in first gear, the all-wheel drive planting the power on the ground, fast, secure, and stable. No snaking about, just the hand of God firmly in your back, pushing you forward—like a Gulfstream G4 on a high-performance takeoff, thundering toward the end of the runway. Then, snick, back on the upshift, and before you can take half a breath you're up a gear, a new takeoff.

Where less-sophisticated transmissions might bang and slam you into the next gear, the Bugatti seems to instantaneously assume you into the following ratio, and off you go, so fast, so unobtrusive. Magic—again.

Before you can say Ettore Bugatti, you're into third and the speedo is climbing to the right. Into fourth . . . .

Except this is someone else's $1.2 million machine. So I eased off as the straightaway ended and the forest surrounded me. Quite pretty, but the wet roads were as treacherous as thin ice. I thought I sensed Ditmar relaxing.

I backed off and let the Bugatti assume its second personality. Because even with all its horsepower and torque, the Bugatti was not only super quick, but also dignified. Civilized.

Those $25,000 carbon brakes did squeal a bit under light braking, but brought the Veyron to a dignified stop from speed quickly. The steering was light enough to make the Veyron quite maneuverable in town while still properly direct at speed.

In the end the Bugatti is mightily impressive, but a bit overwhelming and not necessarily lovable in the manner of a Ferrari or that singular product of genius, the McLaren F1.

When you are with the Bugatti, however, there is the feeling that you are in the presence of greatness. Like being on a high-speed ride with Phil Hill when he's driving a vintage Ferrari. Attending an Eric Clapton concert. Or dropping into your airplane seat (as I once did) to find next to you is Walter Payton, who loved to talk about auto racing.

In a word, magic. ■

From behind it's possible to see two important elements of the Veyron's well-defined aerodynamics package: The rear spoiler in the high handling position, where it can take an angle of 15–27 degrees, and under the back of the Bugatti on either side of the exhaust opening, are the venturis that help draw air from under the car.

CHAPTER 32

Zora Duntov, father of the Corvette, started the first Z06 program in 1963 as a way of creating racing parts for Corvette owners. The performance package name was revived in 2001 and is now in its third iteration, horsepower having climbed from 385 to 505 in the latest version.

199
MILES PER HOUR

CORVETTE Z06 2006

When the revs hit a little over 3 grand, you step off the clutch of the Corvette Z06. After just a bit of spin, the tires bite and in 3.9 seconds you slam the car into second gear. The 7.0-liter V-8 hammers away once again, wham, into third, all of this quite controllable.

Shift at the redline into fourth at 125 miles per hour, and you can barely believe that the digital numbers reflecting in the windshield heads-up display are climbing so quickly. You're smiling.

The reality is that any number of cars will rocket you to 60 in the 4-second area, but few do it with the seeming juice and joy of the Corvette.

As a prime example of the weight saving that took place in creating the Z06, the aluminum V-8 rides on a cradle of lightweight magnesium, the same material that is used for the car's top. Each of the 505-horsepower 7.0-liter LS-7 V-8s is hand-built at GM's new Performance Build Center.

We know a Ferrari F430 will squirt to 60 an eye-blink faster than the Z06 and, for that matter, a Bentley Continental R coupe will do it in 4.4 seconds, but there's something soulful about the way the Z06 does it that is oh, so satisfying. Maybe this is what it's like to be shot from a gun. Not to imply the Corvette's acceleration is crude or hairy, just so explosively satisfying.

Which is one reason why anyone who thinks Chevrolet's Corvette Z06 doesn't belong in a book on exotic cars is dead wrong.

Okay, Corvette's annual production numbers easily cover a decade of output from some foreign exotic carmakers. Base price of the Z06 is a mere $65,000. And the average Corvette-owner's portfolio might be slim next to many Ferrarist's, but don't for a second sell the Z06 short.

Short, as in 3.9 seconds, because that's how quickly a Z06 leaps to 60 miles per hour, which opens the case for this super Corvette.

Case point number one: It goes like hell.

That 0–60 number is just a simple smoky-tire start for the 'Vette. In 8.8 seconds you're at 100 and in 12.2 through the quarter-mile at 120 miles per hour, according to *Road & Track*'s testing. Keep popping through the six gears and by the time the V-8 runs out of breath, the tach needle has come to rest at around 6,300 rpm in fifth gear and you're at 199 miles per hour.

Possibly even more fun is acceleration in intermediate ranges, like from 20–50 or 50–70 miles per hour: you hardly have time to blink an eye.

As always, the heart of a Corvette is a V-8, in the Z06's case a pushrod, 16-valve, all-aluminum powerplant with 505 horsepower at 6,300 rpm and 470 ft-lb of torque at 4,800 rpm. Generous porting allows for easy breathing for the fuel-injected 7.0-liter V-8. *David Kimble cutaway for Chevrolet*

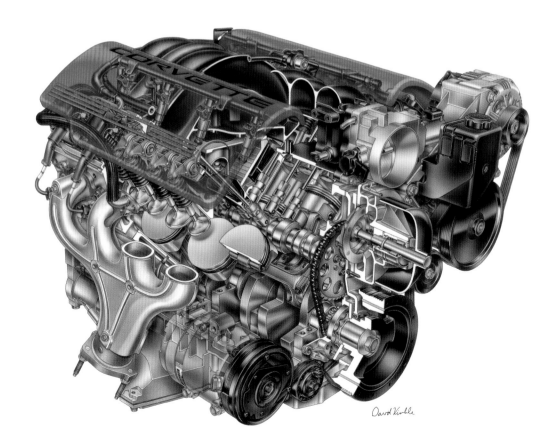

There's more to it than that.

Case point number two: The Z06 is much more than a drag-racing car.

Heck, you could buy an old Plymouth Hemi 'Cuda (which might cost more than a Ferrari F430, by the way) and go like hell, but heaven help you when the road starts to twist and climb. The Z06 loves twisty roads.

Numbers are the first indication, with *Road & Track* generating 0.99 g on the skid pad and an impressive 69.6 miles per hour through its 700-foot slalom test with the Z06. Those examples of the Corvette's agility put it in the same ballpark as the $450,000 Mercedes-Benz SLR (0.97 g, 69.6 miles per hour) and Aston Martin's $110,000 V8 Vantage (0.96 g, 69.6 miles per hour).

Driving the Z06 reinforces the numbers. Sail into a corner with the Corvette and you'll feel light understeer, while on the way out your attitude all depends on how you have set the Active Handling suspension controls and your prowess with the gas pedal. Can be straight out, electronic controls regulating the traction control, brakes, and throttle to keep the car planted and stable. Or it can be in with the tail hung out, the electronic savior systems off. In any event, it can all be well controlled if the driver is competent and using his or her head.

Unlike some older Corvettes, road surface is not a critical matter. Smooth, rumbly, or little potholes, there is a suspension mode on the Z06 that will accommodate all of them without the rear end doing the rumba. And that applies to ride, too, which is surprisingly supple.

In addition to dramatically trimming weight from the Corvette C6 to create the Z06, Chevrolet designers reworked the body. In front there's a larger air intake, a scoop in the nose, and a new lower splitter for channeling airflow. Behind the front wheels are vents to relieve hot air from the engine compartment.

To go with its added power, the Z06 gets a reworked instrument panel with a 7,000-rpm-redline tachometer and a new oil pressure gauge for the increased pressure of the dry-sump oiling system. What matters to the driver is watching those speedo and tach needles wrap quickly to the right under acceleration.

Here's where you stir up all the fun: a highly robust Tremec six-speed manual transmission that is mounted out back with the differential for better weight balance—the same reason the battery is mounted in back. The transmission also has its own oil cooler for added endurance.

Case point number three: Corvette's Z06 is a very sophisticated automobile.

We know that for many years the brilliance of the Corvette was to the credit of engineers who made such enjoyable cars from bins of mundane Chevrolet parts. Not anymore, and particularly with the Z06, which can hold its own on the tech side with many of the Europeans.

Case point number four: The Z06 isn't just a raucous ride meant to replace your testosterone medication, but a very civilized machine.

Done playing? Get on the Interstate, peg the cruise control at 70 (careful, the cops *really* look at this one), and set the Bose sound system to your favorite tunes. The tach needle will settle in around 1,500 rpm and the instant fuel economy reading will climb to 30 miles per gallon.

A good case needs evidence and there's more than enough for the Z06.

The frame and chassis are good starting points because they heavily underline the commitment of the Corvette engineers and their guru, Dave Hill, to put the Z06 up on a technical plain with the Europeans.

Looking for a way to cut serious weight from the Corvette, they went right to its basics. Engineers replaced the steel body structure that is the basis for a standard 'Vette with one done in aluminum. Along its sides are one-piece hydro-formed perimeter rails. Various stampings and extrusions are used to assemble all this into the basic frame, including cast nodes at the points where the suspension attaches to the aluminum.

JAY LENO ON THE *Z06*

For all the foreign exotica in Jay Leno's garage, he has a warm spot for American-made, which is how he can say of the 2006 Corvette Z06, "To me that's one of the greatest, about the only supercar you can use every day. And it's a Chevy, so you fix it with a hammer.

"I find it interesting it is the only 500-horsepower car sold in America that has no gas-guzzler tax. Ferrari can't do it, Lamborghini can't, and that's pretty amazing. People complain that the Z06 has a pushrod engine, blah, blah. Hey, Rocky Marciano was short, but he could still punch, he was still the champion.

"There's no car I have that I can beat on like the Corvette. With the Carrera GT and McLaren F1 there's always a sense that if I have any sort of shunt or accident it's going to be crazy expensive. With the Corvette I can take chances. I know I can get another factory wheel and I don't have to wait 8 weeks.

"People bitch and moan about the interior, well with the extra $100,000 you save buying the Z06, put Recaro seats or whatever you want in it.

"The Z06 is going to be one of the real collectables when we're 80 and 90."

Under that beautiful Corvette bodywork is a very sophisticated chassis. The frame is aluminum, based on one-piece hydroformed rails along its sides with cast-aluminum nodes where the suspension attaches to the frame rails. Making up the passenger compartment floor between the frame rails is a combination of carbon fiber skins and lightweight balsa wood.

As an example of how far Chevrolet has gone with the Z06, the special 'Vette's front fenders are made of strong, lightweight (and expensive) carbon fiber.

Forming the cockpit floors between the aluminum rails is a combo of carbon fiber skins and lightweight balsa wood. The car's front wheelwells are done in carbon composites and bonded to the aluminum.

Even aluminum isn't good enough for the Z06's engine cradle, so it is designed in even lighter magnesium, as is the car's roof.

This rather remarkable replication of the standard steel inner Corvette by an advanced materials twin was for the sake of lightness and weight balance. It seems to have worked, because at 3,130 pounds, the Z06's curb weight is almost identical to the aluminum chassis Ferrari F430.

The rest of the Corvette chassis is just as impressive.

Suspension design was never in question. It has upper and lower A-arm layouts with tube shocks and a now-traditional exception to other supercars, eschewing the expected coil springs for transverse composite leaf springs front and rear. This is a solution to springing and packaging that has been around for decades but is only used on the Corvette these days.

Z06 brakes have 14-inch front/13.4-inch rear rotors that are vented and cross-drilled. The six-piston calipers fore and four-piston aft are somewhat unique in that each piston has its own brake pad, all the better for equalized wear. ABS is part of the system.

Spun aluminum wheels carry the Goodyear 275/35ZR-18 front and 325/30ZR-19 rear tires, which manage the difficult three-way task of generating 1 g on the skid pad, having a reasonable ride, and qualifying as run-flats, so there is no spare.

Guardian angel to all this (and to the driver) is a stability control system, called Active Handling, with three settings. "On" gives the computer complete control to step in with appropriate hits on the throttle, traction control, and brakes to stabilize the car, should you start slipping beyond the limits. "Competition" raises those limits, lets you hang the tail out a bit, while "Off," well, you can figure out what that means. In a car as wonderfully potent as the Z06, it isn't difficult to probe the far reaches of the laws of physics, so you are well advised to work your way up to those limits.

What gets you to those limits is the most powerful production V-8 in the history of the venerable small-block Chevrolet. That's 505 horsepower at 6,300 rpm and 470 ft-lb of torque at 4,800 in an engine that spins happily to its 7,000-rpm redline.

Critics are still bothered by the fact that this engine uses two valves per cylinder with pushrods in a day of four valve heads and overhead camshafts, but we can only say, "Pushrods, smushrods. Who cares?"

Here's what we get: 7 liters in a V-8 with aluminum block and heads. A dry-sump oil system for full lubrication under all cornering circumstances. A forged steel crankshaft with lightweight 464-gram titanium rods connected to aluminum flattop pistons. Generously ported cylinder heads with titanium intake and sodium-filled exhaust valves. High flow going into the straight intake runners, high flow out the other end into exhaust headers that lead to a duo-flow muffler . . . quiet enough to meet noise laws at lower speed, high-flow at high speed for power.

And you get that 505 ready-and-willing horsepower. "Pushrods, smushrods," we say.

Here's an interesting point: While other automakers (spotlight here on "European") pay millions of dollars each year in gas guzzler fines because their high-performance cars can't meet U.S. fuel mileage standards, Chevrolet doesn't pay a penny on any Corvette. The Z06's official Environmental Protection Agency (EPA) numbers: 16 city, 26 highway, 20.5 combined. And we've seen better than that.

Again going for best weight balance, the six-speed manual transmission, of classic stuff with no paddle shifter and no automatic mode, is mounted out back with the limited-slip differential.

Around all this is the recognizable Corvette C6 body shape with detail differences and panels made of fiberglass, but also with carbon fiber front fenders. Seen from the front three-quarter view, you'll note that the Z06 has a scoop for engine air, a generous grille open-

Many of the changes in the newest Z06 were made after consultation with the Corvette race team, which had already proved class winners in the tough 12 Hours of Sebring and 24 Hours of Le Mans endurance events. The Corvette C6-R's toughest rivals are the fast and furious Aston Martin team.

ing, and a lower aero splitter. A duct behind the front wheels draws air from up front, while another ahead of the rear wheels on the wider fenders takes cooling air to the brakes. From the back you'll note a larger tail spoiler with high-mounted stoplights and four shiny stainless-steel exhaust tips.

Chevrolet switched from notchback to the fastback body style for the latest Z06, and that is only one of many changes that came from the Pratt & Miller factory team that races the Le Mans- and Sebring-class winning C6R 'Vettes. Several of the external modifications (flush headlamps, the engine air intake, the aero detailing on the nose, the rear spoiler) were made so the production Z06 could be homologated for racing in the American Le Mans series. Ditto with the engine carrier, though ironically the piece the racers would love to use, the aluminum structure, isn't allowed.

This carryover of production to racing and back again is a natural part of Z06 history. Zora Duntov, godfather of all Corvettes, devised the Z06 package in 1963 as a means of

offering racing equipment, mainly badly needed upgraded brakes and firmer springs and shocks, to owners of the first Sting Rays. After not being used for years, the Z06 tag was revived in the 2001 model for a 385-horsepower third body style for the Corvette. The second-generation Z06 boasted 405 horsepower, so the leap to 505, along with the aluminum structure, is why the latest has deservedly earned praise, even from those with garages full of foreign iron.

And it is why there's a strong case for putting Corvette's Z06 in a book on exotic cars. It was probably eligible in its earlier modern forms, but the technical underpinnings of the newest version, along with the continuing success of the C6R, make it a shoo-in.

At long last the 'Vette sheds its Rodney Dangerfield (don't get no respect) mantle.

Zora Duntov would be proud. ∎

How quick is the Z06? In just 3.9 seconds you're at 60 miles per hour. In 8.8 you pass the 100-mile per hour mark. By 12.2 seconds you've covered the quarter-mile and are going 120 miles per hour. Keep shifting, and at 6,300 rpm in fifth gear the speedo needle registers just shy of 200 miles per hour.

CHAPTER 33

This would be Ferrari's famous test driver, Dario Benuzzi, exercising a 599 GTB. New to this Ferrari is something called Magnetoreological damping control. Applied to the front and rear independent suspensions, the system instantaneously adapts the suspensions to road and driving conditions . . . like sliding sideways at Ferrari's Fiorano test track.

205
MILES PER HOUR

So what has 40 years of exotic cars gotten us?

We began this book with Ferrari's 365 GTB/4 Daytona, with its front-mounted V-12. We end with the newest car from Maranello, another front-engine V-12 GT, the 599 GTB Fiorano. What's the difference?

Back then, the Daytona won our hearts with stunning design, a 0–60-mile-per-hour time of 5.9 seconds, and a top velocity of 173 miles per hour. The equally-stunning 599 hacks that acceleration time to 3.6 seconds and doesn't stop accelerating until it is past 205 miles per hour. Those were pure race car speeds in the Daytona's day.

Where the Daytona was a basic car by twenty-first century standards, the Fiorano is a technological wonder. The gearbox—now called Superfast for good reason—pops off shifts using the steering wheel paddles in only 100 milliseconds.

The 599, successor to the respected 550/575 Maranello that followed up the mid-engine Testarossa, uses a V-12 derived from the Enzo's powerplant and revs to 8,400 rpm. Peak power—611 horsepower by U.S. ratings—comes on at 7,600 rpm and maximum torque is 448 ft-lb at 5,600 rpm.

Under the car is a suspension with electronic controls that constantly monitor car speed and reset shock absorbers and traction control to keep the driver both quick and safe.

A home run for Pininfarina and Ferrari. The 599 GTB consolidates the styling that began with the 612 into a smaller, tighter package. Exciting from any angle, the new Ferrari has optimized aerodynamics, with a coefficient of drag of just 0.336.

Ferrari named the 599 for its 5,999 cubic centimeters of engine displacement. Based on the V-12 used in the Enzo and 612, the twin-cam-per-head engine produces an amazing 611 U.S. horsepower (620 by European rating) at 5,600 rpm, with 448 ft-lb of torque.

Wouldn't you like to just sit there for a while? The leather-upholstered adaptive racing seats are as comfortable as they look. Check out the color on the speedometer (yellow or red is available), while the steering wheel features the START button and a *manettino* that controls everything from suspension settings to launch control.

Pininfarina did the Fiorano body shape in a style as new and distinctive as its Daytona from 40 years ago. The 599 is a new triumph for the design firm, with a modern low coefficient of drag of just 0.336.

A Daytona cost $19,000 new 40 years ago, while a 599 GTB Fiorano will be closer to $250,000.

Such is the price of 40 years of supercar progress. ■